Womanist Forefathers

Womanist Forefathers

Frederick Douglass and W. E. B. Du Bois

GARY L. LEMONS

SUNY PRESS

Published by State University of New York Press, Albany

Printed in the United States of America

For information, contact State University of New York Press, Albany, NY
www.sunypress.edu

Production by Diane Ganeles
Marketing by Anne M. Valentine

Library of Congress Cataloging-in-Publication Data

Lemons, Gary L.
Womanist forefathers : Frederick Douglass and W. E. B. Du Bois / Gary L. Lemons.
p. cm.
ISBN 978-1-4384-2755-3 (hardcover : alk. paper)
ISBN 978-1-4384-2756-0 (pbk. : alk. paper)
1. Douglass, Frederick, 1818–1895. 2. Du Bois, W. E. B. (William Edward Burghardt), 1868–1963. 3. African American feminists—Biography. 4. Male feminists—Biography. I. Title.

HQ1413.D695L46 2009
305.42092'396073—dc22 2008050664

10 9 8 7 6 5 4 3 2 1

First for my pro-woman(ist) godfather, Bishop James Howard—
When I needed you most, you came into my life.
I hear the raspy tone of your voice even now as you called me
by name—"Brother Gary." Years ago, in search of black pro-woman(ist)
forefathers, I discovered Frederick Douglass and W. E. B. Du Bois.
I did not know then that it was you for whom I searched, you for whom
I yearned. You taught me the lessons of feminist fatherhood I needed
to write this book, with all the wise counsel and intellectual
and spiritual insights you brought to our weekly meetings over the course
of two years. Like a mantra, the words you habitually spoke to me have
remained with me: "*You* have something to say."
I have said it—it is done.

And for the feminist/womanist women whose minds, hearts,
and *hands* modeled my vision of pro-woman(ist) black men
and gender justice in the world—
bell hooks, Jacqui Alexander, Kim Vaz,
Aaronette White, Beverly Guy-Sheftall, Alice Walker,
Audre Lorde, Barbara Smith, Rosalyn Terborg-Penn,
Paula Giddings, Angela Davis, Layli Phillips, Fanni Green
(my life partner/wife), and Thelma Jean Lemons (my mother).

Finally, for my children: Gabriel, Elmore, and Danyealah
for allowing me to include your stories to illustrate the
challenges of feminist-womanist fatherhood.

Womanist: A black feminist or feminist of color . . . Committed to survival and wholeness of entire people, male *and* female . . . Not a separatist . . . Traditionally universal, as in: "Mama, why are we brown, pink, and yellow, and our cousins are white, beige, and black?" Ans.: "Well, you know the colored race is just like a flower garden, with every color flower represented." Traditionally capable, as in: "Mama, I'm walking to Canada and I'm taking you and a bunch of other slaves with me." Reply: "It wouldn't be the first time."

Womanist is to feminist as purple to lavender [emphasis added].

Alice Walker (1983, xi–xii)

Pro-woman(ist): employed in *Womanist Forefathers* to describe a gender-progressive black male who supports the social, economic, sexual, and political rights of "woman" transnationally and womanist thinking (as a black feminist or feminist of color) simultaneously.

Contents

Acknowledgments ix

Prologue: Theorizing a Pro-woman(ist) Politics of Gender Justice before, during, and after "The Black Sexism Debate" xi

Introduction: Black Men Writing Ourselves into Pro-woman(ist) Being(s) in the Name of the Black Maternal 1

Part I: Reclaiming Frederick Douglass and W. E. B. Du Bois as Womanist Forefathers

Chapter 1 A Recovered Past Most Usable: Documenting the History of Black Male Gender Progressivism 13

Chapter 2 Frederick Douglass's Journey from Slavery to Womanist Manhood: Liberating the Black Male Self 23

Chapter 3 W. E. B. Du Bois: "The Leading Male Feminist of His Time" and "Most Passionate Defender of Black Women" 53

Chapter 4 Novel for the "Darker Sisters": *The Quest of the Silver Fleece* and W. E. B. Du Bois's Vision of the (Quint)essential Black Woman(ist) 81

Part II: Black Feminist "Sisters," "Brothers," and Fathers: Securing the Womanist Legacy

Chapter 5 On the Power of Contemporary Black Feminist Profession 115

Chapter 6	"Brother"hood Called into Question	127
Chapter 7	A Vision of Pro-woman(ist) Masculinity for a "NewBlackMan(hood)"	145
Chapter 8	Hands-on Practice: Everyday Challenges of Pro-woman(ist)/Feminist Fatherhood	163
Epilogue:	"This is What a (Black Male) Feminist Looks Like" Time Has Brought about a Change	191
Notes		201
Works Cited		205
Index		211

Acknowledgments

When I think about how this book came to be and the years I spent searching for other pro-feminist black men, I must thank all the women in my life who enabled me to write out publicly my personal journey toward womanist/feminist male self-recovery and self-discovery (a simultaneous and interrelated process I have come to signify in this book through the term "self-re(dis)covery." As autobiographical writing has taken up more space in my life in recent years to chart the evolution of my consciousness as a pro-womanist/feminist black man, I thank Fanni, my wife/life partner, for giving me space and time to comb through my past and helping me to know that "womanist" and "feminist" are more than (easily appropriated) labels. She never fails to let me know when my feminist idea(l)s are undermined by masculinist self-interests. For their belief in and support of womanist principles of black male identity and vision for gender-progressive liberation in black communities, I thank Joseph Thompson and Thandabantu Iverson. Iverson is a feminist-identified scholar/activist, and his research on class and fair labor practice testifies to his long-standing commitment to gender justice and black women's struggle for economic independence. I thank him, in particular, for his critical support of my work in this book.

Without the confessional writing of black men engaged in the *profession* of feminism and of other gender-progressive "brothers" (inside and outside the academy) such as Michael Awkward, Mark Anthony Neal, and Kevin Powell, I would have little ground on which to make a case for the contemporary efficacy of the pro-woman(ist) discourse and activism of Frederick Douglass and W. E. B. Du Bois. Moreover, without the historical documentation of black male participation in the woman suffrage movement, the critical foundation for the re(dis)covery would not exist. I have to thank for this crucial reclamation work Rosalyn Terborg-Penn, Angela Davis, Paula Giddings, Beverly Guy-Sheftall, Deborah McDowell, Joy James, and bell hooks. On the subject of contemporary ideas of black men and feminist fatherhood, Aaronette White's research provided me a location to think about its transformative possibilities in black male rejection of patriarchy and of the idealization of the patriarchal father in black communities. I especially thank Kim Vaz, chair of Women's Studies at the University of South Florida for giving me a home in the department to teach and write as a faculty member. Her tenacious struggle to secure my position is only exceeded by her unyielding fight to maintain the autonomous status of women's studies at USF at the departmental level in the face enormous adversity (from within and outside). I could never fully repay her for her efforts to secure this position, for her collegial comradery, and for her continual activist inspiration and vision of solidarity among progressive feminist folk in women's studies across our political differences. I am always indebted to the work of Jacqui Alexander. For more than a decade, inside and outside the academy, she has enabled me to live, write, and work transgressively for the good of the people—they are hungry; they wait for us; they have need of our hands, our hearts, our labor.

Finally, I thank Larin McLaughlin at SUNY Press for her belief in and consistently strong support of my work, from the proposal to the finished book. Once more, I have much gratitude for the efforts of Diane Ganeles, who oversaw the production of this book. I am also especially grateful to Wyatt Benner, Leah Cassorla (for completing the index), and to Jenny Jeddry, my former student, who meticulously edited chapters in part 2 and also provided critical insights concerning many of the ideas I struggled with in the book. Again, Jenny, you demonstrate just how much a student/teacher research/scholarly collaboration can yield.

Prologue

Theorizing a Pro-Woman(ist) Politics of Gender Justice before, during, and after "The Black Sexism Debate"

> It is . . . downright reactionary to resist the criticism that we African-American men have generally adopted a sexist outlook and behavior vis-à-vis our women. Our lack of the power to institutionalize sexism means little because sexism is already embedded into nearly every institution in America. *Regardless of our lack of power, the fact is that we routinely act out sexist behavior and the controllers of society at large condone, seldom punish and even sometimes reward such sexist behavior* . . . [emphasis added].
>
> —Kalamu ya Salaam (in *Black Scholar* 1979, 21)

> If this society ascribes roles to Black men which they are not allowed to fulfill, is it Black women who must bend and alter our lives to compensate, or is it society that needs changing? And why should Black men accept these roles as correct ones, or anything other than a narcotic promise encouraging acceptance of other facets of their own oppression? . . . As Black women and men, we cannot hope to begin dialogue by denying the oppressive nature of male privilege. . . . One oppression does not justify another.
>
> —Audre Lorde (1984, 61–63)

Riding the Waves of Black Feminism

Writing about the politics of gender and race in the 1960s in *When and Where I Enter: the Impact of Black Women on Race and Sex in America*, Paula Giddings refers to that time period as "The Masculine Decade." She writes: "A male-conscious motif ran throughout the society in the sixties. . . . The theme of the late sixties was 'Black Power' punctuated by a knotted fist. . . . Although it may not have been consciously conceived out of the need to affirm manhood, it became a metaphor for the male consciousness of the era" (Giddings 1984, 314–15).

In the early 1970s, during the second wave of the women's movement, black women feminist activists, scholars, and writers began to reclaim the history of black women. As if in direct response to the rising tide of black masculinist in*surge*ncy in the gender politics of the black power movement a decade earlier, in the early 1980s Alice Walker authorized the search for "womanist" foremothers in her groundbreaking book, *In Search of Our Mothers' Gardens*. It showed clearly that the identity and "herstory" of black women were intertwined and that there was an inextricable link between gender and race.

In the late 1980s, having been profoundly influenced by black feminist thought through my introduction to the writings of bell hooks when I was a graduate student in English at New York University, I discovered the name of a special issue of *Black Scholar* entitled "The Black Sexism Debate."[1] The special issue emerged in response to an essay published earlier in the same journal by the noted black sociologist Robert Staples entitled "The Myth of Black Macho: A Response to Angry Black Feminists." Publication of "The Black Sexism Debate" represented a critical historical moment in the discourse on black sexism. According to the *Black Scholar*, the debate showcased the idea that "[b]lack feminists have raised just criticisms of black male sexism . . . to improve . . . the collective black human condition . . . to clarify the nature of black male/female relationships . . . in the process of re-uniting our people and revitalizing the struggle against oppression."[2] In my own response to the historic and contemporary firestorm Staples's article created, I wrote:

> Since . . . "The Black Sexism Debate," controversy continues to rage around the idea of *black* feminism. Black antifeminist men have charged black women feminists with creating a racial/gender rift between black men and women, arising from the feminist positionality they have claimed. Thus, black feminist women have been accused of such Machiavellian plots as conspiring with white feminists against black men, with promoting lesbianism, and selling out black struggle against racism (a move tantamount to black cultural genocide). Stated another way, the single most virulent critique of black women in feminist movement has come with the perception by some black men that "feminism" is itself a racist ideology solely fixed in a manhating ideology ultimately leading to the castration and "feminization" of all black men. (Lemons 1998, 275)

Thirty years after the historical dialogue on black sexism staged by the *Black Scholar*, to underpin the *anti*sexist standpoint of this book I affirm the *pro*-womanist spirit of the "debate." Of the revolutionary voices included in it, two stand out with regard to the aim of this text: Audre Lorde and Kalamu ya Salaam. In sharp reaction to the antifeminist venom Staples spewed, both radically oppose the idea that sexism is a "white" issue. Breaking silence, they expose the dirty laundry of black sexism—that though "[o]ne oppression does not justify another," the fact remains that "[r]egardless of our lack of power" as black men, we still possess the privilege to "routinely act out sexist behavior," a behavior "the controllers of society at large condone, seldom punish and even sometimes reward. . . ." I open the prologue with their words not only to recapture the social and political significance of black dialogue on sexism in the late 1970s, but also to register with urgency its obvious critical relevance today. Recalling the unprecedented pro-womanist response to Robert Staples's antifeminist argument and its personal and intellectual impact on me as a graduate student many years ago, as a committed "professor" of black feminist thought I endeavor to promote ongoing dialogue about ways sexism in black communities works in tandem with white supremacy and racism to undermine the humanity of all black women *and* men.

Against the Historical Tide of Black Sexism

In 1998, in *Men Doing Feminism*, I wrote a response to "The Black Sexism Debate" under the title "A New Response to Angry Black (Anti-)feminists: Reclaiming Feminist Forefathers, Becoming Womanist Sons." It was more than just a critique of Robert Staples's attack on Wallace and Shange. I wrote this piece not only to declare solidarity with gender-progressive black women and men, but also to voice publicly my own antisexist standpoint. Reflecting on the supportive voice of pro-feminist black men in the debate, I said: "Those black men . . . who wrote in solidarity with black women against black antifeminist ideology must today be joined by those of us black men who declare ourselves in feminist alliance with black women—writing, speaking, and acting in comradeship against women's oppression. We must critique sexism perpetrated by black men (as well as other men)—calling out sexism and misogynist behavior wherever we encounter it" (Lemons 1998, 274)

In part, "The Black Sexism Debate" fueled my passion for black feminist politics, and it was the radical, gender-progressive politics of black men such as Kalamu ya Salaam in the late 1970s that led me on a search for others like him during my graduate school years at NYU. Looking to the distant past, as had the black women feminists before me, in the late 1980s I discovered the extensive body of work produced by Frederick Douglass and

W. E. B. Du Bois on female equality and women's rights. In their writings (especially those infused with confessional and autobiographical discourse) on female equality and women's rights, I found a theoretical starting point—a radical discursive location from which to contemplate pro-woman(ist) black male consciousness. Laying claim to the term, I invoke its employment with historical and contemporary specificity. I deploy it in this book as a theoretical gesture to articulate the gender-progressive politics of black men who have aligned (and allied) themselves with the struggle of women against gender oppression.

In light of the history of racism in the first and second waves of women's liberation movement in the United States as well as the history of sexism in African American political movement, I am fully aware of the racial, gender, class, and sexual controversy "feminism" and "womanism" summons up in black communities. Playing on such terms as *pro-woman(ist)* and *pro-woman(ism)* in this text, I accomplish two things. First, these two terms serve to signify and define the radical political beliefs Douglass and Du Bois espoused as long-standing activists for woman suffrage and female equality. Second, the terms imply an ideological affirmation of feminist principles. At the same time, they strategically play within the humanist domain of womanism. Even so, the distinctive terminology I set in place to identify the history of gender-progressive ideas articulated by certain black men creates a more nuanced, named space in which to represent its historical and contemporary particularities. And this is the point of this study: not only to reclaim those pro-woman writings of Douglass and Du Bois, but also to recognize the critically important dialogic dimensions of womanist legacy each man bequeathed to every black male *and* all men of conscience across race/ethnic differences.

In the writings and speech acts of Douglass and Du Bois advocating the rights and equality of women, I found a location to anchor the development of my own womanist/feminist consciousness. Reclaiming the activist work for gender justice these men (and other black males during their respective times) committed themselves to affords me a multidimensional personal/political, scholarly/historical, and inspirational space in which to revisit the debate on black sexism. The point here is to reframe, strengthen, and renew continued dialogue in black communities about the injurious effects of sexism and the healing implications of pro-woman(ism), especially in the lives of black men. With this, as the guiding imperative of this book, I document Douglass and Du Bois's record of sustained advocacy for gender justice. In doing so, I try to forge a vital connection across time and space between black men in the woman suffrage movement and those today who publicly identify as proponents of the rights and equality of all women. This link further enlarges the dialogic space for black men in the herstory of black women's studies.

In the opening decade of the twenty-first century, the legacy of Douglass and Du Bois, embodied in my representation of them as pro-woman(ist) forefathers, models a black male defense of women's rights that defies a masculinist vision of black liberation. It stands in striking contrast to the male-centered rhetoric that dominated the black power movement of the 1960s and more recently the Million Man March of the mid-1990s, which called for a repatriarchalization of black manhood. As black men we should know (better than men born with inherited racial privilege) that in a culture of white male supremacy, race and gender oppression work together with deadly consequences. We need to reflect again upon the courageous outspokenness of Kalamu ya Salaam as he holds all black men accountable with respect to the privilege *and* power we possess as men to act out sexist behavior. In "A New Response" I spoke of the historical significance of his words, which are connected to the task of reclamation this book embarks upon:

> I respond to Salaam's words as a contemporary call for black men to recognize and resist sexism as a misogynist weapon employed to dehumanize all women. I hear his words [in the epigraph which opens the prologue to the present book] as an echo of W. E. B. DuBois' exhortation to black men of his time to take up the cause of woman suffrage and women's rights. For those of us black men already committed to feminist movement, we must begin a more vocal and demonstrative declaration of a "pro-womanist" stand. . . . Whether we name ourselves in solidarity with "feminism" or "womanism," collectively, black men must—as did black men in the woman suffrage movement—actively combat antifeminist thinking that privileges anti-racist work over women's struggle to end sexual oppression (Lemons 1998, 277)

As this book maintains, the legacy of gender justice Douglass and Du Bois passed on to us should inspire every black male who has rejected manhood ideas rooted in heteromasculinist performativity and homophobic denunciation of feminism. It is a legacy that demands reclamation by a new generation of black male activists for gender justice actively speaking and writing against the injurious effects of sexism and patriarchy in black communities. The claims I make on Douglass and Du Bois as pro woman men allow me to conceptualize a contemporary, black male space for writing/speaking our own narratives of *self*-recovery, a recovery grounded in black feminist thought. At the same time, it is a space that responds to my deepest yearning for community with other gender-progressive black men, past and present.

Introduction

Black Men Writing Ourselves into Pro-woman(ist) Being(s) in the Name of the Black Maternal

> The African-American male has been touched . . . by the mother, handed by her in ways that he cannot escape, and in ways that the white American male is allowed to temporize by a fatherly reprieve. . . . [T]he African-American woman, the mother, the daughter, becomes historically the powerful and shadowy evocation of a cultural synthesis long evaporated—the law of the Mother—only and precisely because legal enslavement removed the African-American male not so much from sight as from mimetic view as a partner in the prevailing social fiction of the Father's name, the Father's law. . . . *[T]he black American male embodies the only American community of males which has had the specific occasion to learn who the female is within itself. . . . It is the heritage of the mother that the African-American must regain as an aspect of his own personhood—the power of "yes" to the "female" within* [emphasis added].
>
> —Hortense J. Spillers (1987, 80)

> Doing anything but pursuing black feminist insights would have meant being like my father. I could no more have rejected feminism than I could have chosen not to love my mother. . . . This book [*Scenes of Instruction: A Memoir*] constitutes my risky attempt to circulate the major themes of my mother's narratives, and to demonstrate that I've absorbed their form and content well enough to contribute to feminism's efforts to challenge patriarchy's unabated rule.
>
> —Michael Awkward (1999, 5, 7)

A Laying On of Hands: Recovering the Power of the Black Mother's Touch

Growing up in the black Pentecostal Church, I witnessed the ritual practice of what is called a "laying on of hands." During Friday night and Sunday morning services, the congregation sat with fervent expectation that our pastor (always male) would call us collectively to the altar so that he (and other male clergy under his authority) might place his hands (covered in sacred oil) on our foreheads as a form of spiritual blessing, an anointing. He and those "men of God" who assisted him had been themselves anointed to perform this practice. The power of the sacred touch lay within the hands of the Man of this House. Growing up, I never questioned the order of things. This was the way it was (and always would be) in the black church I knew.

In the epigraph above from "Mama's Baby, Papa's Maybe: An American Grammar Book," Hortense J. Spillers performs a provocative reading on the constitutive devaluation of the black familial in the history of the United States. She inserts a profound revelation about the healing power of the black mother in the face of the shared psychic and physical trauma for black women and men in the attempted dissolution of the black family. In particular, Spillers insightfully marks the historical connection between the "African-American man" and the black mother through the power of her touch. He "has been *handed* [italics added] by her in ways that [we] cannot escape." To comprehend the critically important grammatical (and ultimately the symbolic) nature of the subject/object relationship in this sentence, some basic knowledge of syntax is useful. Note that "the African-American *male* [italics added]" (in the subject position) "has been touched . . . handed" (passive verb forms). He is acted upon by the mother. The passive verbalization of the noun "hand," on one level, suggests physical movement.

On another metaphysical, life-sustaining plane, through the mother's *handedness*, there is a *passing on* of the black feminine spirit here. The laying on of hands/anointing/spiritual blessing is performed by the maternal figure. She has "handed" *her* spirit to him "in ways he cannot escape." He is bound to the spirit of the mother, an untenable condition of the law of patriarchy. Spillers claims the power of the mother's hand is a metonymic sign of "the law of the Mother" (*her* hand upon her children, sons and daughters), activated in the absence of the (African American male) father's hand—hidden from "*mimetic* view" in slavery's annihilation of the black family. Thus, in the "American Grammar Book" of patriarchy, the African American male/father—legally barred "as a partner in the prevailing social fiction of the Father's name, the Father's Law"—stands without hands. He is handless—symbolically cut off—and unable to touch his sons and daughters in the ways of their mother. Not only is he unable to touch them physically, because he is out of view/invisible in their lives, but in the "Grammar Book" he cannot see or speak to them. Not only is he barred from modeling them in his ways of being, he simply cannot *be* outside the power of the ruling-class (white) father/master.

Yet against the annihilating force of white supremacist patriarchy operating to ensure that a black man in the United States will never come to know his family and *himself*, Hortense Spillers remains steadfast in the conviction that black male self-recovery (interconnected to the recovery of whole black families) is inextricably linked to the black feminine (within). Recognizing *and* accepting the distinctive familial tie that the black man "embodies" in his relationship to the mother, wrought in the holocaust that was American slavery, he possesses the ability to understand (with at first *hand*) the experience of *black* female oppression (racially and sexually). It is precisely this history that "has given [him] the specific occasion to learn *who* the female is within itself" in the black community. The overarching challenge for the black American male is to live out this knowledge in everyday practice. But first, he must recover and reclaim "the heritage of the *mother* . . . as an aspect of his own personhood—the power of 'yes' to the 'female' within [him]." I maintain that in a culture of white supremacist patriarchy, it is this acknowledgment that drives the fearful denial in black males of any association with "fe(male)ness"—that fuels the rampant (albeit irrational) exhibition of homophobia in black communities. It has become our number one defense in the face of white male heteropower. In this hegemonic equation, white supremacy = male supremacy.

Thus, in the racially colonized mind of the black male, there can exist nothing in us that can be remotely associated with the feminine—even if it calls for the rejection of our mother, sisters, daughters, and/or other females in our families. To embrace the intrinsic, historical value of the black mother's *hand*/spirit in shaping who we are as men would be to accede to the power of the feminine in our lives. To do otherwise, as I have argued elsewhere, is for the black man to see himself in perpetual despair as a black male victim of racist emasculinization—effeminized, having internalized the myth of white male superiority. Saying yes to the spirit of the black feminine within the constitutive power of "the black community" is not about giving up his manhood. It means that to know him*self*, his "personhood"—what defines him as a human being worthy of self-respect and self-dignity—he "must regain" the wisdom of the mother's *hand* upon him.

For we black men today who have recognized and felt the power of the black mother's hand/spirit in the evolution of our belief in female equality and women's rights, we claim the legacy of Frederick Douglass and W. E. B. Du Bois in writing and speaking as committed pro-woman activists in the movement for woman suffrage—even as they struggled for racial equality. It is, according to Hortense Spillers, the "touching" force of the slave mother in the life of the African American male that distinguishes black male experience (bereft of the black father's presence) from that of his white male counterpart. In the history of white male identity, it is the father who "temporizes" the mother's presence/impact. In light of the psychic damage historically heaped upon the black family—damage normalized through the forced, legalized absence of an African American paternal *hand*—many black males today suffer from its touch. In the labor of the hands and voices of Frederick Douglass and W. E. B. Du Bois, we discover the womanist spirit of their mothers. We contemporary black men committed to a politics of gender justice have recognized its power in the lives of our own mothers and the efficacy of its influence in our lives. Today, we are writing and speaking publicly about its confessional and professional challenges as men embracing womanist thought as a site of liberating self-recovery.

The Joy of Pro-womanist Self-Re(dis)covery for Black Men

Broadly, *Womanist Forefathers* is about black men from the past and present writing and speaking publicly about the power of pro-woman thinking in their lives as a liberatory practice to transgress the boundaries of patriarchy. First and foremost, its attempt to recover the history of black men involved in the movement for woman suffrage, begun in the mid-nineteenth century, undermines the masculinist myth that *race* is the single most pressing issue for black people. Second, its simultaneous effort to theorize, recover, *and* reclaim the history of pro-womanism articulated by black men offers a large critical framework to think about black male identity vis-à-vis sexism, patriarchy, and white supremacist notions of manhood. Through this framework, this book contemplates the personal, self-liberating, and political possibilities inherent in the feminist politics of black male gender progressivism. The retrieval of a pro-woman(ist) black male past represents a form of radical antipatriarchal insurgency that goes beyond the boundaries of the black cultural nationalism formulated in exclusive antiracist principles. Gender-progressive black men (past and present) writing and speaking openly about ways patriarchal domination personally wounds them gets to the core/heart of the case I make for the self-transforming power of black feminist/womanist thought.

As if the joy of discovering and documenting a historical and contemporary shared belief in the equality of women among gender-progressive black men itself was not enough, I also have found in the exploration of it another more deeply rooted connection in pro-womanist, black male thought. At its center is the liberatory vision of *womanism*. I have written about its efficacy more than once and referenced it multiple times elsewhere as a radically gender-inclusive standpoint. Womanist thought (as Alice Walker conceived it in *In Search of Our Mothers' Gardens*, 1984) engages a personal and political vision of liberation dedicated to the "survival and wholeness of entire people, male and female." Fostered in the wisdom of black maternity, its definitional power speaks in an emancipatory tone invoking the history of antislavery struggle of blacks as "[t]raditionally capable, as in: 'Mama, I'm walking to Canada and I'm taking you and a bunch of other slaves with me.' Reply: 'It wouldn't be the first time' " (A. Walker 1983, xi).

What I discovered in my examination of pro-woman(ist) autobiographical texts by black men writing as advocates of female equality and women's rights—from Douglass to Du Bois and beyond—is the centrality of the *black mother*. More often than not in these texts, I have found that she represents the signifying catalyst in the authors' evolving pro-feminist consciousness. I theorize that in the minds of self-professed, womanist/feminist black men, the material condition of the black mother in a culture of white supremacy and under patriarchy (inside and outside black communities) serves with stunning illustrative power these men's (firsthand, experiential) understanding of the simultaneity of sex and race oppression, oppression beginning in childhood. Autobiographical writing becomes a critical space for gender-progressive, black male self-examination in the context of the maternal relation. Before documenting this phenomenon in the autobiographical writings of Frederick Douglass and W. E. B. Du Bois, I begin by drawing upon a contemporary example to illustrate my theory of the germinal connection between the black maternal and the conceptualization of black male feminism. In *Scenes of Instruction: A Memoir*, Michael Awkward offers a deeply moving explanation for his feminist self-identification in complex (albeit problematic) relation to his mother: "To speak extensively about why I am a black male feminist is to expose myself to charges that I have visited upon my mother a discursive violence similar in intensity to the unimaginable physical pain she suffered at my father's hands. But given my experiences, given her experiences, I'm not sure how else I can explain the personal and professional choices I've made. . . . Indeed, how else can I, a self-defined and flawed, black male feminist, justify my love and myself?" (Awkward 1999, 5).

Clearly, Awkward does not lay bare the emotional pain of his relationship with his mother to promote black male feminism as a site for opportunistic self-aggrandizement. Rather, in the creation of an autobiographical space of vulnerability he can openly talk about the critical linkage between his and his mother's experiences. As Awkward reveals, that link not only influenced his "personal and professional choices" over the years, but also acts as the justification of himself as a "self defined *and flawed* [emphasis added], black male feminist." In fact, the experiential connection between mother and son bound up in domestic violence is pivotal to understanding his love for her and himself.

Writing autobiographically about the politics of black male feminist self-identification related to the condition of his mother, Michael Awkward follows in the path of Douglass and Du Bois in condemning black female oppression. While positing the idea of a black maternal presence in the pro-womanism of black men, I make no claim that it is the single source for the development of gender-progressive consciousness in pro-feminist black men. Nevertheless, it remains strikingly clear in the cases of Douglass, Du Bois, Awkward, and other black male proponents of female equality represented in this book that the black maternal acts as a key transforming element in their gender consciousness. In fact, discovering the gender-progressive autobiographies of these men provided me a critical standpoint to begin writing about the condition of my mother as a working-class black female survivor of domestic violence. Moreover, their survival stories represented discursive road maps that aided me as I crafted a womanist writing space to address publicly the wounding effects of patriarchy in the lives of black men, in particular. At the same time, in this space, I began to contemplate the gender-healing power of black feminist thought. It housed the tools to confront the wounding effects of growing up in a culture of white supremacy and the ill effects of black patriarchal domination I experienced as a child. Theorizing the childhood-wounding experience of patriarchy through its impact upon the black mother as a recurring, life-altering theme in gender-progressive black men's personal narratives, I center their critique of patriarchy in the men's personal gender politics. In recounting painful childhood memories of paternal abandonment, I trace Douglass and Du Bois's (non)experience with the place of the father in each man's complex relationship to patriarchy.

As stated in the prologue, when I began a historical search for black men speaking and writing in defiance of patriarchal domination I did not anticipate finding extensive autobiographical material by pro-woman(ist) black men about their fathers. I had little idea then that it would have a major influence in my thinking on black fatherhood, as well as the development and focus of my research on gender-progressive black men. More than this, on a personal level, I also did not anticipate in reading Douglass and Du Bois's autobiographies that their emotional experience as children with(out) fathers would mirror my own in such striking detail. Reading their autobiographies, I came to know the lives of these black men who had, like me, experienced in childhood the traumatic effects of familial dysfunctionality bound up in the father's (mis)behavior.

During their lives, Frederick Douglass and W. E. B. Du Bois produced an amazing body of work on female equality and women's rights that has yet to be fully mined for its political relevance to contemporary dialogue about the relationship between patriarchy, manhood, and fatherhood in black communities. In my early examination of these writings as a graduate student years ago, I idealized Douglass and Du Bois's writings on women as models of black male gender progressivism. How could they be masculinist or patriarchal in their thinking about female equality as committed activists for woman suffrage, for example? In retrospect, perhaps what I wanted most to believe about them was that they were nothing like the patriarchal black men or fathers I had grown up knowing. Over the years, however, I have come to understand Douglass and Du Bois more fully in the context of the lives they lived and the politics of gender, race, and class that shaped them. Whatever idealistic notions I have held on to about the self-transformative possibilities of feminism in the lives of black men, over the years I have become much more (self-)critically aware of the familial politics and the politics of identity informing the very idea of womanist thinking as a mode of self-re(dis)covery for black men.

Writing about the history of black male identity and how it relates to the wounding effects of patriarchy in the black family, I am, indeed, grateful for black feminist critiques of Douglass and Du Bois's gender-progressive thought. In particular, Deborah McDowell's critique of the curious, "troubling presence/absence" of women in the writings of Douglass immeasurably complicates my analysis. Moreover, the distinction Joy James articulates between the masculinism and patriarchal imperatives that underlie the zeal of Du Bois's impassioned plea for the liberation of black womanhood further explains his (*and* Douglass's) drive for *male self*-representation, which is crucial for contemporary pro-feminist black men to understand. James exposes the always possible contradiction or "phallusy" of a black male feminism that is not aware of any competing male-dominated self-interest.

Rejecting a vision of black liberation rooted in the belief that it will be achieved when black men "rightfully" assume the position of patriarchal head, this book is organized in two parts. Part 1 provides an analysis of the multigenre discourse produced by Douglass and Du Bois largely in defense of woman suffrage. Part 2 examines antisexist thinking conceptualized by some of today's most outspoken gender-progressive black men and women. In the critique of patriarchy they advance—formulated in the intersectionality of oppression in black communities—they confront black machismo head-on.

Considering the historical ground on which this book stands, chapter 1 principally records the history of black male support for woman suffrage. It relies heavily upon Rosalyn Terborg-Penn, Angela Davis, and Paula Giddings's finely detailed documentation of the woman suffrage movement. Situating myself in feminist familial connection to Douglass and Du Bois, I try to reveal the depth of their influence on my pro-woman evolution and examine the gender progressive ideas of well-known elite black families from the early 1900s, including the Remonds, Fortens, Pauls, and Purvises. From these and other families, I represent a group of fathers, sons, and sons-in-law who were staunch proponents of gender progressivism among them. They include Charles Lenox Remond, Martin Delany, Robert Purvis, William Whipper, William C. Nell, Alexander Crummell, James Forten Sr., and James Forten Jr. The chapter concludes by mapping the emergence of Frederick Douglass and W. E. B. Du Bois as the major voices of black male, pro-woman(ist) thought in their respective times.

In chapter 2, I discuss how Frederick Douglass made a powerful case for woman suffrage when he boldly declared on May 28, 1888: "I am a radical woman suffrage man," a position based upon the discourse of natural rights and his acute understanding of the similarities between race and gender oppression. A former slave, he compared the evils of slavery to that of female oppression in his speeches and editorials and strategically spoke in opposition to male supremacy. The pro-woman(ist) writings reflect Douglass's capacity to imagine with deep feeling the oppression of women—even as he passionately defended Negro (male) suffrage. Douglass advanced a critique of racism and sexism illustrating his comprehension of the link between white supremacy and male supremacy. As a black abolitionist and pro-woman rights man, he had to navigate the channel of white supremacist, patriarchal political power with great caution, even as he carefully negotiated the rocky terrain of racist attitudes held by liberal white feminists (many of whom were actively involved in the abolition movement).

Douglass was acutely aware of the sensitive nature of his personal associations with white women feminists. He knew there would be race and gender fallout surrounding his decision to campaign for Negro suffrage. Despite the racist attacks that ensued from some of the white suffragists closest to him to the end of his life, Douglass remained a devoted supporter of women's right to vote. While Frederick Douglass communicated his belief in female equality primarily through speeches and editorials (largely excluding personal familial references), Du Bois heavily employed autobiographical narrative to champion black women's political and economic independence. The confessional appears strategically in the pro-woman(ist) writings of Du Bois as a discursive vehicle to express his personal disdain for female oppression. He employs it in multiple forms, including the editorial, exposé, sociological treatise, familiar essay, poetry, and fiction.

Chapter 3 provides a close reading of Du Bois's most articulate statement of his gender-progressive views: the 1920 essay "The Damnation of Women." Stylistically moving between sociological treatise, autobiography, and African mythology, Du Bois crafts, what was, for its time, an amazingly advanced defense of black womanhood against the myth of white supremacy and white female superiority. Moreover, chapter 3 considers the gender progressivism of Du Bois in light of his theory of art, represented in the 1926 essay "Criteria of Negro Art." In it, he boldly proclaims, "[A]ll art is propaganda," and adds emphatically, "I do not care a damn for any art that is not used for propaganda." This chapter examines three early key texts by Du Bois to demonstrate how the theory works: *The Souls of Black Folk* (1903), *The Quest of the Silver Fleece* (his first novel, published in 1911), and a little-known personal essay, "So the Girl Marries" (1918), about the then forthcoming marriage of his daughter, Yolande.

Chapter 4 looks at Du Bois as a writer of political fiction. It details artistic motivations that led him to publish *The Quest*. The novel sprang from the same political agenda as his pro-woman suffrage texts and critical writings about what he believed to be the deplorable condition of black women in the United States. The chapter builds its analysis on Du Bois's attempt to write a political "feminist" novel featuring a dark-skinned protagonist. *The Quest* represents the first work of fiction in African American literary history to feature a dark-skinned female protagonist, a protagonist who becomes the catalyst for female *and* male transformation in the novel. By its end, she, Zora, has become the revolutionary leader for her community. Advancing Arnold Rampersad's assertion that the novel arises from a feminist impulse and Nellie McKay's belief that the narrative is groundbreaking for its feminist representation of the novel's female hero, I argue that Du Bois transgresses the representational limits of black fiction during his time to assert the primacy of a "black" black woman's story rooted in African mythology.

Chapter 5 opens part 2 as a reinforcement of the aim and theoretical underpinning of this book. This chapter works to place contemporary feminist/womanist thought by black males in dialogic relationship with that of Frederick Douglass and W. E. B. Du Bois. Primarily, it reengages the politics of black male feminism as articulated by Michael Awkward, one of today's leading black gender-progressive voices. As stated earlier, one must possess a clear understanding of the black mother's place in it. Amplifying Awkward's employment of *autocritography* (a term popularized by Henry L. Gates) as a "critical concept" to expound upon the professional and academic concerns of the black male feminist critique, I position the chapter as a thematic bridge. Relating the relevance of autobiography in the pro-woman rights "professions" of black men from the nineteenth and early twentieth century (as exemplified in the memoirs of Douglass and Du Bois), I appropriate Awkward's terminology of a black male, self-liberatory narrative expression to frame critiques of patriarchy, sexism, and black fatherhood.

Chapter 6 reveals how the complexities of "name-calling" are related to what it means for contemporary black men to take on the gender-progressive labeling associated with feminism. It insists that for any black man publicly rejecting patriarchal, heteronormative, and homophobic notions of black masculinity, the penalty is certain expulsion from the "(brother)hood." He will most likely be "called out of his name" denigrated by names associated with emasculinization. But as this book sets out to show, as was the case with Frederick Douglass and W. E. B. Du Bois, being a feminist-identified black man is necessarily a risky business.

Chapter 7 chiefly focuses on contemporary narratives of pro-feminist black males interviewed in Johnnetta B. Cole and Beverly Guy-Sheftall's *Gender Talk: The Struggle for Women's Equality in African American Communities* and Aaronette White's *Ain't I a Feminist? African American Men Speak Out*. . . (particulary its chapter "African American Feminist Fathers' Narratives of Parenting"). Through these works, I examine the extent to which antipatriarchal ideas of parenting figure in the formulation of black male feminist thinking. Chapter 8 illustrates the humanizing benefits of pro-womanist/feminist fatherhood. Comprised of my own confessional narratives about the challenges of antisexist manhood and fatherhood opposed to patriarchy, the chapter reveals my personal recovery over a two-year period from what I call a "malehood breakdown." Through a process of "self-inventory" (a critical step in traditional recovery work), I cover what evolved into a soul-searching reexamination of my relationship to feminism. I examine my life as a childhood survivor of domestic violence, its relation to my work as a college professor and a minister (ordained in a Pentecostal denomination), and my experience as a gender-progressive husband and father. I end with the assertion that becoming a pro-womanist/feminist man not only necessitates a commitment to ending sexism as an ongoing political project but also requires unrelenting struggle against patriarchy and female oppression through daily practice. Today, publicly sharing our own narratives of self-transformation about our rejection of patriarchy—whether we identify as "(pro-)feminist," "(pro-)womanist," and/or "antisexist" men—as black men committed to female equality and women's rights, we will do well to reclaim the legacy of gender justice embodied in the writings and speeches of Douglass and Du Bois. Ultimately, in whose *hands* does the work for black male self-recovery against the wounds of white supremacist patriarchy rest? It is a question for which the answer will continue to elude many of us as long as we perpetuate the belief that racism is the biggest obstacle to our identity as black men.

1

Reclaiming Frederick Douglass and W. E. B. Du Bois as Womanist Forefathers

1

A Recovered Past Most Usable

Documenting the History of Black Male Gender Progressivism

In the history of the struggle for women's rights in the United States during the nineteenth century and early twentieth century, most often identified with the woman suffrage movement, a select group of black men actively supported ideas of female equality. They achieved a record of sustained commitment to women's rights. Without the historical vigilance of certain scholars on black male involvement in the movement for women's voting rights, that record would have been lost. Retrieving it, this chapter maps the evolution of black male gender progressivism from the mid-1840s to the rise of Frederick Douglass as a major black male voice for woman suffrage. Douglass's sustained support for women's right to vote would predate Du Bois's unyielding support for the passage of the Nineteenth Amendment in 1920. Beverly Guy-Sheftall underscores the notion that the black feminist struggle to end gender and racial oppression was rooted in the battle for all oppressed people: "The most enlightening aspect of the examination of [nineteenth-century and early twentieth-century] attitudes toward woman suffrage, which was seen as another vehicle for the improvement of the race, is the revelation that some black men and many black women saw as early as a century ago no contradiction in associating themselves with struggles for women's rights (despite the opposition of many whites) at the same time that they were fighting for the emancipation of the race. They saw themselves as fighting for the liberation of all people" (1990, 162).

Douglass and Du Bois produced a body of writings that denounced the subjugation of women. They wrote in multiple genres, including autobiography, speeches, editorials, and creative writing (in the case of Du Bois) These writings offer a critical entry point into the complicated familial, social, personal, and political contexts from which they emerged. On the one hand, they are full of hope and possibility with regard to the transformative power of feminism in men's lives. On the other hand, they are daunting. These texts provide deep insight into the complex relationship between the theory and practice of feminism for men and its personal and the political implications for women, children, and men in a culture founded upon the ideology of male supremacy.

Looking Forward with Eyes Fixed on the Past

From "The Rights of Women" (1848), the first text Frederick Douglass published, to his most impassioned speech, "The Woman Suffrage Movement" (delivered before the Woman Suffrage Association convention in 1888), it is clear that he passionately supported women's rights. These texts (and those others written/delivered between 1848 and 1888) illustrate that his passionate speeches and editorials on behalf of women's liberation were intrinsically tied to the abolition of slavery. Douglass became the key black male figure in the nineteenth-century woman suffrage movement, arguing against the evils of sex and race oppressions strategically through a discourse of gender justice, and W. E. B Du Bois in the early twentieth century succeeded him in becoming the chief male advocate for black women's rights. Paula Giddings in *When and Where I Enter,* her groundbreaking analysis of race and sex in the experience(s) of African American women, asserts that "W. E. B. Du Bois . . . took Frederick Douglass' place as the leading *male feminist of his time* [emphasis added]. . . . His view reflected the consensus: Political empowerment of the race required the participation of Black women" (Giddings 1984, 121). Like Douglass, Du Bois strategically employed his journalistic skills to promote women's rights.

Each man approached the "woman question" from a different perspective. Douglass based his pro-woman rights stance on the ideology of natural rights, believing that all women were "naturally" equal to men and, therefore, deserving of equal rights. Du Bois held that when the black woman attained her freedom, all women would be free. In the discourse on the equality of women each man wrote, however, common themes surface. For each man, personal, firsthand witness of women's oppression acted as the primary catalyst for his feminist development; each man consciously understood the *inter*relationship between women's liberation and black liberation; being black, male, and pro-woman(ist) posed a particular set of gender and racial issues for each man; and each man conceived women's rights within a larger human rights framework.

While both Douglass and Du Bois employed journalistic writing as a major vehicle to promote women's liberation, Du Bois not only represented his gender-progressive views in editorial form, but also drew from and merged autobiography with sociological observation and fiction to produce a hybrid, discursive, womanist form. It spoke personally and poignantly to the gender, race, and class politics of black womanhood. From the publication of *The Souls of Black Folk* (1903) to "The Damnation of Women" (1920) and his tenure as editor of the *Crisis* (1910–35), Du Bois critiqued black female racial and class oppression in ways that set him apart from any man of his day espousing a belief in women's rights. It is Du Bois's particular attention to the condition of black women in the United States that distinguishes his writings on gender justice from those of Douglass. The radical critique of black female oppression Du Bois advanced locates him solidly within the history of black feminism. No other black man, before or after Du Bois, has written with such sustained passion and deep commitment to the liberation struggle of African American women.

In "The Damnation of Woman," an essay in *Darkwater* (1920) that analyzed the status and condition of women in the United States, Du Bois laments their mistreatment. He writes, "I remember four women of my boyhood: my mother, cousin Inez, Emma, and Ide Fuller. They represented the problem of the widow, the wife, the maiden, and the outcast. . . . They existed not for themselves, but for men they were named after, the men to whom they were related and not after the fashion of their own souls. They were not beings . . ." ([1920] 1969, 163). Like those of Du Bois, Douglass's ideas of women and womanhood were filtered through the lens of a childhood experience of female mistreatment. As a black child born into slavery, Douglass's understanding of family was completely shaped in a world of brutal and inhuman violence against the female and male slave. Without certain knowledge of his biological father (who he came to believe was the white slave master who originally owned him and his mother), Douglass knew himself to be a product of miscegenation. I maintain that he was not nearly as disturbed by this racial origin as by having as a child witnessed the brutal/sexualized beating of the aunt who served as his surrogate mother. Neither Douglass nor Du Bois, whose father left him and his mother when he was a young boy, would ever realize the love and nurture of a biological father. I suggest that their long-standing commitment to the struggle for women's rights and equality had its origin in the experience of childhood paternal rejection and abandonment that was replaced by a deep sense of connection to the black maternal figure. Deborah McDowell has argued as much in the case of Douglass.

Documenting the History of Womanist Forefathers, Sons, and Sons-in-Law

Out of a rising black middle class in the North during the 1830s came a number of politically active women and men from such well-known activist families as the Remonds, Fortens, Pauls, and Purvises. Men in these families promoted female education, as well as the involvement of women in public affairs. Early nineteenth-century black men's belief in the priority of women's education exemplified progressive thinking on the equality of the sexes. Paula Giddings notes, "[M]ore affluent Blacks . . . were organized along patriarchal lines. However, their struggle for racial equality sanctioned the non-traditional political activities and education of their wives, sisters, and daughters. . . . Men like James Forten, Sr., and his son James Jr. believed that the women's role in the abolitionist struggle was too important for them to be relegated to their homes. . . . Many Black male activists believed in the fundamental equality of the sexes" (1984, 59). Many of the females in these families actively participated in the struggles for race and sex independence. From these same women's families came husbands, brothers, and sons who took up the cause of women's education and suffrage, as well as political and economic freedom for black people. Sarah Remond, the Fortens (Margaretta, Sarah, Harriet, and Charlotte), and Susan Paul were only a few of the early black female abolitionists to emerge from the black bourgeoisie (Giddings 1984, 59). In the 1850s, Sarah Remond became an international antislavery spokesperson, speaking in England, Ireland, and Scotland. And Charlotte Forten, a noted educator (A. Davis 1983, 65), and Hattie Purvis became well-known voices in the abolitionist movement (Giddings 1984, 66).

In fact, all of the children of James Forten Sr. were members of the female antislavery movement. In 1836, James Forten Jr. voiced before the Ladies Anti-Slavery Society of Philadelphia his opposition to male abolitionists' sexism in the movement. His brother-in-law, Robert Purvis, and his wife, Harriet Forten, worked together as conductors on the Underground Railroad. They also worked with whites to bring about recognition of women's equality in the antislavery movement (Terborg-Penn 1978, 32–33). In 1837, at a meeting of the American Moral Reform Society, Purvis and William Whipper (a black pro-woman supporter from Philadelphia) sponsored a resolution maintaining the divine justice of women's right to education: "Resolved that these women who are now pleading the cause of humanity, and devoting their time, talents, and industry, to the cause of universal Freedom, deserve the blessings of Heaven and the gratitude of posterity" (Terborg-Penn 1978, 32). An early vocal advocate of female equality, Purvis believed that "[w]oman [was] not a mere dependent of man. The relation is perfectly reciprocal. God has given to both man and woman the same intellectual capacities, and made them subject to the same moral argument" (Giddings 1984, 59). As Paula Giddings remarks, "It was a stunning position for the early nineteenth century." Giddings notes that it would have been politically wrongheaded for black men to continue to bar black women from political work, considering the racial oppression both faced (59). Producing a complex picture of black men's reactions to the idea of women's equality, Terborg-Penn shows that black men responded in a variety of ways. She states:

> [Black men] tended to perceive the problems of black women primarily in terms of the struggle against racism rather than as a struggle against sexism. To some black men, however, legal and social discrimination against all women was a primary concern. . . . On the whole during the antebellum period, black male leaders were more sympathetic to woman's rights than white male leaders. . . . Black men were therefore inclined to be sensitive to the demands of other groups similarly disfavored. In reacting to the "woman question" on the basis of their own images of women in general and black women in particular, some Afro-American men perceived women as being in need of male protection, *while most perceived them as equal to men* [emphasis added]. Some sought to uplift the women of the race, while others included women and men in the uplift process. Some viewed black women as particularly vulnerable to attacks by white society, while others viewed the problems of black women in a white-dominated society as quite similar to the problems of black men. (Terborg-Penn 1978, 28–29)

Well before the "woman question" arose, Terborg-Penn argues, black men and women organized together, and while some black men displayed sexist attitudes toward black women in their organizations, such feelings were considerably milder than those of their white male counterparts. In fact, an examination of some of the predominantly black antislavery and reform societies during the antebellum period indicates that black male reformers usually included the rights of women within the struggle for human freedom. They empathized with the plight of women because much of the legal and political discrimination that black men suffered was shared by all women as well (29).

One of the earliest black antislavery organizations, the Union Society of Africans of Newport, Rhode Island, an association formed to assist fugitive slaves, in 1789 listed among its members Bess Browning and Rebecca Folger. Black women and men led the New England Freedom Association. Three women served among the thirteen officers. In 1848, William C. Nell, one of the organization's leaders, would speak before the Woman's Rights Convention at Rochester, New York, where he praised the involvement of women in the antislavery movement and espoused his belief in the equality of women. Also, black women and men who were excluded from white societies in the temperance movement before the Civil War came together to form their own organizations. "As a result," says Terborg-Penn, "the numbers of black men and black women who cooperated together in racially separate organizations through the North was high." Though black women continued to struggle for equal recognition in black organizations, "male resistance to such participation seemed short-lived and less hostile than white male opposition" (29).

Generally speaking, the exclusion of black men in white reform organizations led them to sympathize with women's experience of sexism. In the 1840s, Martin R. Delany and Frederick Douglass advocated female education, particularly that of black women. "Although these men viewed the 'woman question' from two different perspectives, they both perceived women as equal to men in the struggle" (Terborg-Penn 1978, 31). In his writings, Delany exhorted blacks to adopt a more progressive position toward women. He thought their education was necessary for racial progress, and he called upon black men to support black women in securing education as a means to rise above the level of service workers for whites. "His pleas for adequate schools for black women and career goals above that of domestic predated the woman's rights movement" (Terborg-Penn 1978, 31). Douglass also spoke of the right of women to education in the *North Star* (first published in 1847, becoming the most well known of the abolitionist newspapers) and *Douglass' Paper* (Terborg-Penn 1978, 32). Supporting from its inception the inclusion of women in the reform movement, the *North Star* printed the "Address of the Anti-Slavery Women of Western New York" and ran a continuous column (from March 24 to August 11, 1848) on its proceedings. It also published the proceedings of the historic Woman's Rights Convention in Rochester that same year. The paper argued that a female "has a right to the same intellectual cultures as man; her sphere should be bound only by her power" (qtd. in Terborg-Penn 1978, 32).

Attending some of the organization's meetings, Douglass made known his belief that black men should be involved in women's rights agitation. He based this idea on the need for joint struggle and pointed to the similarity between black male oppression and that of women (Terborg-Penn 1978, 31–34). For Delany the plight of black women was interconnected to that of black men through the common experience of racial oppression. Douglass, however, viewed the struggle of "woman" as an issue of gender oppression. In *The Condition, Elevation, Emigration, and Destiny of the Colored People* (1852), Delany wrote about the need for black men to support black women in the efforts of the latter to seek education.

Engendering a Movement for Black (Female) Liberation

In the 1840s and 1850s, ruling-class white men of the North heavily policed white women's activism whether on behalf of themselves or on behalf of slaves. Terborg-Penn maintains that "during [this period] white males were more adamant in excluding white women from their reform societies. White males often criticized [them] when they attempted to speak publicly" (1978, 30). From the beginning of the antislavery movement, white men attempted to exclude white women's participation. White women resisted by forming the Philadelphia Female Anti-Slavery Society. White men claimed their involvement betrayed the cult of true womanhood. Bettina Aptheker suggests that abolitionist societies, dominated by white males, were generally not open to women on the basis that, "[i]t violated all manner of Victorian procedure for women to assume a public stance on any issue, much less speak, petition, or organize in defense of it. More to the point, their activities undermined the patriarchal structure of a society in which woman had been rendered the property of men" (Aptheker 1982, 15). She further points out that the backlash white women experienced in the organization came from religious groups such the Council of Congregationalist Ministers of Massachusetts, the most influential group in the state. When in 1838 white women were granted equal participation in the New England Anti-Slavery Convention, in protest a Rev. Amos A. Phelps countered by organizing an all-male group—the Massachusetts Abolition Society. It was among the first of a number of other white male organizations that barred women (Aptheker 1982, 15).

Lucretia Mott, Sarah Grimke, and Angelina Grimke, early antislavery white activists, often experienced public censorship. Mott and Elizabeth Cady Stanton were excluded from participation in the World Anti-Slavery Convention, held in London in 1840. However, Charles Lenox Remond (one of the most celebrated black orators of the nineteenth century) with William Lloyd Garrison (president of the American Anti-Slavery Society) and Nathaniel Roger (editor of the *Herald of Freedom*) denounced the act of exclusion by not taking their seats on the floor with the larger delegation. They sat with the women delegates, who were permitted to sit in the balconies. Remond criticized the action in the *Colored American*, and the piece was later printed in the *Liberator*. Remond also acknowledged the support of the three female antislavery organizations that had funded his trip, thanking the women who defended his antislavery efforts (Terborg-Penn 1978, 30).

Just as some white men acted to silence and exclude the political agency of white women, so there were those black men who resisted the participation of black women in politics. Giddings contended that "[t]here is no question that there was greater acceptance among Black men of women in activist roles than there was in the broader society," but she points out that "[t]his did not mean that sexual equality always prevailed—at home or in the political arena (Giddings 1984, 59). As stated earlier, while in some of the earliest black organizations women's participation was not an issue, there were many that did exclude women from holding office or even having input in decision-making processes. Despite the prevalence of patriarchal thinking among black men, when the National Convention of Colored Freedmen (an organization that had traditionally excluded women from its proceedings) met in Cleveland in 1848, both Douglass and Delany were integrally involved in getting women seated as delegates. Delany officially called for female inclusion. He declared before the convention: "Whereas we fully believe in the equality of the sexes, therefore, resolved that we hereby invite females hereafter to take part in our deliberations." A number of the delegates opposed this, but Douglass reminded them that the convention had agreed to allow "all colored persons" to become delegates. He suggested that "persons" be changed to "women." They finally agreed (Terborg-Penn 1978, 34). After 1848, women attended as convention delegates on a regular basis without contention.

By 1854, twenty-four women, including Delany's wife, Catherine, became full participants at the National Immigration Convention. The New England Convention of Colored Citizens in 1859 elected four women to offices of importance. Mary Ann Shadd Cary, a black journalist and women's rights activist, was one of the first women to hold a seat at a Negro convention (Terborg-Penn 1978, 29). When the National Colored Labor Union was organized in 1869, headed by Isaac Mayers, black women protested the nonresponse of the convention to issues concerning their labor problems. In an effort to respond to black women's demands, the NCLU reduced its convention dues so more females could join. Eventually, the NCLU would call for more female participation in its proceedings. Cary was the first woman to address the convention. She spoke on women's rights. Her speech persuaded the NCLU to grant women the power to organize cooperative societies. On this issue, the NCLU proved more responsive to the concerns of women than its white counterpart (Giddings 1984, 69). From the early nineteenth century and the rise of the antislavery cause in the North to the height of the woman suffrage movement in the early twentieth century, race and gender remained contested issues in both arenas. Of those black men whose names became associated with both, one stood above the rest: Frederick Douglass.

"I am a radical woman suffrage man": Frederick Douglass and the Power of the Speech Act

Frederick Douglass passionately spoke the words "I am a radical woman suffrage man" in a speech given before a woman suffrage meeting in Boston,

Massachusetts, on May 28, 1888. His rise to recognition and esteem in the woman suffrage movement represents a complex interworking of race, gender, sexual politics that was filtered through his close and longtime relationship with Elizabeth Cady Stanton, Susan B. Anthony, Julia Griffiths, and Ottilia Assing, among others. Douglass had a charisma that few people (male or female) could resist. In an 1845 review of *Narrative of the Life of Frederick Douglass, An American Slave*, William Lloyd Garrison described him as "in physical proportion and stature commanding and exact—in intellect richly endowed—in natural eloquence a prodigy—in soul manifestly 'created but a little lower than the angels'—yet a slave . . ." (Gates 1990, 62). When the intellectual acumen of Douglass became the topic of discussion, seldom were his physical attributes left out. And these did not go unnoticed by his women's rights companions, according to the biographer William McFeely.[1] The combination of his keen intellect and verbal eloquence, set off by his striking physical appearance, gained him entrée into the inner circles of white male and female abolitionists, and many of the women were also staunch woman suffragists. In 1874, Celia Logan (a reporter for the *New York Daily Graphic*) wrote about her impression of Douglass after an interview with him, "The play of his fine features made a little thrill run through me. The dignity of his attitude, *the majesty of his stature made Frederick Douglass look every inch a man*" (qtd. in Franchot 1990, 145).

The first official acknowledgment of Douglass as a woman suffrage advocate came in 1848 at the Convention on Woman's Rights at Seneca Falls, when he cast the deciding vote in favor of woman suffrage. Male support for woman suffrage in the nineteenth century was an exception rather than the rule. Antiwoman suffrage rhetoric during the time had little good to say for men who participated in the women's rights movement. Reporting on male attendance at one of the early woman suffrage conventions, the *New York Herald* referred to men there as "long-haired men, apostles of some inexplicable emotion or sensation . . ." (S. J. Walker 1973, 26). Undoubtedly, the comment indirectly made reference to Douglass, who not only frequently attended woman suffrage meetings but in most instances was a featured speaker. For Douglass, the convention at Seneca Falls had proved a watershed moment in his early alliance. Two months after Seneca Falls, Douglass and Martin Delany sponsored a resolution expressing their commitment to female equality at the National Convention of Colored Freedmen. It passed. With this resolution the NCCF sent a definite message regarding black male support of the rights of black women. In Philadelphia the convention of blacks passed a resolution to include as delegates both black and white women. Lucretia Mott, one of the white women in attendance, wrote to Elizabeth Cady Stanton on the convention's proceedings: "We are now in the midst of a convention of the colored people of the city. Douglass and Delany—[Charles Lenox] Remond and [Henry Highland] Garnet are here—all taking an active part—and as they include women and *white* women too, I can do no less, with the interest I feel in the cause of the slave, as well as of woman, than be present and take a little part . . ." (A. Davis 1983, 60). Frederick Douglass and other black male advocates of the rights of women had been spurred on by the spirit and resolve of the historic Seneca Falls Convention to press for woman suffrage. Douglass's push to break down sexist barriers for the inclusion of women in "men-only" organizations was emblematic of his future role in the movement for woman suffrage.

While early black male, pro-woman activists like Martin Delany, the Fortens, and Purvises forged a race/gender alliance articulated in more nationalist terms, Frederick Douglass moved across racial boundaries to argue for a gender coalition with white suffragists. This standpoint defined his long (and sometimes controversial) participation in the woman suffrage movement. Speaking at the 1850 Woman's Rights Convention in Rochester, Douglass said, "In reference to the enfranchisement of women, it need not be questioned whether she would use the right or not; man should not withhold it from her." It is important to note here that he was not the only black man who attended the predominately white female gathering. Also, in 1853, at the New York Statewide Woman's Rights Convention at Rochester, delegates elected Jermain W. Logan and William J. Watkins (black abolitionists) vice president and secretary, respectively (S. J. Walker 1973). It was Douglass who would be credited with bridging the political aims of abolitionism in time with the cause of women's equality. Shortly after the Seneca Falls convention, the *North Star* carried an article by Douglass entitled "The Rights of Women." In it he declared: "In respect to political rights, we hold women to be justly entitled to all we claim for men. We go further, and express our conviction that all political rights which it is expedient for men to exercise, it is equally true of woman, and if that government only is just which governs by the free consent of the governed, there can be no reason in the world for denying to woman the exercise of the elective franchise, or a hand in making and administering the law of the land" (Foner 1950, 321).

Elizabeth Cady Stanton had acknowledged Douglass for his continued support of woman suffrage in the face of much opposition at the 1848 Seneca Falls convention and at the convention in Rochester, New York, one month later. She would again recognize his commitment to the struggle for women's equality forty years later, in 1888, at a national convention of the Woman Suffrage Association. Marking the significance of his work to unite the struggle for female equality with the battle for black liberation, Angela Davis asserts that Douglass "was . . . responsible for officially introducing the issue of women's rights to the Black Liberation Movement, where it was enthusiastically welcomed" (A. Davis 1983, 51).

2

Frederick Douglass's Journey from Slavery to Womanist Manhood

Liberating the Black Male Self

> When I ran away from slavery, it was for myself; when I advocated emancipation, it was for my people; but when I stood up for the rights of woman, self was out of the question, and I found a little nobility in the act.
>
> —Frederick Douglass ([1892] 1962, 472)

> The emancipation struggles of slaves and women became increasingly symbiotic as the tactics and ideology of antislavery began to function as a primary basis for those of women's rights. . . . The argument for woman's emancipation, like that for the slave's emancipation, constituted an integral component of the larger struggles for human rights. . . .
>
> —Waldo E. Martin (1984, 137)

> The incomparable Frederick Douglass did many things of which I am proud, but there is nothing he ever did in his long and brilliant career in which I take keener pleasure and greater pride than I do in his ardent advocacy of equal political rights for women, and the effective service he rendered the cause of woman suffrage sixty years ago [i.e., at the 1848 Seneca Falls Convention.]. . . . I am glad that it was to a large extent due to Douglass' masterful arguments and matchless eloquence that it [the resolution for equal political rights for women] was carried, in spite of the opposition of its equally conscientious and worthy foes.
>
> —Mary Church Terrell (1908, qtd. in Foner, 176–77)

"To be denominated a woman's-rights man"

In the final volume of his autobiographical trilogy, *Life and Times of Frederick Douglass, Written by Himself: His Early Life as a Slave, His Escape from Bondage, and His Complete History* (1892), Frederick Douglass would write, "Observing woman's agency, devotion, and efficiency in pleading the cause of the slave, gratitude for this high service early moved me to give favorable attention to the subject of . . . 'woman's rights' and *caused me to be denominated a woman's-rights man* [emphasis added]" ([1892] 1962, 472).

In the statement above (written toward the close of an illustrious career of abolition and woman suffrage activism), Douglass recalls his longtime association and service to the cause of woman suffrage. This chapter asserts that his status as "a woman's-rights man" was strategically interconnected to his standing as a liberated *black* man. The link between these liberatory positions manifests itself in his discursive ability to (re)present himself as a "self-made man" in the autobiographies and as a "Negro" in his discourse on woman suffrage—both representations responding to a society that had denied him the rights and privileges of citizenship and manhood. As a political strategist, he found the argument for "woman's rights" a perfect vehicle upon which to build his case for the defense of black liberation.

Upon a closer analysis, however, the emancipatory agency Douglass writes about as a black man in the movement for woman suffrage is not as simple as the statement above implies. A number of black feminist scholars have documented the racist treatment he, as well as other black women and men, endured within the movement.[1] Interestingly enough, while Douglass writes passionately against white (male and female) resistance to the idea of Negro suffrage, particularly in his discourse on woman suffrage, he says little about the gendered effects of racism on black women in relation to black men and/or white women. In fact, over time Douglass writes little about the political struggle of black women apart from the nongendered heading "Negro."

This chapter asserts that Frederick Douglass's gender progressivism, represented in his passionate commitment to woman suffrage, placed him in an untenable racial position, as he struggled to navigate the political minefield surrounding the "woman question" and the "Negro question." Conceptualizing a discourse of gender and racial expedience, his support for woman suffrage is strategically linked to his defense of suffrage for the Negro. However, what becomes clear in the pro-woman(ist) texts is that neither "woman" nor "Negro" embodies the position of the black woman. In this way, despite Douglass's lifelong devotion to female liberation and ongoing battle for black independence, black female subjectivity is edited out of the text of black male feminist representation. Ironically, the black woman's presence is constructed in the textual space of absence. One may argue that Douglass (in light of the overt racist *and* classist politics of middle-class white suffragists) found himself between the rock of race and the hard place of gender.

Black feminists and gender-progressive black male scholars examining the politics of gender and race in the woman suffrage movement have shown that black women's battle for equality as women was neither sufficiently addressed by it nor by the campaign for Negro (male) suffrage. Pointing to the history of black women's discursive invisibility in feminist discourse, bell hooks notes:

> No other group in America has so had their identity socialized out of existence as have black women. We are rarely recognized as a group separate and distinct from black men, or as a present part of the larger group "women" in this culture. *When black people are talked about, sexism militates against the acknowledgment of the interests of black women; when women are talked about racism militates against a recognition of black female interests. When black people are talked about the focus tends to be on black "men"; and when women are talked about the focus tends to be on "white" women* [emphasis added]. Nowhere is this more evident than in the vast body of feminist literature. (hooks 1981, 7)

Deborah McDowell has argued that the autobiographical writings of Douglass display a "troubling presence/absence of women." She offers a compelling investigation into the gender politics of a man who spent the greater part of his life involved in the struggle for female liberation.

On the "Troubling Presence/Absence of Women" in the (Con)text of Douglass's Autobiographies

> The troubling presence/absence of women in the 1845 *Narrative* [*Life of Frederick Douglass*] becomes all the more puzzling, given Douglass's active and lifelong involvement in the movement for women's rights. . . . Although women are largely relegated to walk-on parts in Douglass's autobiographies, he left a substantial record of speeches and editorials defending their rights. . . . The contradictions and disjunctions between Douglass's autobiographies and his speeches and editorials illustrate the importance of evaluating his legacy in the round and resisting the stubborn simplification of Douglass the legend and hero.
>
> —Deborah McDowell (1999, xxiv–xxv)

> There is not, beneath the sky, an enemy to filial affection so destructive as slavery. *It had made my brothers and sisters strangers to me; it converted the mother that bore me, into a myth; it shrouded my father*

> *in mystery, and left me without an intelligible beginning in the world* [emphasis added].
>
> —Frederick Douglass ([1855] 1994, 157)

Few historians or feminist critics considering the woman suffrage activism and pro-woman(ist) writings of Frederick Douglass have contested his long-standing commitment to the woman suffrage movement and belief in the equality of women. Yet, as William S. McFeely, Jenny Franchot, and Deborah McDowell demonstrate, the marginal appearance of women in the autobiographies is indisputable. I have argued that there remains a curious absence of *race* related to Douglass's argument for the rights of "woman" in his discourse on female equality as well as his autobiographies. In the introduction to the Oxford World Classics edition of the *Narrative Life of Frederick Douglass: An American Slave* (1999), Deborah McDowell connects the "troubling presence/absence of women in the *Narrative*" directly to the gendered politics of Douglass's representation of himself as a self-made *man*.

Concerning the discursive presence/absence of the black female slave in the term "woman" inside and outside the (con)text of Douglass's autobiographical representation, I hold to McDowell's cautionary statement about "evaluating his legacy in the round and resisting the stubborn simplification of Douglass the legend and hero." While his legacy of commitment to the equality of women remains unparalleled—even compared to W. E. B. Du Bois's pro-feminist standpoint—it is clear the representation of women in the autobiographical (con)text he constructs demands a complex reading. The pro-woman "contradictions and disjunctures" McDowell pinpoints are ones that strike deep into the core of Douglass's being and selfhood. They are related to his continual witness of the racist and sexist brutalization of the black female slave. As Jenny Franchot has argued, Douglass's reaction to the slave master's mistreatment of the woman who served as his surrogate mother (his aunt Esther) "obliterates any integral selfhood and imposes the new ontology of slavehood" (1990, 142). As most male critics of *Narrative* have contended, Douglass becomes a *man* at the precise moment when he resists the authoritative and physical force of his master. McDowell believes that the assertion of "self" this "new black man" creates (as the *author* of his *own* liberation) not only becomes a male model of the slave's freedom, but is a self that stands in for that belonging to the female slave. At the same time, beyond his 1845 *Narrative*, as the major black male voice against slavery, Douglass marks the horrors of it through its damnable impact on her body. According to McDowell, "Douglass's 'freedom'—narrative and physical alike—depends on narrating black women's bondage. He achieves his 'stylistic signature' on the backs of black women, as it were. . . . *Women, especially slave women, remain trapped in the physical, in the body, excluded from language and symbolic activity*" [emphasis added] (McDowell 1999, xxiv–xxv).

For years I have struggled to understand the "presence/absence" paradox of black female representation in the pro-woman(ist) writings of Douglass. In public antislavery speeches, he argued for the abolition of slavery with great eloquence, and based his argument on the inhuman treatment of the female slave as a strategy to gain support from liberal middle-class whites in the North. But he did not write extensively about the depth of inner trauma it caused him as a child (particularly regarding his mother). Douglass "objectively" recalled the horrors of slavery (on the backs of black women) in the service of the abolition movement, even as he publicly concealed the depth of its painful personal memory.

In *My Bondage and My Freedom*, written in 1855, ten years after the *Narrative*, Douglass shares with the reader the all too brief bond he shared with his mother, a bond that caused him a lifetime of grief. One discovers in his expression of it an almost indescribable level of sadness. For Douglass his mother held both a "myth[ic]" and iconic place in his life:

> I cannot say that I was very deeply attached to my mother, certainly not so deeply as I should have been had our relations in childhood been different. . . . The slave-mother can be spared long enough from the field to endure all the bitterness of a mother's anguish, when it adds another name to a master's ledger, but *not* long enough to receive the joyous reward afforded by the intelligent smiles of her child. *I never think of this terrible interference of slavery with my infantile affections, and its diverting them from their natural course, without feelings to which I can give no adequate expression* [emphasis added]. (Douglass [1855] 1994, 152)

Before his mother's death (when he was a boy of eight years old), Douglass had only seen her a few times. Yet on one of those occasions, she seems to have rescued him from being severely punished by one Aunt Katy ("the cook of old master's establishment") (153). He "found himself in the strong, protecting arms of a mother, a mother who was, at the moment (being endowed with high powers of manner as well as matter) more than a match for all his enemies. . . . That night," he says, "I learned the fact, that I was not only a child, but *somebody's* child" (152). That night would be the last time he would see his mother. "The heartless and ghastly form of *slavery* rises between mother and child, even at the bed of death" (155). While a cloud "shrouded [his] father in mystery," his mother had made him feel like he was "*somebody's* child" (if only in that one instance). *Slavery* had not only created a cloud of mystery regarding his paternal lineage and caused an estrangement from his siblings, but had mythologized his mother, which "left [him] without an intelligible beginning in the world."

I maintain that the repression of the feminine in Douglass's autobiographies began with the death of the biological mother, which occurred some years before the brutal whipping of Aunt Esther, as Jenny Franchot asserts. This is by no means a small point. The Douglass who writes in such striking nonemotional terms about the "simple truth" of his mother's death is the same man who would also in reflection admit, "Her personal appearance and bearing are ineffaceably stamped upon my memory. . . . It has been a life-long, standing grief to me, that I knew so little of my mother; and that I was so early separated from her. The counsels of her love must have been beneficial to me. The side view of her face is imaged on my memory, and I take few steps in life, without feeling her presence; but the image is mute, and I have no striking words of her's [*sic*] treasured up" (Douglass [1855] 1994, 151–52, 155).

While as a child, upon hearing of his mother's death, Douglass felt "no strong emotions of sorrow for her," her physical being is "ineffaceably stamped" and "imaged" on his memory, creating "a life-long, standing grief to [him]." Yet the image does not speak. What would she have said? As her encounter with Aunt Katy indicates, she was "more than a match for all his enemies." More than this, he tells us, she could read (a fact he discovered after her death)—"she was the *only* one of all the slaves and colored people in Tuckahoe who enjoyed this advantage" (156). Though she left no words for him (not even the name of his father), she bequeathed to him an astounding gift that would not only change the course of his life, but also would impact the course of the abolitionist movement and the movement for woman suffrage. Douglass's mother left him a love for the *word*. Astonished by the power of literacy she possessed, he states:

> That a "field hand" should learn to read, in any slave state, is remarkable, but the achievement of my mother, considering the place[,] was very extraordinary; and in view of that fact, I am quite willing, and even happy to attribute any love of letters I possess, and for which I have got—despite of prejudices—only too much credit, *not* to my admitted Anglo-Saxon paternity, but to the native genius of my sable, unprotected, and uncultivated *mother—a woman, who belonged to a race whose mental endowments it is, at present, fashionable to hold in disparagement and contempt* [emphasis added]." (Douglass [1855] 1994, 156)

As an adult looking back on his childhood, Douglass is clear about one thing—parental influence, but "*not*" from his white father. We witness in the autobiographical (con)text of Frederick Douglass's life the germinal place the black mother's image holds in it. It is something integrally connected to the power of literacy, freedom for the slave, and the representation of the self-made (black) man. For Douglass the image transforms into an honorific representation of universalized woman(hood) in his texts on women's rights, transcending the discursive boundaries of racial signification. Even so, as Deborah McDowell and William McFeely have argued, in his autobiographies "women are largely relegated to walk-on parts." Neither, however, contests his lifelong devotion to and involvement in the movement for woman suffrage. Douglass viewed his work as a "woman's rights man with the highest regard even to the very end of his life." As McDowell notes: "Perhaps there is not greater testament to Douglass's feminist allegiances than the fact that he died on 20 February 1895, after delivering a rousing speech at a women's rights rally" (1999, xxv). But even as Douglass advocated for the equality of "woman," the ideology of racism that permeated the largely white female movement for woman suffrage was evident in the nonrepresentation of black women in his feminist texts.

And then there was the politics of his own representation of self. As many scholars of the nineteenth century have pointed out, Douglass built his career as a black liberationist and woman suffragist on the principle of the self-made man. Henry Louis Gates maintains that for Douglass, the journey from slavery to freedom represented the path to the achievement of manhood. But what Gates finds problematic about the protean, self-made image the former slave creates—not only in his autobiographies, but also in his political speeches and editorials—is its relative nonrelation to black womanhood. Douglass is virtually silent on the subjugated status and condition of the black female. In "From Wheatley to Douglass: The Politics of Displacement," Gates argues that Douglass's literary status in history exists in part because of forces beyond his control but also in part because his own determination *to write* himself into history as the "father" of black intellectual expression. To begin with, Gates cites the case of James Williams, a slave whose narrative of his experiences had been published seven years before Douglass's *Narrative*. Until controversy arose in 1897 over the authenticity of his story, abolitionists had touted Williams "as their resplendent instance of African intellection" (Gates 1900, 57). Gates remarks, "[B]ut for an accident of history [James Williams] might very well occupy the place in African-American letters that Douglass has occupied since the middle of the nineteenth century" (57).

Gates offers the striking example of how Douglass may have viewed himself in relation to Phillis Wheatley. Apparently he did not have her in mind when a man named M. A. Major requested him to submit names for a forthcoming volume entitled *Notable Negro Women*. In a letter to Major (dated August 26, 1892), Douglass gave an assessment of black people's intellectual achievement generally and that of black women specifically:

> We have many estimable women of our variety but not many famous ones. It is not well to claim too much for ourselves before the public. Such extravagance invites contempt rather than approval. *I have thus far seen no book of importance written by a Negro woman and I know of no one among us who can appropriately be called famous* [emphasis added].
>
> This is in no way a disparagement of the women of our race. We stand too near a former condition to have any famous work in science, art or literature, expected of us. It is not well to ship the paddle wheels before we have steam to move them. You will therefore pardon me if I do not find it consistent to enlarge the list of famous Negro women. Many of the names you have are those of admirable persons, cultivated, refined and ladylike. But it does not follow that they are famous. Let us be true and use language truthfully. (Gates 1990, 51)

Gates is quick to point out that "[b]etween 1773 and the middle of the nineteenth century, Phillis Wheatley virtually *was* the canon of black American letters. What's more, virtually all commentators thought so, and were proud of that fact. Her poems and letters, her book and books about her life, were reprinted widely, reviewed prominently, and praised roundly as the work of the founding 'genius' of African-American letters" (49).

Wilson J. Moses has also suggested that Douglass in the transformation from slave to free *man* was quite aware of the politics of self-promotion. In fact, Moses asserts that the major life conflict for the master statesman had to do with the self-image he constructed as a spokesman for black liberation and the attempt to "deracialize" his writing to make it palatable for "white liberals"—particularly the discourse on gender equality (Moses 1990, 68). Moses observes, "[On the one hand] Douglass's literary act of self-representation was skillfully engineered to produce desired effects on certain sets of white liberals [particularly in the case of white feminists]. On the other hand, he aspired to the position of a world historical figure. . . . Douglass, like his contemporaries Ralph Waldo Emerson, Abraham Lincoln, and Phineas T. Barnum—all cunning manipulators of their public images—was both a product and a casualty of his own self-promotion" (68). Moses speaks to the pressures under which Douglass continually labored when he took up the pen (as former slave, abolitionist, woman suffragist, journalist, and autobiographer). The "white liberals" Moses referred to in the earlier quotation were the same individuals who had helped Douglass establish himself on the antislavery circuit as its major speaker.

Given the complex location he occupied in both the abolitionist and woman suffrage movements, and in the light of his own personal and political aspirations as a representative Negro man, Douglass labored under enormous pressure to remain in good standing with the powerful white men and women who (more often than not) desired to control how he should (re)present himself in both. Thus, the politics of (re)presentation in Douglass's autobiographical, woman suffrage, and Negro suffrage texts invites the reader to question who gets written into (and/or out of) the categories "slave," "woman," and "Negro." While posing an unequivocal challenge to the white patriarchal order, Douglass viewed it through the existing lens of white *male* (and female) bourgeois notions of manhood that prevailed then. His personal struggle for manhood and the battle he waged for black liberation and woman suffrage are integrally related to a "cult of true manhood" ideology. Moses asserts, "Like Emerson, Lincoln, and Barnum, [Douglass] interpreted his life as a moral precept, inviting his contemporaries to learn from his experiences and to weave them into the developing web of American values. His life symbolized the myth of American [male] individualism" (69).

Just as Douglass had exhorted women to "take" possession of their own rights, so he had successfully exerted his right to be a ("woman's-rights") *man*. The perfection of Douglass's skill as a writer and orator was the perfection of his manhood. The abolitionist Wendell Phillips said, "[L]anguage, taste, fancy eloquence, vigor of thought, good sound common sense, [and] *manliness* are all his" (Gates 1990, 61). Douglass consciously fashioned his writing for self-promotion, and he capitalized on the uniqueness of his position as a Negro *male* woman suffragist. For a black man in the United States during the nineteenth century whose escape from slavery propelled his beliefs in human rights, a political alignment with feminist ideas provided a path to the possibility of becoming a *new* and distinctive kind of man (in the support of woman's rights). That Douglass could so convincingly argue for women's equality, while successfully writing *his*tory as a black man in the woman suffrage movement, attests to his power with words and acumen as a political strategist. Understanding this sheds considerable light on the position Douglass took as an honored guest speaker at the 1888 convention of the Woman Suffrage Association. It provides the reader with a deeper insight into and context for his gratitude toward the woman's movement. After a nearly thirty-year involvement in the cause, he aimed to acknowledge publicly those women at the convention who influenced his decision to support woman suffrage. Without having succumbed to the movement's racist practices, Douglass never lost faith in the idea that was the driving force his vision of a struggle for gender and racial liberation: the idea of the "natural" right of freedom for all humanity.

"Negro" (Male) Rights versus "Woman's" Rights

> Look at this all of you. And hear me swear that I will cut off this right arm of mine before I will ever work for or demand the ballot for the Negro and not the woman.
>
> —Susan B. Anthony (qtd. in S. J. Walker 1973, 28)

> The first white women's rights advocates were never seeking social equality for all women; they were seeking social equality for white women. . . . When white women reformers in the 1830s chose to work to free the slave, they were motivated by religious sentiment. They attacked slavery[,] not racism. . . . While they strongly advocated an end to slavery, they never advocated a change in the racial hierarchy that allowed their caste status to be higher than that of black women or men. In fact they wanted that hierarchy to be maintained.
>
> —bell hooks (1981, 124–25)

Having become the leading black voice of the times for woman suffrage and Negro suffrage, Frederick Douglass had to write with multiple audiences in mind. Considering the political power elite white men possessed to determine the lives of white women and all black men and women, he had to adopt a discursive voice and tone that did not alienate those white men and women who had supported the abolition of slavery or offend white woman suffragists, many of whom had also been abolitionists as well. bell hooks maintains: "The fact that the majority of white women reformers did not feel political solidarity with black people was made evident in the conflict over the vote. When it appeared that white men might grant black men the right to vote while leaving white women disenfranchised, white suffragists did not respond as a group by demanding that all women and men deserved the right to vote. They simply expressed anger and outrage that white men were more committed to maintaining sexual hierarchies than racial hierarchies in the political arena" (hooks 1981, 127).

Precisely because Douglass remained sympathetic to the struggle of white women suffragists, he strategically employed the discourse of human rights to argue for race and gender equality. Envisioning possibilities for a unified struggle against racism and sexism, his theory of a coalition between the struggles for black liberation and women's equality (based upon an analogous relationship of sexual oppression and racial oppression) appears reasonable in the abstract logic of human rights. Yet the seamless *nature* of the two forms of oppression that Douglass describes in the human rights discourse continually betrays a very obvious and real discursive erasure of black women's subjectivity. As hooks and other black feminists have pointed out, the discursive erasure of black women is so commonly exercised (across race, ethnicity, class, gender, and sexuality, as well as other unnamed categories) that such a practice appears natural. It is precisely the universalized/deracialized "woman" and the degendered "Negro" in Douglass's pro-woman(ist) writings that reflect the racist and sexist politics of his day that continue to make feminism such a hotly contested topic in black communities.

In the feminist writings of Douglass, the white middle-class woman remains the universal signifier of womanhood, and the black male nearly always stands in as the iconic representative of "Negrohood." Strategically, as Wilson Moses has stated, Douglass constructed an equal rights discourse that primarily appealed to a white, liberal, educated female audience. What becomes clear in the texts on women's equality is that there is no distinction in his mind between the oppression of black women and that of poor and middle-class white women. Discursively, Douglass continually negotiated the racism and sexism of elite white men and the racism and classism of elite white women to maintain their support for black liberation. As hooks shows, racism and sexism were constantly mediating the political relationship between woman suffrage and Negro suffrage: "White suffragists felt that white men were insulting white womanhood by refusing to grant them privileges that were to be granted black men. They admonished white men not for their sexism but for their willingness to allow sexism to overshadow racial alliances. [Elizabeth Cady] Stanton, along with other white women's rights supporters, did not want to see blacks enslaved, but neither did she wish to see the status of black people improved while the status of white women remained the same" (hooks 1981, 127).

A critical dialogue between Anthony and Douglass illustrates the ideological race and gender stakes that grounded their suffrage positions:

> ANTHONY. Mr. Douglass talks of the wrongs of *the Negro* [emphasis added] how he is hunted down . . . , but with all the outrages that *he* [emphasis added] today suffers, he would not exchange his sex and take the place of Elizabeth Cady Stanton.
>
> DOUGLASS. I want to know if granting you [i.e., white women] the right of suffrage will change the nature of our [respective] sexes.

> ANTHONY: It will change the pecuniary position of women. It will place her where she can earn her own bread. She will not then be driven to such employment only as man chooses for her. (qtd. in Lutz 1959, 163)

While Susan B. Anthony and Elizabeth Cady Stanton had acknowledged the contribution of Douglass to the woman suffrage movement, Anthony admitted to employing racial expedience as a tactic to win Southern white women's support, even if it meant validating racist attitudes (some of which she shared). For example, on one occasion, fearing Southern white women would object to his presence, she requested that he not attend the National American Woman Suffrage Association (NAWSA) convention convened in Atlanta, Georgia, in 1894. Discussing the matter with Ida B. Wells-Barnett (organizer of the first black woman's suffrage club), Anthony defended her actions as follows: "In our conventions . . . he [Douglass] was the honored guest who sat on our platform and spoke at our gatherings. But when the . . . Suffrage Association went to Atlanta, Georgia, knowing the feeling of the South with regard to Negro participation on equality with whites, I myself asked Mr. Douglass not to come. I did not want to subject him to humiliation, and I did not want anything to get in the way of bringing the Southern white women into our suffrage association" (qtd. in A. Davis 1983, 111).

Wells-Barnett rejected Anthony's strategy, saying, "I felt that although she made gains for suffrage, she had also confirmed white women in their attitude of segregation" (qtd. in A. Davis 1983, 12). In 1893, the National American Woman Suffrage Association had made its sentiments public: "[W]ithout expressing any opinion on the proper qualifications for voting, we call attention to the significant facts that in every State there are more men who can read and write than all Negro voters; more American women who can read and write than all foreign voters; so that the enfranchisement of such women would settle the vexed question of the rule by illiteracy whether of home-grown or of foreign-born production" (A. Davis 1983, 115–16).

Even before this pronouncement, Anthony had denied several black women in the association the right to organize suffrage clubs on the grounds that it would have inflamed Southerners and hurt the NAWSA's recruitment efforts in the South. She maintained this position until she stepped down as president of the NAWSA in 1900 (Giddings 1984, 126). In spite of overt racism against blacks in the organization, Douglass had maintained an allegiance to the movement. He fervently believed in suffrage for women but passionately held on to the idea that voting rights for black men would improve the general condition for black males and females. He said, "*I am now devoting myself to a cause [if] not more sacred, certainly more urgent, because it is one of life and death to the long enslaved people of this country, and this is: Negro suffrage* [emphasis added]. . . . [H]is claims may be preferred by me without exposing in any wise myself to the imputation of narrowness or meanness towards the cause of men" (qtd. in Diedrich 1999, 267).

On May 9, 1865, Frederick Douglass declared, "Slavery is not abolished until the black man has the ballot" (McFeely 1991, 268–69). In making this proclamation, he formally announced his commitment to fight for Negro (male) suffrage. It would test the solidity of a formal coalition founded the next year between proponents of black liberation and woman suffrage. Leading members of both causes—including Douglass, Anthony, Stanton, and Wendell Phillips, among others—established the American Equal Rights Association (AERA) in 1866. When it became clear that the struggle for Negro suffrage was gaining support among Northern, radical, white male Republicans, white woman suffragists in the association (most vocally Susan B. Anthony) vehemently objected. Her resistance, among that of other whites, to its growing support exposed a virulent strain of racism. "She [Stanton], who had been steadfast in her opposition to slavery, crossed the line into racism when she said that women were more intelligent than the black men who, she now saw, were competing with her and her fellow women for the vote. That competition resulted in the one of the saddest divorces in American history. . . . Now a breach was in the making, and it has never fully healed" (McFeely 1991, 266). Never before had the relationship Douglass had with Susan B. Anthony been so strained as when she led female members in AERA in protest against black male suffrage. Feeling Douglass had betrayed them in shifting his campaign toward Negro suffrage, most white female members left the association in 1869 (to start the National Woman Suffrage Association). After an unsuccessful struggle to include woman suffrage in the Fifteenth Amendment, the NAWSA completely disassociated itself from the black suffrage movement (Terborg-Penn 1978, 35).

Black women were divided on the issue as well. Some viewed the amendment as grounded in the attempt by black men to further oppress them. For others, the issue had little to do with black men securing the vote over women but rather with strategies that could best help black women achieve the rights as women they sought. Sojourner Truth and Frances E. Harper's positions on the matter exemplified the political split between black women. Though Truth and Harper agreed on issues of the black liberation struggle and women's equality, they disagreed on their feelings about the Fifteenth Amendment. Sojourner Truth voiced her disagreement at an 1867 AERA meeting, stating that black men's achieving voting rights would further the subjugation of black women: "There is a great stir about colored men getting their rights, but not a word about the colored woman . . . and if colored men get their rights, and not colored women theirs, you see the colored men will be masters over the women, and it will be just as bad as it was before" (qtd. in Giddings 1984, 65).

Though Harper was aware of sexist oppression by some black men, she felt that what stood in the way of black women's rights was not black men but racism—not only that of white men but that of white women. In 1869, two years after the speech by Truth before the AERA, Harper spoke in support of the Fifteenth Amendment (Giddings 1984, 60). Harper, standing with Douglass against Elizabeth Cady Stanton and Susan B. Anthony, said at the 1869 convention, "If intelligence, justice, and morality are to be placed in the government, then let the question of woman be brought up first and that of the Negro last." Harper held the opinion that racial solidarity was more important, stating, "[W]e [black women] let the lesser question of sex go. But the white women go all for sex, letting race occupy a minor position" (Giddings 1984, 60). For Harper womanhood was not enough to create solidarity between black and white women.

Harper perceived white suffragists' alliance with blacks (black men in particular) in the AERA as a matter of political expediency rather than of racial solidarity. As an officer of AERA, she had observed the politics of expediency at first hand. Over a period of three years, the fifty officers in AERA included only five blacks. And, while Harper and other black women critiqued black male sexism, Anthony and Stanton launched a vitriolic campaign against black men. Anthony wrote in the *Revolution*, the leading white feminist newspaper of the day, that "[w]hile the dominant party have with one hand lifted up TWO MILLION BLACK MEN and crowned them with the honor and dignity of citizenship, with the other they have dethroned FIFTEEN MILLION WHITE WOMEN—their own mothers and sisters, their own wives and daughters—and cast them under the heel of the lowest orders of manhood" (Giddings 1984, 66).

In addition to the explicit racist attitudes both Anthony and Stanton displayed, their campaign to defeat the Fifteenth Amendment was classist and anti-immigrant as well. Stanton, running for a congressional seat in New York, said that middle-class (white) women should be given voting rights to offset the political influence of poor immigrants: "In view of the fact that the Freedman of the South and the millions of foreigners now crowding our shores, most of whom represent neither property, education, nor civilization, are all in the progress of events to be enfranchised, the best interest of the nation demands that we outweigh this incoming pauperism, ignorance and degradation, with the wealth, education, and refinement of the women of the republic" (qtd. in Giddings 1984, 67). With its prerequisite education requirement for citizenship, Stanton not only excludes poor immigrants and all black men but also poor white women and men, as well as all black women in favor of wealthy, educated, and refined (white) "women of the republic." When criticized for her position, Stanton simply replied in the *Revolution*: "We prefer Bridget and Dinah at the ballot box to Patrick and Sambo" (Giddings 1984, 67).

Douglass defended his pro-Negro suffrage position before the AERA in 1869 on the grounds that the oppression of "women" had not reached the severity of that experienced by black men: "When women, because they are women, are dragged from their homes and hung upon lamp-posts; when their children are torn from their arms and their brains dashed out upon the pavement; when they are objects of insult and outrage at every turn; when they are in danger of having their homes burnt down over their heads; when their children are not allowed to enter schools; they will have an urgency to obtain the ballot" (Giddings 1984, 61). Douglass's political savvy is evident. He emphatically defends his position through an appeal to white suffragist sympathy for the plight of black men. In other words, if white women were in the same position as black men, as Douglass graphically illustrates, they too would "have an urgency to obtain the ballot." But as he insists, white women were not in the same position as black men. In soliciting white female support for black male suffrage, without directly offending white women on the grounds of racism, Douglass deracializes "women," while omitting a direct reference to black men as the objects of racist violence. In the passage above, deracialization works to mediate the rocky terrain of cross-race alliance. Only when someone (most likely black and female) in the audience where Douglass recited the lines above queried him about their application to black women did he revise his statement: "Yes, yes, yes, it is true of the black woman, but not because she is a woman but because she is black" (Giddings 1984, 67).

Douglass was partially correct in his response: race was a pivotal factor in black women's experience(s). However, what he failed to do was to link critically the impact of racism with the realities of their gender oppression. The debate on Negro suffrage continued until the passage of the Fifteenth Amendment in 1870. That year, at the National Women's Suffrage Association meeting held in Washington, D.C., Robert Purvis defended the woman suffrage position, demanding "for his daughter all he asked for his son or himself." Mary Shadd Cary, Charles Remond, and Sojourner Truth agreed with Purvis. Purvis's son Charles, with Frances E. Harper, sided with Douglass. At the same meeting, white women attacked black men on the grounds that their stance oppressed black women. Douglass and others saw this as a strategy to splinter the coalition between black men and women, and they held to the belief that rights for black women (struggling against the double oppression of race and sex) could be gained faster if they were tied to those of black men (Terborg-Penn 1978, 36). To maintain unity in the black liberation movement, the majority of black pro-womanists, certainly aware of the sexist implications of Negro suffrage rhetoric, supported Douglass. They, as Frances E. Harper had said, chose racial solidarity over female gender allegiance. Ruling-class white women's undeniably racist stance on the Fifteenth Amendment further plagued any notion of gender coalition across racial boundaries.

While Sojourner Truth's pro-woman stance on the Fifteenth Amendment created tension among black liberationists, black men and women continued to view her as a radical force for antiracist agitation. She was a delegate at the first National Convention on Women's Rights held in Worchester, Massachusetts, in 1850. There, amid the racist resistance of white women and men, she made her now famous "Ain't I a Woman?" address. She became the embodiment of the struggle of black women against sexist and racist oppression (A. Davis 1983, 60). Douglass (true to his word once black men had the vote) began campaigning for a sixteenth amendment that would guarantee woman's suffrage. He said, "[W]e know of no truth more easily made appreciable to human thought than the right of woman to vote . . ." (Foner 1952, 231). As a leading figure in the Negro suffrage campaign, Douglass had to curtail his woman-suffrage speaking engagements. A letter declining an invitation to speak at a woman suffrage meeting (addressed to Josephine Griffing, who had invited him) serves to reveal his skill in diplomacy, as he defends the political choice he made: "I am impelled by no lack of generosity in refusing to come to Washington to speak in behalf of woman's suffrage. The right of woman to vote is as sacred in my judgment as that of man and I am quite willing at any time to hold up both hands in favor of this right. It does not however follow that I can come to Washington or go elsewhere to deliver lectures upon this special subject" (McFeely 1991, 268).

Douglass, sensing the dilemma he placed himself in by rejecting the offer to speak before the convention of women, adopts a tone of high seriousness to underscore the high moral purpose of woman suffrage, and contrasts its "sacred" status to the harsh reality of the black American male who "is mobbed, beaten, shot, stabbed, hanged, burnt and is the target of all that is malignant in the North and all that is murderous in the South . . ." (McFeely 1991, 269). Douglass continues, "As you very well know, woman has a thousand ways to attach herself to the governing power of the land and already exacts honorable influence on the course of legislation. She is the victim of abuses, to be sure, but it cannot be pretended I think that her cause is as urgent as . . . ours" (269).

Presumptuously, Douglass assumed that all white women shared the same privilege and class power. Ironically, he concludes the letter to Griffing by criticizing Anthony and Stanton's position on Negro suffrage: "Their principle is: that no Negro shall be enfranchised while woman is not. Not considering that *white men* have been franchised always and *colored men* [emphasis added] have not. The conduct of these *white women*, whose husbands[,] fathers[,] and brothers are voters does not seem generous [emphasis added]" (McFeely 1991, 269). This passage highlights black women's absence in the complaint against racism and sexism he lodges. "White men," "colored men," and "white women" visibly act; black women remain invisible. William S. McFeely (commenting on what he believes is "patriarchal assurance" in the letter's tone) says, "[P]atriarchal or not[,] this was a realistic appraisal of the realities of 1868" (269). McFeely is correct.

Douglass's Discursive Relationship to Black Women

> Throughout his life, Douglass was obsessed with an eagerness to know about his origins—to know who he was.
>
> —William McFeely (1999, 8)

While Douglass abhorred the oppression of "woman," he was unwilling to sacrifice the political opportunities suffrage held for black men (and black women by default). As stated before, seldom in the woman suffrage texts did Douglass make any gender distinction between black female oppression and male oppression. The autobiographies reveal little about the lives of women (black or white) in his intimate life—though white women figure prominently in them politically. For example, in *Life and Times* (1885), he heralds the contribution of "woman" to black liberation. Clearly, in this instance "woman" does not include black woman: "When the true history of the Anti-Slavery cause shall be written, women will occupy a large space in its pages; for the cause of the slave has been peculiarly woman's cause. Her heart and conscience have supplied in large degree its motive and mainspring. Her skill, industry, patience, and perseverance have been wonderfully manifest in every trial hour . . . but her deep moral convictions, and her tender humane sensibilities, found convincing . . . expression by her pen and her voice" (Douglass [1892] 1962, 427).

The autobiographies span a period of forty-seven years (from the first publication of the *Narrative of the Life of Frederick Douglass, An American Slave* in 1845 to the final version, *Life and Times of Frederick Douglass*). Douglass biographers have noted that black women played a significant role in his personal life. For instance, his mother, Harriet Bailey, and his grandmother, Betsy, were women who impressed upon him their strength and resilience in withstanding the inhumanity of slavery. "His ascription both to [his grandmother] and to his mother of a bearing that would have fit men of dignity and accomplishment, is significant. . . . For the rest of his life Douglass looked to women as confidantes, companions, and sources of strength. They rather than men could be comprehended and counted on to be able" (McFeely 1991, 9).

The biographer William S. McFeely asserts that generally Douglass wrote little about women in the autobiographies—even about Anna, his wife of over forty years, who financially supported his escape from slavery. McFeely notes, "In the autobiographies she is introduced—and she is the first woman other than a relative or a child that we meet—virtually as an afterthought. . . . Douglass's books are barren of any hint about the development of his early emotional relationships with women other than relatives, real or surrogate" (66).

However, Jenny Franchot makes an incisive point about Douglass's relationship with black women having to do with his childhood recollection of their brutal treatment in slavery and the psychic violence it wreaked upon him as a young, impressionable child: "As he declares in his disturbing account of Aaron Anthony's whipping of Aunt Esther (Hester), his stunned childhood witness of the whipping has the force of 'revelation.' . . . A surrogate figure for Douglass's mother, Aunt Esther provides the author retrospective access to the recalcitrant interior of the past that closed within itself the parental relation. If slavery leaves him [in Douglass's own words] 'without an intelligible beginning in the world,' Esther's punishment, 'struck . . . with awful force,' obliterates any integral selfhood and imposes the new ontology of slavehood" (Franchot 1990, 149).

Franchot suggests that women's presence in the autobiographies diminished as Douglass became more self-conscious of his status as a public figure: "This shift from often impassioned descriptions of women in slavery to virtual silence about them in the comparative freedom of the North testifies to the repression of the feminine required by the *middle-class virility* [emphasis added] that Douglass emulated" (149). Not only did bourgeois notions of class respectability impact upon his ideas of manhood, but race was a germinal factor in a culture of white supremacy. As a slave, Douglass was barred from selfhood and manhood. In a patriarchal world where manhood and manliness were synonymous with self-possession, he had to escape slavery to become a man, literally (and literarily). Citing his growing contempt for life as a slave and preparation for escape, he writes in the first autobiography: "I began, with the commencement of the year, to prepare myself for a final struggle, which should decide my fate one way or the other. . . . I was fast approaching manhood, and year after year had passed, and I was still a slave" (Douglass [1845] 1982, 122). About the meaning freedom held for Douglass, the biographer Maria Diedrich writes,

"[H]e was a man who had invented himself, proving to the world that the victim could still be the agent of her or his personal history. He liked to see himself not only as an exceptional, as a self-made man, but also as a personification of all his race could achieve, of the potential of his race. An attitude combining egalitarian humanism with elitism, belief in human potential with disgust at human failure, had characterized Douglass' public statements since the beginning of his career . . ." (Diedrich 1999, 265).

From the early writings of the 1850s to his most mature statements on the equality of women through the 1890s, Douglass formulated a liberatory discourse as much about himself as about freedom's benefits, personally and politically. He argued for black male voting rights and equality for women, and in the process he created a discursive platform on which to display the qualities that characterized the persona of the self-made man he struggled to achieve. According to William Lloyd Garrison, Douglass possessed all that was needed to attain "manliness" (allowing him entrée into the inner circles of white liberals).

The qualities Garrison named not only qualified Douglass as a model of black manhood, they represent the same attributes he crafted to fuel the oratorical power of the woman suffrage texts. His first public, pro-woman speech, "Let Woman Take Her Own Right" (delivered on October 24, 1850, as an address given at the National Woman's Rights Convention in Worcester, Massachusetts) illustrates Douglass's "precept-by-example" approach to political agency. There, before Sojourner Truth, William Lloyd Garrison, Lucretia Mott, and others, Douglass asserted the idea that individuals must seize their due rights as he had done. Exhorting women to explore new territory, he said, "Let woman take her rights, and then she shall be free" (Blassingame et al. 1982, 249). From then on, his pro-woman texts embodied this call for self-determination, especially with regard to woman suffrage.

In 1853, Douglass gave a speech entitled "The Property Rights of Women" at a women's convention in Rochester, New York. It laid out the basic tenants of woman's rights—namely, that the oppression of women counteracted the principles of a democratic society, that sexism and racism worked against a system of universal natural laws governing human activity, and that sexism and racism stemmed from the same source of oppression, the disregard for human equality. Asserting his belief in woman suffrage, he underscored the importance of women's economic independence in marriage. Yet, he disagreed with a convention resolution calling for joint ownership of property between husband and wife. Douglass objected on the grounds that there were women who would take advantage of their (in)dependent status. In other words, he felt that women who relied on the security of their husbands' labor had no right to an equal share of their property (Blassingame et al. 1982, 249). Douglass did not clarify how an equitable structure of property disposition would operate for women who did not work outside the home.

In view of nineteenth-century pro-domestic views of women's place in society, Douglass (in exhorting women to seek economic independence) implied that women who labored in the home did not deserve the same rights as those who worked outside it. On the surface, his support of women's economic independence appeared incontestable. Yet, upon closer examination, the "fair treatment" speech of Douglass was rooted in traditional patriarchal notions of property ownership. Ironically, without stepping outside the boundaries of patriarchy, Douglass still challenged women (many who favored men's complete control of property matters) to question the nature of patriarchal laws on property rights. He believed, however, that women had to earn a living outside the home to receive equitable treatment in property disposition.

"Woman Suffrage," the next major statement of Frederick Douglass on women's rights, came after the breakdown of the American Equal Rights Association over the issue of Negro suffrage in 1869. "Woman Suffrage" appeared (on October 20, 1870), in the *New National Era*, the newspaper Douglass founded in 1870, which became the vehicle for his renewed campaign for woman's suffrage. The first edition carried its motto: "Right is of no sex." "This slogan," Waldo Martin says, "encapsulated Douglass's ethical, civic, and political rationales for sexual equality" (1984, 145). The text begins by undermining the logic of slavery and emphasizes the importance of the antislavery movement, advocating the general rights of all Americans to have voice in government affairs. Martin remarks, "Douglass's feminism, like his abolitionism, signified a struggle to foster human emancipation as a means toward human understanding and unity" (249). From the broad discussion of human rights, the thematic emphasis of "Woman Suffrage" shifts to a discussion of the basic logic of women's right to vote and then to its similarity to the right of blacks to be free. Appealing to reason, Douglass says, "Now we know of no truth more easily made appreciable to human thought than the right of woman to vote, or in other words, to have a voice in the Government under which she lives and to which she owes allegiance. The very admission that woman owes allegiance, implies her right to vote . . ." (Foner 1955, 231–32).

That women are governed without consent constitutes what Douglass sees as unjust and inhumane treatment. Taking into account the rightness of woman's suffrage, he establishes his argument in a belief in the "natural" order of things. The proof of women's qualifications to vote was evident in a system of natural laws, which superseded patriarchal ones that were themselves the source of women's oppression. To Douglass, the universe was constructed on a system of "great truths," based on three principles: individuality, rationality, and accountability. In these, women's right to vote has legitimacy (Foner 1955, 232). Given the fact that woman (like man) is a rational, moral being and possesses the ability to choose, she then has a natural right to vote, because the ability to choose constitutes a natural function in human beings. Douglass says, "Our natural powers are the foundation of our natural rights, and it is a consciousness of powers which suggests the exercise of rights" (Foner 1955, 232). He employs the appeal to reason as a rhetorical stance to defend the logic of women's rights. According to Douglass, human rights have validity in their "Naturalness." Supporting Douglass in this argument, Waldo Martin observes, "Woman's exclusion from the United States government constituted a blatant violation of the Lockean contractual view of human government as a compact entered into freely and explicitly by individuals to protect their natural rights. The United States was obviously not a democratic republic with respect to the rights of women" (Martin 1984, 149).

In his appeal to reason as the correct path to comprehending the right of woman suffrage, again Douglass makes an emphatic link between the disenfranchisement of woman even under a governing system of benevolent patriarchy and the benign power wielded by "good" slave masters:

> A despotism is no less a despotism because the reigning despot may be a wise and good man. The principle is unaffected by the character of the man who for the moment may represent it. He may be kind or cruel, benevolent or selfish, in any case he rules according to his own sovereign will—and precisely such is the theoretical relation of our American Government toward woman. It simply takes her money without asking her consent and spends the same without in any wise consulting her wishes. It tells her that there is a code of laws which men have made, and which she must obey or she must suffer the consequences. She is absolutely in the hands of her political master: and though these may be kind and tender hearted, (*the same was true of individual slave masters, as before stated,*) . . . [emphasis added]. (Foner 1955, 232)

"Woman Suffrage" displays Douglass's command of logic, refined rhetorical skill, and expertise as a political strategist. As a self-possessed man of high intellect, Douglass writes to make a case for the rationality of women's rights and, at the same time, to justify himself as a model of black manhood. While a critique of white male privilege is never overtly present as such in the text, he wrought a subtle critique of patriarchy that interrogated the political power elite white men held over all white women as well as over black women and men. Obviously, Douglass wanted to avoid a clash with white men who opposed voting rights for women but supported the antislavery movement (and Negro suffrage when the time came). Rather than lodging a direct protest against white male supremacy, Douglass defended the worthiness of women to participate in politics. Women's ability to make intelligent choices indicated the principle of accountability: it "gives [them] a *natural* right to choose the legislators who are to frame the laws under which [they are] to live, and the requirements of which [they are] bound to obey" (Foner 1955, 233). He maintained that this could not be disputed, because it already possessed validity in reasonable deduction.

By justifying the right of suffrage for woman as a human right, Douglass by implication set up the debate for the "naturalness" of black male suffrage. The following passage is an apt example: "[T]here can be no natural prohibition of such action on [women's] part. Usage, custom, and deeply rooted prejudices are against woman's freedom. They have been against man's freedom, national freedom, religious freedom, but these will all subside *in the case of woman as well as elsewhere* [emphasis added]. The thought has already been conceived; the word has been spoken; the debate has already begun" (Foner 1955, 233).

Douglass knew his readers would know the case for freedom could be applied "elsewhere"—namely, to the black liberation struggle. The final pronouncement of "Woman Suffrage" is an appeal to truth: "[N]obody need fear [its] result. The truth can hurt nothing which ought not to be hurt, and it alone can make men and women free" (Foner 1955, 233). Having founded the justification for woman suffrage upon the indisputable laws of nature, rather than upon those legislated by elite white men, Douglass redefined the *nature* of gender laws—revealing the governance of a universal higher power. Every individual, according to Douglass, had a right to draw on it.

One week after the publication of "Woman Suffrage," Douglass published "Woman and the Ballot" (October 27, 1870), a continuation of the earlier text. Further expounding upon the need for woman's suffrage, he used an analogy based on society's right to cause or protect itself from injury: he compared the exclusion of women from the voting process to an individual's self-infliction of injury. To exercise such a right did not inform nor exhibit "enlightened reason" (Foner 1955, 235). Douglass applied the same set of principles to the sexist prohibition of woman suffrage. His argument exposed the fallaciousness of a position held by a society that knowingly cripples itself by refusing to grant women the right to vote.

"Woman and the Ballot" continued a subversive critique of white male power and elaborated on the idea that natural laws are superior to man's and constitute the most just guides to human behavior. The word "nature" (or some form of it) appears in fifteen different instances in the essay—*naturalizing* "human rights," "power," "respect," "dignity," "law, "gentleness," and "forbearance." Douglass redefines these terms according to a more just consideration of humanity, particularly in the case of women. Suggesting women's superiority to men, he attributed to womanhood the power of "natural" instinct, which he said men lacked because they were not as close to nature as women. On the one hand, Douglass asserted the idea to affirm women's right to suffrage. On the other, the same statement could be marshalled against women rights, by using it to argue women's inferiority. His defense of feminine instinct rests on the premise that women, to be equal to men, must be superior to them by possessing inherent qualities that men do not. Like other woman suffragists of his day, Douglass did not fully challenge the sexist ideology inherent in Victorian notions of womanhood. Waldo Martin makes a similar observation: "Given the omnipresence of sexual inequality, it was understandable, albeit ironic, that nineteenth-century feminists, like Douglass, used what they interpreted as natural differences between male and female personalities as arguments to promote sexual equality. This advocacy of sexual equality extended widely over the political and social terrain without seriously calling into question the crux of woman's oppression: her inability to escape the confines of her familial and domestic identity" (Martin 1984, 142).

A number of women in the movement for female equality during the time objected to the patriarchal notion that woman's place was in the home. Some of the most outspoken opponents of women as "naturally" domesticated came from black women. The rise of the black Women's Club Movement (in the last decade of the nineteenth century) had a significant impact in dismantling the cult of true womanhood. A survey of 108 black women club members showed that most of them were educated, and the majority of the educated ones were teachers or businesswomen. Though three-fourths were married, only one-fourth had become mothers. They believed in the career-oriented woman. According to Anna Julia Cooper, working outside the home "renders woman less dependent on the marriage relation for physical support (which by the way, does not always accompany it)" (qtd. in Giddings 1984, 108). Cooper without reserve said that women should not be "compelled to look to sexual love as the one sensation capable of giving tone and relish, movement and vim to the life she leads. Her horizon is extended" (qtd. in Giddings 1984, 109). The National Association of Colored Women's periodical, the *Woman's Era*, in 1894 declared that "not all women are intended for mothers. Some of us have not the temperament for family life. . . . Clubs will make women think seriously of their future lives, and not make girls think their only alternative is to marry" (Giddings 1984, 108).

Douglass stood on much surer ground when he shifted his argument to a defense of woman suffrage predicated upon her intellectual fitness and its connection to the aims of democracy. He reasoned that the "grand idea of American liberty" (Foner 1955, 236) is compatible with the idea of universal suffrage, which is indicative of universal intelligence. "Without the latter," Douglass said, "the former falls to the ground; and unless suffrage is made co-extensive with intelligence something of the natural power of society to its guidance and well-being is lost" (Foner 1955, 236). He believed that the nation had failed to govern its citizens intelligently, and in "Woman and the Ballot," as in "Woman Suffrage," he made allusions to the injustices of slavery as examples of the absence of intelligence and reason in the very existence of the institution. And as Douglass had done before, he alluded to slavery to make a stronger defense for woman suffrage.

Once again, the strength of the woman suffrage discourse Douglass employed resides in its power to illustrate the analogous relationship between the inherent racism of slavery and the indisputable wrongheadedness of sexism in the denial of women's voting rights. His view of the state of the world and its problems was directly related to men's exclusion of women from the governing process: "Man in his arrogance has hitherto felt himself fully equal to the work of governing of the world without the help of woman. . . . He has made human history a history of war and blood even until now" (Foner 1955, 236). According to Douglass, women's participation in government could have had a significant impact on the course of history. However, when discoursing on gender difference, he took a more traditional, patriarchal position: "To nothing more than war is woman more *instinctively* [emphasis added] opposed" (236). He also says, "The vote of woman is essential to the peace of the world. Her hand and voice *naturally* [emphasis added] rises against the shedding of human blood" (237). That women "instinctively" and "naturally" objected to war was another myth perpetuated in the cult of womanhood ideology.

Douglass also appealed to "weaker sex" logic in his critique of Southern white women's racism. He believed their racist attitudes were the result of "slavery impart[ing] something of its own blood-thirsty spirit to women in the South . . . [having] led some women to consent to the slaughter of their children and to the destruction of themselves . . ." (237). He observed this to be the exception to women's general behavior and felt that Southern women's attitude toward war did not alter "the *natural* [emphasis added] gentleness and forbearance of the sex as a whole. She [woman] naturally shudders at the thought of subjecting her loved ones to the perils and horrors of war, and her vote would be a peace guaranty to the world" (237).

It is clear that Douglass addressed sexual difference in a manner that advantaged woman by placing her on a higher moral plane than man. In reality, he was more convincing in "Woman and the Ballot" when applying *natural* principles to the cause of human rights than those of women's rights. Moreover, he built a more valid case for woman suffrage in arguing against society's ill reasoning in denying voting rights to women than in his argument for female moral superiority. The argument against denying voting rights to women reveals the relationship between the essential right of women to vote and the power of elite white men to withhold it. "To deny woman her vote," he continued, "is to abridge her natural and social power, and deprive her of a certain measure of respect" (Foner 1955, 237). He believed a lack of self-respect and feelings of inferiority plagued women as a result of their exclusion from the voting process.

While "Woman and the Ballot" maintains there is an analogy between the struggle for black liberation and the battle for woman suffrage (waged by middle-class white women), it did make clear certain differences between them, particularly when Douglass defended the cause of the slave. He wrote, "Woman has not fallen so low as the slave in the scale of being, (her education and her natural relation to the ruling power rendering such degradation impossible)" (Foner 1955, 237). In this passage, Douglass's audience could only be middle-class white women. Few black women in the nineteenth century shared the same relationship "to the ruling power" as certain white women. In fact, the lack of black women's "natural" relation to that power rendered their "degradation" possible. Douglass did not interrogate gender difference between black men and black women's oppression; nor did he question economic differences between white men and white women. Yet "Woman and the Ballot" makes a sound case for women's political self-representation: "Let her represent herself. This is the simplest and surest mode of representation. The old slave-holders used to represent the slaves, the rich landowners of other countries represent the poor, and the men in our country claim to represent woman, but the true doctrine of American liberty plainly is, that each class and each individual of class should be allowed to represent himself—that taxation and representation should go together" (Foner 1955, 238). Douglass not only rejected the idea that all women were protected and represented adequately through the existing voting rights, but also refused the idea that they should determine the destiny of black people. This was the reasoning behind his stand on black male suffrage—a major step in black liberation. While he called into question "woman's" obvious lack of representation under patriarchy in agitating for Negro suffrage, he knew that it would have been political suicide to criticize white male supremacy openly. He knew that his allegiance to the woman suffrage movement could have alienated potential white male supporters for black male voting rights (given that elite white men were the ones who had created the laws that excluded white women from the voting process). He also knew that radical white male Republican support for Negro suffrage had provided him the necessary power to secure its passage. Diedrich says, "Douglass had forced an alliance, and the radical Republicans had found a powerful and loyal companion who would campaign well for them and the policy on race relations they represented—however reluctantly. . . . How else could he maintain his personal dignity; how else could he wield political influence; how else could he continue the civil rights battles that needed to be fought? It was a tactic of survival for a man who knew that the battle could not be fought by African-Americans alone" (Diedrich 1999, 272).

The fact that the Constitution excluded women from consideration did not concern Douglass nearly as much as the desire to obtain suffrage for black men, who in his mind would (after securing it) be in a better position to help black women. But Douglass could not assure black women that by coalescing with white women, they would have a better chance of obtaining the vote. After all, white woman suffragists had shown discrimination against black women in the movement prior to the passage of the Fifteenth Amendment. Hazel Carby notes: "Individual white women helped publish and promote individual black women, but the texts of black women from ex-slave Harriet Jacobs to educator Anna Julia Cooper are testaments to the racist practices of the suffrage and temperance movements and indictments of the ways in which white women allied themselves not with black women but with a racist patriarchal order against all black people" (1987, 6).

There were black suffragists (female and male) who were skeptical about benefits the Fifteenth Amendment would hold for black women. However, Douglass believed that obtaining the right to vote for black men was better than having no voting privileges for blacks at all. He ended "Woman and the Ballot" with a gesture of conciliation urging black support for woman suffrage: "[O]nly recently [were blacks] lifted into the privileges of complete American citizenship . . ." (Foner 1955, 238).

Douglass and the Question of Men's Place and Voice in Woman(ist) Space

After the publication of "Woman Suffrage" and "Woman and the Ballot," perhaps the most important address Douglass made was before the 1888 Woman Suffrage Association convention. Between 1870 to1888, Douglass had revised much of his thinking on women and their struggle for equality. His address "The Woman's Suffrage Movement" (which appeared in the *Woman's Journal*, April 14, 1888) displayed certain readjustments in the pro-woman stance Douglass adopted, recognizing the power of male gender privilege. Infused with a tone of humility, the address focuses on a reconsideration of his and other men's place in the struggle for women's equality. Critically pointing out the presence of men at the convention, Douglass publicly revealed his uneasiness about men being there. Even as he perceived the presence of men as an encroachment upon a space made for women, he qualified his own inclusion by noting that he had been invited to speak. He, nevertheless, reiterated that men should have close to nothing to say or do in this woman-identified location: "Men have very little business here as speakers, anyhow[,] and if they come here at all *they should take back benches and wrap themselves in silence* [emphasis added]. For this is an International Council, not of men, but of women, and woman should have all the say in it. This is her day in court" (Foner 1955, 449). For the first time in his writings on the equality of women, Douglass admitted that the idea of a *male* woman suffragist posed certain problems, particularly in men speaking on behalf of women.

The vulnerability Douglass exhibited in "The Woman's Suffrage Movement" makes it the most self-revealing text among his pro-woman writings. The speech shows a more insightful Douglass consciously struggling to question privileges he has gained in the woman suffrage movement as a male ally. Rather than the *self*-promoter, we observe a man who is critically thinking about how even his presence might be a barrier to female solidarity. In "The Woman's Suffrage Movement," Douglass seems to have realized that the voice of male authority in the earlier woman suffrage writings had sometimes detracted from the power of their argument, though he does not provide us with specific references. Perhaps, more than anything, Douglass had come to understand that as much as he believed in women's equality, he had not been its best spokesperson.

Reaffirming the importance of women's self-representation, Douglass repeated from "Woman and the Ballot" a slightly altered version of the statement on who should speak for women. Douglass said, "Woman knows and feels her wrongs as man cannot know and feel them. . . ." He added, "She is her own best representative. We can [not] speak for her . . ." (Foner 1955, 449). "The Woman's Suffrage Movement" is free from many of the masculinist trappings of the earlier texts, but Douglass's continued commitment to woman suffrage remained fixed on its relevance to the black liberation struggle. "I say of her as I say of the colored people: 'Give her fair play, and hands off' " (Foner 1955, 449).

The rhetorical movement of this last address proceeds with Douglass reminiscing on the early stages of the woman suffrage movement, back to the 1848 Seneca Falls convention. It had been then that Douglass believed the movement needed the help of men most. "Now," he said, "it can afford to dispense with me and all my sex" (Foner 1955, 449). Acknowledging Elizabeth Cady Stanton and Susan B. Anthony, both present at the convention,

Douglass praised Stanton as president of the Woman Suffrage Association and attested to his admiration of her work. In this way, his speech took on a twofold purpose. The first was to praise the perseverance of the association and its leaders in developing the cause women's equality beyond the stage of proof to a place of "firm and inflexible assertion" (450). The second was to show himself in a different, more self-introspective light. At this point, the speech shifted to a celebratory tone as Douglass marked the occasion as the fortieth anniversary of the first woman suffrage convention. In so doing, he elevated the woman suffrage struggle above other movements for peace, temperance, and even the abolition of slavery. His justification was that women's oppression manifested itself in forms much more subtle and pervasive than any other. In the following passage, Douglass describes woman's state of "innocence" under patriarchal domination: "[E]verything in her condition was supposed to be lovely, just as it should be. She had no rights denied, no wrongs to redress. She herself had no suspicion but that all was going well with her. She floated along on the tide of life as her mother and grandmother had done before her, as in a dream of Paradise. Her wrongs if she had any, were too occult to be seen, and too light to be felt" (Foner 1955, 451). Woman emerges from "this delightful dream" through the guidance of a "daring voice and determined hand awake[ning] her from this delightful dream and call[ing] the nation to account for the right and opportunities of which it was depriving her" (451).

The scene focuses on Stanton as the liberator of women. Praising himself among women suffragists Douglass continues, "It was well understood at the beginning that woman would not thank *us* [emphasis added] for disturbing her by this call to duty, and it was known that man would denounce and scorn us for such a daring innovation upon the established order of things. But this did not appall or delay the word and work" (Foner 1955, 451).

In this moment, more than anything in life (with black male suffrage having been obtained) he wanted to be remembered in history as a devoted supporter of the woman suffrage movement. And from this standpoint he concluded his speech by directly addressing Stanton herself:

> There are few facts in my humble history to which I look back with more satisfaction than to the fact, recorded in the history of the Woman Suffrage Movement, that I was sufficiently enlightened at that early day, and when only a few years from slavery, to support your resolution for woman suffrage. I have done very little in this world in which to glory except this one act—and I certainly glory in that. When I ran away from slavery, it was for myself; when I advocated emancipation, it was for my

> people; *but when I stood up for the rights of woman, self was out of the question, and I found a little nobility in the act* [emphasis added]." (Foner 1955, 452)

"The Woman's Suffrage Movement" would be the last speech Douglass would deliver before a convention of woman suffragists. He concludes it in reflection on the course of his life—as a runaway slave (to gain freedom), as an abolitionist (speaking on behalf of the necessity of freedom for all blacks in the United States), and as a man advocating woman suffrage (a position from which he denounced the oppression of women). Of all that he had done and had become in life, Douglass found his place as "a woman's-rights man" in the struggle for woman suffrage to be one of his greatest and most humbling achievements. Connecting the sense of himself as a "self-made man" to the idea of being a committed supporter of woman suffrage, Douglass not only came to believe that the liberatory power of the movement for women's equality was as important as the freedom he had attained in escaping the institution of slavery, but also conceived to be inextricably linked to black liberation.

With W. E. B. Du Bois, the *black* mother holds an esteemed place of endearment, and the same is true with Douglass. However, the place of the "father" in the mind of both men constitutes an image of absence. There is no presence of the father figure in the feminist writings of Douglass or Du Bois except in the critique of patriarchy and of the use of male power against women. In the autobiographical (con)texts of Douglass and Du Bois, the *black* woman is idealized in the image of motherhood. While on the political level, the pro-woman(ist) texts of both men argue eloquently *for* the equality of women, on the personal level they speak to Douglass and Du Bois's passionate regard for the *black mother*. For both Douglass and Du Bois, the feminist impulse informing the position they held on the necessity of women's rights is traceable to the *presence* and deep signification of the *black feminine* in their formative years. However, as the next chapter and the two following it demonstrate, in the gender-progressive texts of Du Bois the ideology of race is inseparable from the gendered condition of the black woman/mother.

3

W. E. B. Du Bois

"The Leading Male Feminist of His Time" and "Most Passionate Defender of Black Women"

> [T]he race question is at bottom simply a matter of the ownership of women. . . .
>
> —W. E. B. Du Bois (1922, 201–2)

> All this of woman,—but what of black woman?
>
> —W. E. B. Du Bois ([1920] 1969, 165)

> The uplift of women is, next to the problem of the color line and the peace movement, our greatest modern cause. When, now, two of these movements—woman and color—combine in one, the combination has deep meaning.
>
> —W. E. B. Du Bois ([1920] 1969, 181)

Frederick Douglass did not live to see the passage of woman suffrage in 1920. W. E. B. Du Bois would. While both wrote extensively on the necessity of women's right to vote, their approach differed significantly. Whereas Douglass had previously perfected a discourse of woman's "natural right" suffrage that simultaneously deracialized and universalized "woman," Du Bois strategically concentrated on black women's battle for racial equality. As this chapter demonstrates, in "The Damnation of Women," his most passionate defense of black womanhood, he crafted a vision of women's liberation that simultaneously examined and denounced both gender and racial oppression. From this overtly racialized standpoint, Du Bois addressed the impact of sexism on all classes of women.

In *When and Where I Enter: The Impact of Black Women on Race and Sex in America*, Paula Giddings declares that "W.E.B. Du Bois . . . took Frederick Douglass's place as the *leading male feminist of his time* . . . [emphasis added]" (1984, 121). And in *Daughters of Sorrow: Attitudes toward Black Women, 1880–1920*, a text whose title comes from Du Bois's 1920 essay "The Damnation of Women," Beverly Guy-Sheftall records the germinal place of his work in her own: "This study was inspired by my reading of W. E. B. Du Bois who was, in my opinion, the most passionate defender of black women, to whom he referred as 'daughters of sorrow' . . ." (1990, 13). Moreover, she states, "Only Du Bois, the most outspoken feminist among the group [of black men] examined, felt compelled to devote his life's work to the emancipation of blacks *and* women" (161).

Du Bois and the Vindication of Black Womanhood

W. E. B. Du Bois never ceased to champion the right of women to vote. He launched a campaign for women's rights devoted to the political, social, and economic empowerment of black women. Not only was his conception of antiracist resistance feminist-inspired, but his worldview was profoundly influenced by black women. Nellie McKay examines the personal impact they had upon Du Bois and concludes, "More than any other black man in our history, his three autobiographies demonstrate that black women [were] central to the development of his intellectual thought" (1990, 229).

In 1920, the year women won the right to vote, he published what surely may be taken as his womanist manifesto on the rights of women, "The Damnation of Women." In it Du Bois proclaimed, "To no modern race does its women mean so much as to the Negro nor come so near to the fulfillment of its meaning" ([1920] 1969, 173). In these words, he directly echoed (as well as quoted directly in the text) the revolutionary proclamation of the black feminist activist Anna Julia Cooper, who in 1892, over thirty years before, articulated the necessity of a conjoined struggle for black liberation: "Only the black woman can say when and where I enter, in the quiet, undisputed dignity of my womanhood, without violence and without suing or special patronage, then and there the whole Negro race enters with me" (173). In the spirit of her pronouncement, Du Bois would say, "Every argument for Negro suffrage is an argument for woman's suffrage; every argument for woman's suffrage is an argument for Negro suffrage; both are great movements in democracy" (*Crisis* 9 [April 1915]: 285). At the core of this statement lies the principled foundation of Du Bois's feminist standpoint: the belief in the coterminous relationship between democratic movements for race and gender rights.

Just as Du Bois was influenced by Anna Julia Cooper, so a generation of black men committed to the eradication of sexism have had their vision of womanhood, manhood, and masculinity changed by black women feminist/womanist scholars, teachers, mothers, sisters, friends, and lovers. Thus, as pro-woman(ist) men, the antisexist activist work we perform is historically linked to that of Du Bois. His work as a womanist/feminist and the unyielding support of equal rights for black women he voiced exemplifies the depth of his political commitment to them. The extraordinary manner in which Du Bois employed the antiracist movement to press the case for woman suffrage had not been witnessed in the black liberation struggle since the campaign Frederick Douglass had begun in the 1870s. Douglass also surely inspired Du Bois, as Jean Fagan Yellin notes in "DuBois' *Crisis* and Woman's Suffrage": "The coupling of rights for women with rights for black people was not new. Du Bois educated his readers in the history of the struggle for the franchise by both groups in September, 1912, in the first special issue of *The Crisis*. His central theme is suggested on the cover, which features a portrait of Frederick Douglass and the message, 'Woman's Suffrage Number' " (1973, 367).

As the founding editor of *The Crisis*, from 1910 to 1935, Du Bois envisioned a movement for black liberation struggle in which gender and racial oppression were to be fought on equal fronts. Over the course of twenty years, *The Crisis* functioned as a political platform from which Du Bois launched a sustained attack against racism and sexism as they impacted the lives of both black and white women. As stated earlier, unlike Frederick Douglass, Du Bois strategized woman suffrage and female equality from a standpoint grounded in the lived experiences of black women. "[W]hen the triumph of woman's suffrage was imminent," Yellin observes, "DuBois repeatedly addressed himself to black women, urging them to prepare themselves to vote" (374). And it is "The Damnation of Women" that articulates the foundational ideas of his womanist beliefs. Relating an affinity for African goddess mythology to the deep affection he bore for black women, Du Bois imaginatively recoups the idea of ancestral female power to construct a vision of modern black womanhood. The essay at once laments the condition of black women he had known from his childhood, while celebrating the heroic achievement of black women in U.S. history. It praises black motherhood, while elaborating the devastating interrelated effects of race and sex discrimination on all mothers. Defying Western ideas of female beauty, it exposes their damning consequences on black and white women, while asserting the superiority of an African feminine mystique.

"The Damnation of Women" reads as a personal narrative of the evolution of a black man's journey toward the advocacy of women's rights through the politicization of the personal. In the childhood recollection of four women, Du Bois laid the foundation for a sustained critique of all women's oppression. And the adult views he held on womanhood have much to do with how he perceived the ways race and sex had determined the experience of his own mother as a black woman. "There can be little doubt that Du Bois's remarkable regard for women, especially black women, had its roots in his deep regard for his mother," asserts Arnold Rampersad ([1976] 1990, 4). The vindication of black motherhood and its liberatory relation to the idea of "woman" form a central trope in the evolution of a Du Boisian feminist nationalism. Its use as a political location from which Du Bois could call out the racial and economic subjugation of the black mother reminds us how crucial her representation was in the formation of his African-centered ideology concerning the black woman. For him, motherhood embodied the essence of black womanhood, which he idealized in the form of the mythological African goddess Neith, his universal symbol of maternality.

In fact, Du Bois's critique of women's oppression originated in a cultural nationalism rooted in African mythology popularized in the early 1900s.[1] By the early twentieth century, black women liberationists had articulated their platform in the concept of "racial uplift," frequently alluding to Africa as a source of inspiration. During the Harlem Renaissance, Amy Jacques Garvey, the feminist writer for the *Negro World*—the official journal of the Universal Negro Improvement Association (founded by her husband Marcus Garvey)—voiced an African nationalist stance to protest what she saw was a lack of black male political agency: "Mr. Black Man watch your step! Ethiopia's queens will reign again, and her Amazons protect her shores and people. Strengthen your shaking knees and move forward, or we will displace you and lead on to victory and glory" (qtd. in Matthews 1979, 12). Her symbolic representation of black women (as Ethiopian queens protecting the land) placed them in a heroic position, one that Du Bois replicated in his version of feminist nationalism.

Few black feminists of his day would have taken issue with an African-identified portrayal of themselves. They had already begun to redefine black womanhood in nationalist terms in the late nineteenth century. Critically aware that gender-based inequity operated across racial, political, and economic divisions, he spoke both universally and in racially specific terms when necessary. But Du Bois never lost sight of the race/gender oppression black women experienced. Never assuming the universality of the meaning of "woman," he asked: "All this of woman,—what of black woman?" ([1920] 1969, 165).

Where the Personal, Political, and Poetical Merge: Du Bois and the Idealization of the Black Mother

> Their beauty,—their dark and mysterious beauty of midnight eyes, crumpled hair, and soft, full-featured faces—is perhaps more to me

than to you, *because I was born to its warm and subtle spell* [emphasis added]; but their worth is yours as well as mine.

—W. E. B. Du Bois ([1920] 1969, 185–86)

Despite the struggle for women's rights . . . the majority of black men, like their white male counterparts, were reluctant to challenge accepted notions of True womanhood. Doing so would free black women to develop their full potential. Instead, they wished that black women could climb on the pedestal and take their rightful place beside white women.

—Beverly Guy-Sheftall (1990, 160)

In writing "The Damnation of Women" to marshal an incisive critique against the racist and sexist treatment of black women, Du Bois used his critical acumen as a sociologist, journalist, litterateur, and cultural critic to challenge the damaging effects of racism and sexism in the lives of women. Stylistically, the essay may be characterized as a womanist pastiche that illustrates the writer's rhetorical skill in blending literary forms. Couched in autobiography, the treatise on the rights of women strategically integrates sociopolitical discourse with poetic prose to create a more intimate form to politicize the condition of women in Du Bois's personal life. In this manner, the autobiographical and political become one, producing a style often associated with a number of feminist writers today.

Du Bois frequently lifted images of heroic black women from his extensive body of autobiographical texts. He put to use cultural and political history to create his own brand of literary social realism, as represented in his first novel, *The Quest of the Silver Fleece* (1911), perhaps the feminist-inspired source of "The Damnation of Women." The portraits of women open the essay. Their sensuous, poetic stylization is reflected in the emphasis on their skin color ranging from dark to light. While differing in skin tone, they share in common their oppression as women. They represent the dispossessed, powerless, and *self*less—women Du Bois recalled from his childhood:

I remember four women of my boyhood: my mother, cousin Inez, Emma, and Ide Fuller. They represented the problem of the widow, the wife, the maiden, and the outcast. They were, in color, brown and light brown, yellow with brown freckles and white. *They existed not for themselves, but for men; they were named after the men to whom they were related and not after the fashion of their own souls* [emphasis added]. They were not beings, they were relations and these relations were enfilmed with mystery and secrecy. We did not know the truth or believe it

> when we heard it. Motherhood! What was it? We did not know or greatly care. ([1920] 1969, 163)

In the passage above, he began a critique of the devaluation of womanhood and motherhood through the relationship of domestic subjugation. Questioning the foundation of patriarchal power and its relation to the family, Du Bois argued that female *self*-possession lay sacrificed to the will of the "father." In other words, a woman's worth and status in society was always already measured by her domestic and maternal service. But even as Du Bois mounted a strategic attack against the devaluation of motherhood and the racist dehumanization of the black mother, like other black and white feminists in the woman suffrage movement he remained wedded to the cult of true womanhood. "Though very few men in the history of America were as opposed to male supremacy as was Du Bois," Guy-Sheftall maintains, "even he was not totally free of conventional ideas about women's roles, especially where domesticity was concerned. Du Bois can also illustrate how one can be in favor of equal rights for women but still hold tenaciously to the ideology of motherhood" (1990, 72).

But Du Bois held to the notion that women should not have to choose between a career and motherhood. As much as he extolled the virtues of the maternal, he staunchly supported the economic independence of women. Acknowledging the limitations of conventional motherhood, he maintained that for women who chose it, it most often meant "[the] sacrifice of intelligence and the chance to do their best work. . . . This is the damnation of women. All womanhood is hampered today because the world on which it is emerging is a world that tries to worship both virgins and mothers and in the end despises motherhood and despoils virgins" ([1920] 1969, 164).

He also denounced the prevailing attitude that a woman had to choose one over the other; he believed she had the right to achieve economic security through her own work and the right to become a mother if she so desired. "The future woman," he insisted, "must have a life work and economic independence. She must have the right of motherhood at her own discretion" (164). He cited poverty as the main determining factor in her victimization, and boldly asserted that the path to female self-autonomy was obstructed by three things: marriage, prostitution ("to what men call shame"), and "to that which is more evil than nothing"—the refusal of men to accept women as capable of being intelligent, productive individuals as well as being mothers at the same time (164).

Yet the fact remains that the womanist politics of "The Damnation of Women" reside in a defense of black womanhood rendered almost entirely through the idealization of motherhood—sometimes liberatory, at other times not. Filtered through childhood memories of black mothers, the representation of maternal womanhood in the text was drawn chiefly from the iconographic image of his mother: "with all her soft brownness—the brown velvet of her skin, the sorrowful black-brown of her eyes, and the tiny brown-capped waves of her midnight hair as it lay parted on her forehead" (168). Repeatedly, black womanhood and femininity are measured against the maternal in the text. Du Bois's understanding of it rested on an unwavering respect for black women. For him, their "instinctively pure" nature originated in a familial relationship that was female-identified: "I have known the women of many lands and nations,—I have known and seen and lived beside them but none have I known more sweetly feminine, more unswervingly loyal, more desperately earnest, *and more instinctively pure in body and in soul than the daughters of my black mothers* [emphasis added]" (186).

Black women, "the daughters of my black mothers," are depicted here as models of womanhood, standing above all other women. "The Damnation of Women" is a paean to black motherhood defying its racist exploitation. Working against white supremacist notions of womanhood, Du Bois constructs a black nationalist version of the maternal. Attesting to the courage of black women in the face of slavery's horrific effect upon their lives, he declares, "I most sincerely doubt if any other race of women could have brought its fineness up through so devilish a fire" (171). Well aware of the fact that even after the end of slavery black women exercised little control over their bodies, either as workers and/or childbearers, he praised their resiliency: "They [were] asked to be efficient, to be strong, fertile, muscled, and able to work" (184). In praising black women's will to survive, Du Bois elevated the black mother to a mythic level, creating a racialized reversal of the pedestalized Southern belle. In dismantling one stereotype, however, Du Bois reified another in the myth of the "superwoman," a symbol of strength, self-sacrificing, and long-suffering.[2]

Du Bois sets up a (race/class) double standard between black and white women in which he views the maternal as "instinctively" black, Southern, lower-class, and innocent. Ultimately, for Du Bois the question of female liberation is one integrally connected to "married motherhood," a preferred condition for women religiously and morally: "God send us a world with woman's freedom and *married motherhood* [emphasis added] inextricably wed, but until He sends it, I see more of future promise in the betrayed girl-mothers of the black belt than the childless wives of the white North, and I have more respect for the colored servant *who yields to her frank longing for motherhood* [emphasis added] than for her white sister who offers up children for clothes" ([1920] 1969, 184). Comparing the life of a married white woman of the North to that of an "[unwed] colored servant" from the South, Du Bois has nothing but admiration for her "yield[ing] to her frank longing for motherhood." There is only castigation for her childless "white sister" who chooses materialistic pleasure over that of motherhood. In both instances, he ironically glosses over the economic implications of childbearing for a woman—wed or unwed, black or white. Furthermore, the reinscription of certain racist as well as sexist notions of childbearing onto the bodies of black women undercuts any attempt to create a truly liberatory image of them. But rather than a further interrogation of the impact of class on motherhood across race, Du Bois privileges cultural nationalism, mythology, and symbolism over women's material condition in order to protect the image of black womanhood from racist denigration.

Thus, in "The Damnation of Women" the affirmation of black women comes as praise for their status as mothers, precisely because Du Bois believed that they had suffered most in this capacity.[3] In her critique of Du Bois's and other black men's idealization of the black mother, Guy-Sheftall calls into question the root of its formulation. She observes that while these black men were "opposed to the abuse of black mothers in white households, they nonetheless embrace the ideology of motherhood, for they believe in the fundamental values associated with the mammy—home, nurturance, and maternal influence. In other words, black mothers should be removed from white homes so that they can devote themselves full time to the needs of their own homes" (1990, 84).

While Du Bois based his argument for the veneration of black womanhood on the defense of the ideology of mother, he firmly supported the idea of women's work outside the home. Unlike other black men who simply wanted to redress the exploitation of black women by placing them upon a pedestal—keeping them completely powerless—Du Bois envisioned a time in which female labor outside the domestic space would be justly compensated. Looking to a future of women's equality, he affirmed the right of black women to enter the workforce and emphatically called for universal suffrage, while upholding the preeminence of motherhood as the surest means of black people's survival: "Out of a sex freedom that today makes us shudder will come in time a day when we will no longer pay men for work they do not do, for the sake of their harem; we will pay women what they earn and insist on their working and earning it; we will allow those persons to vote who know enough to vote, whether they be black or female, white or male; and we will ward race suicide, not by further burdening the over-burdened, but by honoring motherhood . . ." [1920] 1969, 184–85).

Informed by a prophetic message of female economic independence, "The Damnation of Women" is both a defense of black motherhood and an homage to the heroism of black women as women, mothers, workers, and revolutionary womanists. It stands as a testament to Du Bois's devotion to black women and supreme admiration for their courage. He wrote "No other women on earth could have emerged from the hell of force and temptation which once engulfed and still surrounds black women in America with half the modesty and womanliness that they retain. I have always felt like bowing myself before them in all abasement, searching to bring some tribute to these long-suffering victims, these burdened sisters of mine, whom the world, the wise, white world, loves to affront and ridicule and wantonly to insult" (186). "If these comments seem exaggerated," Guy-Sheftall maintains, "one should be reminded of the prevailing stereotypes of black women that Du Bois and others were attempting to counteract. . . . The attempt to place black women on a pedestal should be seen against the backdrop of the elevation of the white woman. Black men wanted their women to be worshipped in the same manner" (1990, 63). Thus, Du Bois transforms Harriet Tubman and Sojourner Truth into the daughters of Neith, whom he imagined as the African mythical mother of all civilization. Besides offering historical background of their lives as slaves and freedom fighters, he profiles other black women of heroic stature. They include Phillis Wheatley, a poet; Kate Ferguson, a homeless children's advocate and founder of the first Sunday school in New York; Mary Shadd Cary, a teacher, editor, and lecturer, as well as a recruiting officer for black soldiers out West; and Louise De Mortie, who in 1877 established a home for orphans (Du Bois [1920] 1969, 960–63). Black women's achievement and contribution to racial uplift, according to Du Bois, surpassed that of black men: "As I look about me today in this veiled world of mine, despite the noisier and more spectacular advance of my brother, I instinctively feel and know that it is the five million women of my race who really count . . ." ([1920] 1969, 179).

Describing the attainment of his "brother" as "noisier and more spectacular" (adjectives which in this case are not to be read as necessarily complimentary), Du Bois is obviously more impressed with the achievements of "five million" black women. In foregrounding the public accomplishments of outstanding black women, he states: "All the way back in these dim distances it is mothers and mothers who seem to count. . . ." Men, on the other hand, as fathers "are shadowy memories" (168). In fact, *fathers* are figuratively and literally almost absent in "The Damnation of Women." They function more as patriarchal specters, whose "shadowy" presence, in the course of history, has "count[ed]" less than that of mothers. The missing figure of the father in the text may be partly accounted for by the absence of him in the childhood of the author. According to the Du Bois biographer David Levering Lewis, he "almost surely came to suspect years later that his father was something more than a well-meaning, romantic rakehell, 'indolent, kind, unreliable,' who came and soon departed from the valley (Great Barrington, Connecticut) and his family, only to die shortly thereafter" (1993, 21).

In the text, the "ghost" of the father is supplanted by the power of the embodied, self-sacrificing mother—the symbolic center of the womanist ideas Du Bois supported. Yet in the romanticization of motherhood, coupled with an unyielding desire to celebrate a history of black female heroism, his critique of women's oppression reveals an unresolved ambivalence between an uncompromising belief in the freedom of women and a devotion to the maternal. His support for women's economic independence is progressive, even emancipatory, but the womanist sensibility exhibited in this position is repeatedly undercut by a strong allegiance to the "cult of motherhood," couched in language affirming a woman's choice not to bear children.

Nevertheless, we should not lose sight of the principled aims "The Damnation of Women" puts forward as a pro-woman suffrage text. First and foremost, it asserts the necessity of women's right to vote. Second, while it affirms motherhood, it seeks to dismantle sexist attitudes that pitted the maternal against the economic empowerment of women. As a womanist testament to the courage and achievement of black women in light of the nearly insurmountable racial, sexual, and economic odds facing them, the text rejects the racist ideology of the cult of true womanhood that positioned the white woman as the universal representative of the feminine. But most aggressively, it is the wrong against the black mother that Du Bois is determined to correct above all, writing in defiance of the historical racist and sexist devaluation of black motherhood. Despite the limits of the (domestic) feminism Du Bois espoused, he, like other black and white feminists during the time "The Damnation of Women" was published, convincingly argued for the self-governance of women as mothers and workers—as independent, autonomous individuals. In the end, it is the visionary belief that no woman should have to choose between motherhood and a career outside the home that stands as the hallmark of the feminist ideas he expressed. Boldly he would assert, "We cannot abolish the new economic freedom of women. We cannot imprison women again in a home or require them all on pain of death to be nurses and housekeepers. . . . *The uplift of women is, next to the problem of the color line and the peace movements, our greatest modern cause—woman and color—combine in one, the combination has deep meaning* [emphasis added]" ([1920] 1969, 181).

Du Bois and the Masculinization of Feminism: A Quagmire of Contradiction

By expanding critical theoretical frameworks, Du Bois demystified racism and class elitism. Unfortunately, at the same time, he also mystified the agency of African-American women. Du Bois's sexual politics suggest that

> he navigated between increasingly nonclassist and democratic ideologies and a moribund gender progressivism into a quagmire of contradictory progressive and paternalistic racial-sexual politics.
>
> —Joy James (1997, 35)

While the pro-feminism of Du Bois (and Douglass) offers contemporary black men a remarkable window into the complexity of male pro-woman(ist) identity, it also presents a historical testing ground for an analysis of the existence of masculinist egocentricism in it. As scholars critical of Douglass's depiction of women concur, their "presence/absence" signals a conflict between male self-representation and feminist presentation. In the previous chapter, I argued that in the discursive realm of Douglass's speeches and editorials on woman suffrage, racial signification is omitted, eclipsing its relation to the condition of the black woman. However, in this opening chapter on Du Bois's pro-womanism, it is indisputably clear that he is most interested in passionately defending her, as Beverly Guy-Sheftall maintains. Yet, as Deborah McDowell argues in the case of Douglass, when one compares the autobiographical (con)text of Du Bois's representation of women with that of the pro-woman(ist) political writings, one discovers a similar minefield of discursive "contradictions and disjunctions." Like McDowell, Joy James—whose critique of Du Bois's "profeminism" calls into question its unequivocal progressive nature—demands a thorough analysis of the "masculinist worldview [that] influences his writing to diminish his gender progressivism" (James 1997, 35).

As much as I press my case for the pro-feminist legacy of Frederick Douglass and W. E. B. Du Bois, I acknowledge its limits. Joy James in *Transcending the Talented Tenth: Black Leaders and American Intellectuals* offers a revealing critique of the "profeminist" positionality Du Bois espoused both in autobiographical and political (con)texts. On the one hand, as James contends, Du Bois's political writings on the equality of women and the rights of black women, in particular, convey an antisexist standpoint. On the other, she suggests that they employ a "masculinist framework that presents the male as normative" (35–36). While James distinguishes "masculinism" (not necessarily advocating male supremacy) from patriarchy, she concludes that it is rooted in the patriarchalization of male identity without being against women rights: "For instance, Du Bois argued against sexism and occasionally for the superiority of women. However, even without patriarchal intent, certain works may replicate conventional gender roles. Du Bois's fictional portraits of African-American women emphasize and romaticize the strength of black women. . . . [H]is nonfiction minimizes black female agency. Without misogynist dogma, his writings naturalize the dominance of black males in African-American political discourse" (36).

Convincingly, James demonstrates how fictional romaticization of black womanhood by Du Bois contradicts the marginalized treatment of real-life black women in the political treatises on them he writes, particularly with regard to their political agency: "In theory and practice Du Bois opposed women's subjugation. But his political representations of and relations with influential female leaders reflect a considerable ambivalence toward black women's political independence" (37). James cites his relationship with Anna Julia Cooper and Ida B. Wells-Barnett as examples. Time and time again, she points to textual moments when it would appear Du Bois could have named them specifically but did not. Without doubt, in autobiographical and political (con)texts, he referenced women in his life who influenced him: "his mother, familial women as well as personal friends and acquaintances." Yet as James contends, through "a censorious revisionism [he obscures] the pioneering works of Cooper and Wells-Barnett. The diverse and conflictual nature of these relationships point to a 'double consciousness' muddled with the contradictions of his gender politics" (41).

Joy James performs a careful reexamination of the pro-feminist politics Du Bois espoused, and she includes critiques of it by other critics such as Patricia Morton and Nagueyalti Warren. They, like James, point to the mythic stature of black woman Du Bois constructs of the black woman. It was, they say, often rooted in stereotypes either of black feminine superiority or of total victimization. These criticisms provide a more nuanced assessment of the contradictions of his gender progressivism, without dismissing Du Bois's devotion to women rights and black female liberation. James's final assessment of it revolves around the idea of "nonspecificity and erasure" in Du Bois's political writings on black women. In the autobiographical (con)text, his creation of "types" of black women to be celebrated for their strength and long-suffering obtains through a lack of specificity. In the political writings, his decision (on multiple occasions) to omit the name or failure to give credit to the work of such women as Anna Julia Cooper and Ida B. Wells-Barnett signals an overt attempt, according to James, to erase their political agency. Her cautionary note to contemporary (male and female) gender progressives is well taken: "If we address black women as a generic topic without their specificity, we obscure the radical dimensions of black politics and history. If we portray African-American women in an aggregate as victims, icons, or the embodiment of a cause, we project the notion that political change transpires without black female independence and leadership. If we assert black women's leadership in theory but minimize the empirical record of African-American women leaders, we masculinize black agency and implicitly elevate men to a superior status as intellectuals" (54).

In the remaining chapters on the gender-progressive texts of Du Bois, both nonfiction and fiction, as I further consider his pro-feminist pronouncements, I do so with Joy James's critical perspective in mind. She contends that we gender-progressive black women and men, as "heirs of Du Bois," must interrogate his legacy of pro-feminism "to transcend" its limitations (56).

Womanism in the Name of the "Father": Du Bois and the Politics of Patriarchy, Race, and Art

As the intellectual architect of the Talented Tenth and political and artistic arbiter of the Harlem Renaissance, W. E. B. Du Bois held to the belief that black creative expression should be guided by a political imperative to enhance "the right of black folk to love and enjoy." The idea that "all art is propaganda" remained a dominant feature of his political and literary production. In "Criteria of Negro Art," published at the height of the Harlem Renaissance in 1926, Du Bois set forth his ideas on the character and purpose of black art. This chapter traces the evolution of his artistic convictions as illustrated in several key texts, from the publication of *The Souls of Black Folk* in 1903 to the issue of his first novel, *The Quest of the Silver Fleece* (1911) and to the public release of a little-known personal essay entitled "So the Girl Marries." As principal examples of Du Boisian propaganda, these texts exemplify the strength of the author's conviction. He would declare passionately, "I do not care a damn for any art that is not used for propaganda."

Du Bois's ideas on the power of art as propaganda originated in *The Souls of Black Folk*, which appeared more than twenty years before "Criteria for Negro Art." *The Souls of Black Folk* was written in service to the development of a black aesthetic whose fundamental aim was to "uplift the race." I argue that *The Souls* functions as a womanist prototype for Du Bois's later attempts at fiction and the personal essay. Striking for their portrayal of black female identity, early writings such as *The Quest* and "So the Girl Marries" embody the author's woman-identified vision of black liberation. In *The Quest*, Du Bois creates a protagonist whose physical, intellectual, and spiritual maturation is integrally tied to the survival of an entire community—especially that of its female members. My aim in discussing the novel in this chapter is to locate its genesis in *The Souls*. As for "So the Girl Marries," it acts as an early platform for Du Bois's pro-woman(ist) ideas. Its analysis reveals its link to his larger propagandistic intention, which was invested in racial progress. The essay reads as an intimate family portrait in which Du Bois candidly writes about the personal and symbolic meaning of the education, maturation, and forthcoming marriage of his daughter, Yolande. In "So the Girl Marries," she comes to exemplify the ideal of black womanhood: the quintessential womanist.

The image of his real-life daughter as an archetypal figure in Du Bois's propaganda of black liberation may be traced back to the creation of his feminist hero in *The Quest*, Zora Creswell. Her depiction epitomizes the Du Boisian notion that models of superior womanhood could be inculcated into people through art. *The Quest* functions as one of its author's most successful deployments of propaganda as a tool to uplift black womanhood and the race. I maintain that both the first woman-identified novel of Du Bois and the little-known essay on the personal recollection of his daughter's wedding are ideologically linked through *The Souls*. I will discuss *The Souls of Black Folk*, *The Quest of the Silver Fleece*, and "So the Girl Marries," in the order of their publication, but to provide a critical backdrop for Du Bois's ideas on the relationship between art and propaganda let me first discuss "Criteria for Negro Art."

Art for the Sake of the Race

Conscious that to many "purists" he would be committing literary heresy in his politicization of "art," Du Bois boldly defended an aesthetic of art as propaganda. It not only determined his own artistic production but imbued it with political agency, an agency particularly demonstrated in the interplay of poetic prose styling and political intent in such major works as *The Souls*, *The Quest*, and "The Damnation of Women." To Du Bois, the aesthetic value of his art and its effect as propaganda were one and the same. In other words, Du Bois believed that artistic production by black people should be created primarily for black people and their cultural edification, thus "gaining the right of black folk to love and enjoy."

Du Bois was the proselytizer of a new black humanism during the Harlem Renaissance, and he most thoroughly developed this persona with regard to his theory of black art. The "Criteria of Negro Art" (1926) is his most passionate statement on the subject. Couched in nineteenth-century romantic notions of truth and beauty, Du Bois situates himself as a "humble" storyteller and "disciple of art," "one who tells the truth and exposes evil and seeks with Beauty and for Beauty to set the world right. That somehow, somewhere eternal and perfect Beauty sits above Truth and Right I can conceive, *but here and now in the world in which I work they are for me unseparated and inseparable* [emphasis added]" (1926, 293). Almost as a disclaimer to the art-as-propaganda position Du Bois so ardently espoused in the passage cited earlier (also from "Criteria of Negro Art"), in the quotation above Du Bois (re)frames his black aesthetic theory after a Eurocentric model of art (which for him is art with a capital A). In an "apolitical" poetic vision, Du Bois has little trouble imagining "Beauty" functioning as the prime arbiter of moral justice "to set the world right . . . sit[ting] above Truth and Right."

In the reality of the world in which Du Bois writes, he sees beauty, truth, and *right* as "unseparated and inseparable." First of all, in his discourse on aesthetics Du Bois reconfigures the nature of art. "Right," as the agent of political and social change, becomes the necessary complement to beauty and truth. Second, he deconstructs the hierarchical relationship between the three to establish the validity of art as propaganda, to Du Bois a much more powerful vehicle for artistic expression than the restrictive notion of "art for art's sake." The politicization of art in Du Bois's mind lent itself to the construction of a distinctly black cultural milieu, free from the pressure of having to please a white audience. Perhaps the most critically self-conscious statement on the artistic representation of black people made by Du Bois in "Criteria of Negro Art" had to do with intraracial censorship. Articulating what he perceived to be the major barriers to black artistic expressivity during the Harlem Renaissance, Du Bois located them in an exploitative system of white patronage and a black sensibility invested in classist provincialism. "[I]t is important," says Arnold Rampersad, "to insist that Du Bois was no part of the clamor by certain middle-class and aristocratic members of the black intelligentsia for a literature set in the middle, *to show whites that some blacks, at least, were capable of refinement* [emphasis added] . . ." (1985, 51).

The religious and moral conservatism in black communities during the period had its effects upon black artists. What "hemmed in" younger black artists of the period, Du Bois suggests, was the intraracial pressure upon them to self-censor artistic representation of black experience(s). "Criteria of Negro Art," as an exhortation to "our new young artists to fight their way to freedom," echoes Langston Hughes's essay on art, "The Negro Artist and the Racial Mountain." Similarly, Hughes called for the "new young [black] artists" to rebel against convention and the ideological conservatism of the black bourgeoisie. An "artistic manifesto" of the Harlem Renaissance, "The Negro Artist and the Racial Mountain," was published in June 1926, only four months before the Du Bois essay. Both Hughes and Du Bois advocate a "shameless" representation of black people in art, free from race and class restraints. But Du Bois, before the publication of "The Negro Artist," had set up the "call" for a "response" such as Hughes's. In "A Questionnaire," featured in the Opinion column of *The Crisis* (February 1926), Du Bois generated a series of questions specifically related to the problematics of black art, questions that he would go on to address in "Criteria of Negro Art."[4]

The Souls of Black Folk as Urtext and the Making of a Pro-woman(ist) Novel

Du Bois had already begun to address such questions fourteen years earlier in the *The Souls of Black Folks*. As the site of germination for a "womanist" novel, *The Quest* embodied in its protagonist a composite of "Ethiopian" nationalism and feminist idealism. The liberatory ideas of black womanhood and black women's liberation evident in the pro-woman texts written by Du Bois after 1911 all point back to *The Quest* as their precursor. In writing a novel in which a black woman rises to become the leader of her people, its author consciously constructed her in opposition to the existing racist and sexist myths of black womanhood. After *The Souls of Black Folk*, *The Quest* was the only extended fictional account of the postslavery South that Du Bois would write. As an interrogation of racial oppression in the South, the result of capitalist exploitation of Southern black labor in the production and commercialization of the cotton industry by the white ruling class, the novel prefigures the pro-woman(ist) standpoint Du Bois established in "The Damnation of Women."

We first encounter the source of the subject matter of *The Quest* in an essay in *The Souls* entitled "The Quest of the Golden Fleece," a text that weaves together nonfiction and fiction. It is framed as a sociological discourse on the condition of blacks in the postbellum South, and Du Bois would draw upon the social reality portrayed in it some eight years later in his construction of *The Quest*. The title of the essay and the novel is based on the story in classical mythology of Jason's search for the Golden Fleece and the modern South's quest to make cotton the "Golden Fleece" of its economic structure through the exploitation of slave labor. Du Bois, trained as a sociologist, infused poetry into the language of sociology, creating the prose style that characterizes *The Souls*. The first paragraph, which opens with "Of the Quest of the Golden Fleece," is a striking example of this socioliterary style. It foreshadows the development of his career as a novelist:

> HAVE YOU EVER SEEN A COTTON-FIELD white with the harvest,—its golden fleece hovering above the black earth like a silvery cloud edged with dark green, its bold white signals waving like the foam of billows from Carolina to Texas across that Black and human Sea? I have sometimes half suspected that here the winged ram Chrysomallus left that Fleece after which Jason and his Argonauts went vaguely wandering into the shadowy East three thousand years ago; and certainly one might frame a pretty and not far-fetched analogy of witchery and dragon's teeth, and

> blood and armed men, between the ancient and the mother Quest of the Golden Fleece in the Black Sea.
>
> And now the golden fleece is found; not only found, but, in its birthplace, woven. For the hum of the cotton-mills is the newest and most significant thing in the New South to-day. All through the Carolinas and Georgia, away down to Mexico, rise these gaunt red buildings bare and homely, and yet so busy and noisy withal that they scarce seem to belong to the slow and sleepy land. Perhaps they sprang from dragons' teeth. So the Cotton Kingdom still lives; the world still bows beneath her scepter. ([1903] 1994, 83–84)

The Souls of Black Folk, one of the earliest treatises by Du Bois on the experiences of black people in the United States, was the ideological germ out of which a pro-woman position developed. Prefiguring Jean Toomer's *Cane* (1923), which was to come some twenty years later, *The Souls* defies categorization. Houston Baker says, "[I]t is virtually unclassifiable. . . . I think the phrase 'cultural performance' is perhaps the most apt classification" (1987, 17).

As a "cultural performance" of African-American artistic expression, the multigenre text Du Bois writes collapses literary categories, allowing the writer a larger landscape in which to interpret black life in the South before, during, and after Reconstruction. Du Bois moves between fiction and nonfiction and between private and public spheres without diminishing the factuality of his sociological observation. Prior to the publication of *The Souls*, he had already published several essays ("The Freedmen's Bureau," "The Evolution of Negro Leadership," "A Negro Schoolmaster in the New South," and "The Relationship of the Negroes to the Whites in the South") that contained important ideas that would reappear in the book and subsequently become a chief source in the composition of *The Quest*. In *The Souls* he addresses the issue of black illiteracy and female sexual oppression in "Of the Meaning of Progress," an autobiographical narrative about the tragic life of a young woman named Josie, who "had about her a certain fineness, the shadow of an unconscious moral heroism that would willingly give all of life to make life broader, deeper, and fuller for her and hers" (1903, 98). Her desire for education, "[t]he longing to know, to be a student in the great school at Nashville, hovered like a star above this child-woman amid her work and worry, and she studied doggedly" (99).

Because Josie is black, female, and poor, her chances for success are severely diminished. In the course of her brief life, hope and ambition give way to more work and finally despair. She "worked on, with the vision of schooldays all fled, with a face wan and tired,—worked until, on a summer's day, some one married another; then Josie crept to her mother like a hurt child, and slept—and sleeps" (104). Suffering from complete physical exhaustion, coupled with the frustration of an unfulfilled life, Josie cannot go on. Du Bois ends the story with a question: "How shall man measure Progress there where the dark-faced Josie lies?" (108). In other words, if racism, sexism, and poverty crushed the dream and life of a young black woman who possessed the desire and potential to succeed, what room is there for optimism about the progress of black people as a whole?

The irony of the story's ending rests in the fact that Du Bois, having returned South (ten years later) to the community where Josie lived, departs on a train in which he had to sit in the Jim Crow car. The racism that confronted Du Bois in this instance had also confronted Josie—only multiplied by the obstacles of sex and class. Josie's story illustrates the life-threatening effect the triple oppression of race, sex, and class has on a black, poor, uneducated woman. The belief in women's education and economic empowerment becomes the chief basis of his pro-woman suffrage discourse written after the publication of *The Souls of Black Folk*. Nellie McKay refers to Du Bois as "an anomaly" as a black male, pro-feminist writer in the decades leading up to the ratification of the Nineteenth Amendment. Certainly he was the first African-American male writer to focus a novel-length narrative on black female self-development. Du Bois's construction and employment of a female "hero" (Zora Creswell) in *The Quest* speaks to the unique nature of the project. Arnold Rampersad, author of *The Art and Imagination of* W. E. B. *Du Bois* (1976), views the novel as a feminist predecessor to "The Damnation of Women." As the first of five novels (the others include *Dark Princess*, 1928, and the *The Black Flame Trilogy* [*The Ordeal of Mansart*, 1957; *Mansart Builds a School*, 1959; and *Worlds of Color*, 1961]), *The Quest* embodies the feminist platform on which his later woman suffrage writings evolve.

If the "deformation of mastery" that characterizes *The Souls of Black Folk* is the modern counterpart of Booker T. Washington's *Up From Slavery*, as Houston Baker argues, *The Quest* exists as the "deforming" text of the black male fictive tradition. The novel's narrative impulse continually subverts the notion of a male-identified hero in Zora. She—not Bles Alwyn, the major male character in the novel—propels its narrative force and drive toward a vision of black people's empowerment. It was in *The Souls* that Du Bois had sought to achieve racial self-determination by creating a cultural nationalism rooted in an African heritage. In *The Quest* he puts into place an African mythological framework as a source and informing base from which his representation of black female power comes. In this way, Africa itself takes on metaphorical implications in the story of Zora Creswell's development as a black woman and *feminist* leader. This theme resurfaces as the underpinning of the political platform on which "The Damnation of Women" succeeds in its black (male) feminist nationalism. *The Quest for the Silver Fleece*, thematically conceived in the deformative mastery of *The Souls of Black Folk*, represents the fictional counterpart of Du Bois's developing modernist vision of the reconstruction of the black American psyche in an African ethos. The Afrocentricity of *The Quest*—it is located in an African version of the black feminine—makes the "deforming" qualities of the novel even more radical than the experiment with form and style Du Bois engaged in with *The Souls*.

That Du Bois represents Zora Creswell with dark skin reflects his aim to politicize color. Of particular importance is the fact that he constructs her as a dark-skinned black woman, during a period when her opposite dominated the fictional portrayal of black women by African American female and male writers. Arthur P. Davis notes that *The Quest* ended the tradition of the mulatto heroine with the image of Zora Creswell.[5] Of the many "mulatta" heroines who come before and after her, Iola Leroy, the heroine of Frances E. Harper's novel by the same name published in 1893, is the light-skinned counterpart of Zora, prefiguring her paradigmatically as a black feminist race leader. In the "black" body of Zora, Du Bois evokes an association with racial "purity" (meant to contrast with the "impurity" of her sexual exploitation by white men). He also means her dark skin to signify undenatured ancestral power. Blackness itself, particularly with regard to racial pigmentation in the novel, repeatedly underscores the centrality of black womanist nationalism. In "The Poetics of Ethiopianism: W. E. B. Du Bois and Literary Black Nationalism," Wilson J. Moses observes that Du Bois was working in two traditions (one rooted in Africa, the other in the West) in the nationalism he adopted (Moses 1985, 92). This doubleness can be seen as the governing narrative strategy of *The Quest*.

Moses perceives the employment of a dual literary tradition in Du Bois's creative writing as a manifestation of a "double-consciousness." Moses characterizes the African tradition as "Ethiopianism." The Ethiopian tradition, he says, "sprang organically out of a certain shared political and religious experiences of English-speaking Africans during the late eighteenth and nineteenth centuries" (92–93). As such, it found expression in the slave narratives and the folk tales and slave songs. Literarily, according to Moses, it became an essential aspect of the sermons and political tracts written by members of the black middle class. Pivotal to the tradition's foundation is biblical scripture. Many black writers (Henry Highland Garnet, Frances

E. Harper, Paul Lawrence Dunbar, and others) referenced the Bible as an integral source of their discourse on racial progress. The most popular scriptural citation of the day proved to be Psalms 68:31—"Princes shall come out of Egypt; Ethiopia shall soon stretch out her hands unto God." Out of this scripture came the "rising Africa theme," the core formulation of Ethiopianism (Moses 1985, 94). Another defining element was the idea of a declining West, emphasizing a dichotomy between Caucasians and Ethiopians. While he was the editor of Atlanta University Publications in 1905, Du Bois wrote "The Moon," a poem about the racial destinies of whites and blacks. Guided by "tropical dreaminess, *feminine aestheticism* [emphasis added], and a childlike love of nature" (Moses 1985, 96), Du Bois favors the future of blacks. He associates these qualities with signs of "African genius." In *The Quest*, Du Bois privileges the relationship between dreams and nature as a complement to Zora's development from girlhood to womanhood to feminist revolutionary. She is a "dreamer" who spends much of her life in nature. The spiritual and intellectual growth of Zora occurs, however, on American soil. Her search for self-understanding and purpose is represented in a coterminous relationship between being African and being American.

And while Ethiopianism is one of the most salient political features of *The Quest*, Moses points to the fact that its organizing myth locates itself in a classical Greek legend. I read the novel as a dialectic between the author's socialist ideas and the more traditional ones of Christianity, interwoven with a feminist legitimation of the right of a black woman to liberate her people. Reconstituting the past through different cultural/racial mythological traditions and interposing them between social and religious critique, Du Bois challenges conventions of race, gender, and literary form.

Leading up to the publication of *The Quest*, Du Bois had gained a reputation as a social scientist. By 1910, he had lost interest in sociology per se. While his sociological treatises stood as master studies on black American experiences, he moved away from the scientific discourse that characterized them toward more imaginative writing. According to Moses, "He turned—and it would seem with more satisfactory results—to the power of imagination as his chief instrument for changing public morality. He became a crusading journalist, a novelist, and a poet of Ethiopianism, dedicated to embodying his view of history in mythical form" (1985, 102–103). Arnold Rampersad notes that Du Bois had expressed aspirations of writing fiction early in his life. When he was twenty-five Du Bois had written in his journal, "These are my plans: to make a name in science, to make a name in art and thus to raise my race." In publishing *The Quest*, Du Bois both "ma[d]e a name in art and thus raise[d his] race"(Rampersad 1985, 58).

From Art to Life: On the Marriage of Art and Politics in "So the Girl Marries"

When men advocate the equality of the sexes, women's rights, and feminism, it necessarily implies a political relation to women. In *Maternal Thinking*, Sara Ruddick maintains that the act of mothering when performed by a man inherently calls into question the social inscription of masculinity and the power of patriarchy as he "to some extent takes on the female condition and risks identification with the feminine"(1989, 45). I employ Ruddick's statement on men and mothering to begin a discussion of the womanism W. E. B. Du Bois professed and its effect upon his family—particularly on his first wife, Nina, and their daughter, Yolande. Picking up on the "feminine" problematics of men mothering Ruddick raises while thinking about W. E. B. Du Bois as a feminist-identified man and its complex relation to motherhood, I work through one of his most revealing personal essays—"So the Girl Marries," published in the *Crisis* (1928)—to set into play a critique of Du Bois as a "feminist father."

I begin a critical discussion of this little-known essay by posing several general questions having to do with feminist men, motherhood, and familial relations that lead into an analysis of male feminism and the politics of patriarchy in the Du Bois family. How, for example, do men embracing feminism negotiate the privileged position they inherently occupy in a male supremacist society? In a sexist, patriarchal culture where manhood exists in opposition to womanhood and most things associated with it—mothering notwithstanding—notions of masculinity are culturally, socially, politically, sexually, and economically bound up in the hegemony of patriarchy. How do men claiming feminist positionality construct a political and personal alliance with women in a feminist movement that challenges forms of male domination?

The issue that informs my reading of "So the Girl Marries" has to do with the way Du Bois employs mothering to erase the position of the "Mother" (Nina) in the text—effectively silencing her voice in the parenting of her daughter. What happens to the position of Nina as the mother of a daughter whose "feminist father" assumes almost total control over the social and intellectual development of their daughter to the point where neither mother nor daughter has any say in who the daughter's marriage partner will be? While the essay's tone is jovial and lighthearted, its familial politics suggest a sentiment on the part of Du Bois that was far from humorous. The feminist ideas of black womanhood and mothering of the ruling patriarch relegate Nina to a trivial role, making her only a surrogate for the true mother—Du Bois himself. I will argue that not only did he govern the intellectual and social destiny of his daughter, but also attempted to mold her into his own image of black womanhood idealized. Nina Du Bois functioned as a live-in companion for Yolande—traveling and accompanying her wherever she was to be whether abroad at school or at a social affair. Du Bois, rather than sharing parental duties with his wife, takes on the role of maternal figure to her exclusion. In "So The Girl Marries," male feminist idealism gives way to patriarchal dictum.

In his position as a preeminent black male feminist and as the twentieth century's most ardent proponent of the "racial uplift" philosophy, Du Bois imagined black womanhood as the prime location where race progress would be cultivated. But it was not womanhood alone that he thought would bring African Americans into a state of ascendancy—he thought its destiny resided in the virtues of motherhood. Having previously vindicated the womanhood of black women through the idealization of motherhood in "The Damnation of Women" (1920), in "So The Girl Marries" (published eight years later) Du Bois brings "mothering" under scrutiny. Examining closely the position Nina and Yolande occupy in the grand project of "racial uplift" Du Bois conceived, I pinpoint the various ways that ideas of racial progress and feminist ideals come into sharp contrast in the domain of the domestic space. In considering how the feminist standpoint of W. E. B. Du Bois impacted his wife and daughter, I make inquiry into the interplay between feminism, patriarchy, and the family. Examining the political, social, and personal life of Du Bois, I argue that even as a man who embraced feminism, writing extensively in support of woman suffrage, the liberatory nature of his discursive practice, more often than not, in the context of the family, worked to reinscribe patriarchal privilege and practice.

From the public arena of woman suffrage activism to the personal location of the domestic, I track the feminist movement of Du Bois, observing ways the political, social, and personal overlap, interrelate, and merge in his pro-woman texts. He not only exercised tremendous influence in the struggle for woman suffrage, but as a "feminist father" also determined to a large extent the lives of his wife and daughter. Reading the feminist writings of Du Bois, one gains significant insight into the operation of feminism in the family. "So the Girl Marries"—like "The Damnation of Women" and *The Quest of the Silver Fleece*—is representative of a feminist discourse in which he seeks to idealize black womanhood. Some of the same qualities he employed to portray the "dark-skinned" heroine of *The Quest* are reconfigured in the textual image of his daughter. Yolande becomes the "modern black woman," as Zora Cresswell had in *The Quest*. Beauty, sophistication, and intelligence, among others, were the qualities Du Bois believed defined the ideal black woman, and he worked to refine them in the "Girl."

From her childhood on, Du Bois determined how his daughter would be educated. To him private education in America and abroad was the most appropriate way to ensure that she would receive the best. Presumably, it was associated with taste, culture, and class. At age ten, after the family moved to New York, Yolande attended the Ethical Culture School. Du Bois's long-range educational plan for her included preparing her as a black woman to deal with racism, but his elitist notions of private education reveal a rather naive, classist attitude toward racial oppression. The belief that a private school education, particularly one abroad, would best prepare his daughter to struggle against racial oppression in America reflected a middle-class provinciality.

How Du Bois relates Yolande's development is particularly interesting when one considers the way he speaks about the role of his wife in her life. The way Du Bois presents it, of the two parents he was actually closer to their daughter, and he seems to have exploited that relationship for reasons, we come to understand, that had little to with either Yolande or Nina. Du Bois was going about the work of "racial uplifting." If his daughter could aid in the process by marrying the "ideal" man, so be it. Nina's role in the matter as travel companion and chaperone ensured that nothing would impede race progress. She, as Du Bois portrays her in the text, had no *active* voice or hand in Yolande's development. The "Mother," after having lived with her daughter away from the "Father" for two years in England, remains voiceless in response to the changes Du Bois said had taken place in Yolande. We only hear the "Father's" reaction: "The Girl had grown. She was a reticent stranger with whom soul-revealing converse was difficult. I found myself groping for introductions" (Du Bois 1928, 192).

Considering the fact that Du Bois chose not to include his wife's voice here, questions arise around his characterization of the "Mother." Why are her thoughts on her daughter's life absent from the text for the most part? Might her ideas have conflicted with her husband's? As one reads through the essay, there persists the feeling that Du Bois purposely positioned the "Mother" outside the text and in an exclusionary relation to their daughter. I suggest that when Nina speaks in the text, her words are trivialized. She is virtually excluded from the decision-making process regarding her daughter's wedding, and left out of the "Grand Idea(s)" her husband conceived for their daughter's future. Du Bois's notions of a refined and cultured woman had to do in large part with the importance he placed on college education (the basis of his Talented Tenth theory). To his consternation, Yolande was not remotely interested in attending college. But the "Father" insisted, so she went. His argument had great merit, however. "I have," he says to the "Girl," "told 12 millions to go to college—what will they say if you don't go?" (193). He believed the experience would make her self-sufficient, even as it would be "furnishing [her with] topics of conversation in the long years to come" (193). What Du Bois meant by "self-sufficient" is ambiguous here, in light of the statement that follows it. He appears to suggest that a college education for women had to do with little more than acquiring interesting topics to talk about.

Just as Anna Douglass had trouble contending with an "educated" daughter, so it seems with Nina. Yet, Du Bois says that during the four years Yolande was away at college, she came to "enshrine" (207) the "Mother." From the text, we are led to believe that Nina and Yolande did not engage in intellectual conversation. Du Bois characterizes it as something more suitable for "Father" and daughter. Having produced a college-educated daughter meant that his "Grand Idea" had been accomplished. Yolande became the intellectual companion for Du Bois that Nina was not. Du Bois said himself upon Nina's death in 1950 (after fifty-five years of marriage) that "[h]er great gift was her singularly honest character; her *passion for cleanliness and order* [emphasis added] and her loyalty" (Diggs 1974, 296). He revealed that his marriage to Nina Gomer was at best one based on duty and allegiance ("loyalty"). According to Du Bois, neither spouse complemented the other. He, like Douglass, spent long periods of time away from home and admitted that it took a toll on his marriage and family. He said, "I was not, on the whole, what one would describe as a good husband. The family and its interests were never the main center of my life" (1928, 170).

Du Bois characterized her as "a slip of a girl, beautifully dark-eyed and thorough and good as a German housewife" (Diggs 1974, 296), and we have no words from Nina to suggest otherwise. Furthermore, it would appear that she may have been more at home in this capacity. Whether or not it was in Nina's nature to challenge the banal existence of her everyday life as a homemaker actually is not the issue here. Du Bois's conventional notions of Nina as housewife and "Mother" actually exacerbated what may have been a problem of incompatibility. Though he framed it are a lack of intellectual comradery in the marriage, Du Bois himself failed to see the degree to which he completely dominated and silenced his wife.

Again, Du Bois acknowledged that his being away from home so frequently did little to allow Nina the opportunity to explore and develop beyond the context of the home. "[A]lways," he says, "I was ranging away in body or in soul and leaving the home to my wife. She must often have been lonesome and wanted more regular and personal companionship than I gave" (1928, 206). Indeed, Du Bois was correct in saying that his wife did not have it in her to break free of the need to clean and do housework, but it made his life easier not to change hers. Implicit in Du Bois's statement above is the notion that he had to be the center of her life as a companion. The guilt he felt might have diminished had he encouraged his wife to find other sources of companionship. That Du Bois allowed himself to occupy such a dominant role in Nina's concept of herself is contrary to his notion in "The Damnation of Women" that a woman must have the freedom to choose whether even to be a mother or homemaker. How could Nina Du Bois exercise any movement beyond the confines of her home, when it was clear that her husband supported the barriers that kept her framed within its boundaries?

Implicit in Yolande's treatment of the "Mother" is the suggestion in "So the Girl Marries" (which may be interpreted as an antifeminist text) that Yolande also found her mother intellectually, socially, and physically uninspiring. Commenting humorously on the excessive importance the "Girl" invested in physical appearance (considering her expensive tastes in clothes), Du Bois notes a rather revealing exchange between mother and daughter. It focuses on the "Mother's" appearance and what her daughter took it to represent. On the one hand, the brief dialogue sounds playful, even trivial—perhaps as the writer intended. On the other, Du Bois places Yolande's reaction in a most "unfilial" space. "So the Girl Marries" marginalizes the place of the maternal, putting the "Father" in the "Mother's" position. The essay is, therefore, not so much about the author's anxiety around the maturation of his daughter and the political, social, and racial implications of her marriage as it is about the playing out of patriarchal mastery and domination.

Du Bois recognized and lamented the lonely life Nina led. He, like Douglass, failed to understand his role in it. In "So the Girl Marries," "Mother" is represented as a self-isolated, uninteresting, nonstimulating, anal-retentive homemaker. Her "inabilities" enable the "Father" to operate in a position of complete control. "Father" knows best. Even in the role of traveling companion and chaperone "Mother's" power is undercut. To her daughter and her daughter's friends (both female and male), Nina often served as a matriarchal trickster. When she was not cleaning house, she spent her time "hanging" with Yolande. In the Du Bois family portrait, the "Mother" is not only a meticulous homemaker but a perennial "joke" maker. Her position as chaperone was a role Du Bois rarely (if ever) performed, either because he was not available or (more likely) because "[i]t was a bore." As he himself said, the "Father, of course, was busy with larger matters and weightier problems, including himself." In this sentence, Du Bois refers to himself (the "Father") in the third person. Clearly, he separates the concerns of the patriarch from the "boring" duties of the "Mother."

The most important concern for the "Father" in "So the Girl Marries" is *his* daughter's wedding. For Du Bois, it marked the "end of an era—a sudden break and beginning" for which he had to "readjust [his] soul." He continues, "*I* [emphasis added] planned frantically" (1928, 208). From beginning to end, as the wedding preparations and ceremony are described, it is the "Father" who positions himself at the center of activity. Du Bois used the event to make a larger, more political statement about the black middle class. There was more at stake for Du Bois than the marriage of two individuals—it was what they represented. Yolande epitomized black womanhood idealized; Countee Cullen was "a living exemplar of Talented Tenth values," and by 1926 had been acknowledged as "Harlem's poet prodigy" (Lewis 1979, 75). The couple's union (symbolized by the ceremony itself) represented the future of black America.

Rather than emphasize the importance of specific individuals included in the wedding party, he focuses on them in a collective sense. They stand as the living testament of his Talented Tenth. The bridesmaids and groomsmen were educated at some of America's most prestigious colleges and universities. This group also included the black avant-garde, the prized elite of the black artistic and intellectual communities. To Du Bois, these young men and women bore in them the unique qualities and ideas that would distinguish the artistic, cultural, and literary accomplishment of African-Americans. He employs the theme of Ethiopianism in "So the Girl Marries" to describe them, as he had in *The Quest of the Silver Fleece*. Du Bois had used it paradigmatically to characterize Zora Creswell and Bles Alwyn as the leaders of a new generation of black cultural nationalists, and now he used it to evoke the "essence" of their real counterparts. Moreover, he would note, as if in praise, the daring behavior some of the party's female members displayed by smoking cigarettes—improper conduct for refined young ladies during the time.

The "Father" rejoiced in the symbolic magnitude of the event because it brought together some of the black elite's most talented and brightest younger members. Du Bois invested the marriage ceremony with a purpose and sense of power black people had not known before. Its orchestration and completion was man's work. The political and social implications of his daughter's wedding were too important, Du Bois must have concluded, to be placed in the hands of his wife. As the father of the "Talented Tenth," he believed himself best qualified to direct it. He concludes "So the Girl Marries" suggesting that he has yielded to his daughter's "will." Yet when one hears what he has conceded to, it is just the trivial wish for loud music and people dressed in cheerful apparel. There is no doubt that Du Bois planned, organized, and supervised his daughter's wedding. The text quite clearly illustrated that the "willing" soul was not hers but his. Throughout the wedding, Du Bois exerted a form of patriarchal dominance that left little or no room for female interrogation of the "Father."

"So the Girl Marries" is an important text to examine how Du Bois's public, woman-identified voice contradicts the private one, which was articulated through a much more male-identified, hegemonic discourse. As a feminist, as a race spokesman, and as one of the primary voices in the shaping of the intellectual, artistic and literary movements of the Harlem Renaissance, Du Bois was a man whose ideas on the progress of black people proved more liberatory outside his home than in it. The text provides a revealing window into the problematics of gender and "male" pro-woman(ist) thought. Through it, we see how its author exploits his patriarchal power to shape his daughter into his image of the ideal modern, educated, independent-thinking black woman. To achieve this end, Du Bois took on the role of *feminist* "Mother/Father."

There is no doubt that Du Bois was a man finely attuned to the complexity of black women's oppression, but his zeal for racial progress (so much resting on the race and cultural symbolism of the marriage) seems to have foreclosed any moment of self-conscious recognition. The "play" of patriarchal power in the Du Bois house enacted an erasure and subjugation of female autonomy. Thus, for the two black women closest to him, the role they played in the wedding production could only express itself as an extension of the father's will. In the end, mother and daughter are sacrificed for the good of the race. Even while he advocated women's rights in speeches, articles, editorials, essays, and fiction, Du Bois remained wedded to a vision of racial uplift. In "So the Girl Marries," a patriarchal imperative conjoins with a patriarchal practice to produce a form of "benign" male domination that operates to subjugate and devalue the maternal while appropriating its nurturing power. From *The Souls of Black Folk* to *The Quest of the Silver Fleece* to his most compelling feminist critique of black female oppression in "The Damnation of Women," Du Bois created a powerful pro-woman(ist) discourse, across discursive boundaries, melding sociological observation with creative insight in nontraditional disciplinary form. For Du Bois, the personal was indeed political. Employing the essay form, autobiography, fiction, and nonfiction, he constructed a womanist critique of racism. Though they are prefigured in *The Souls* and *The Quest*, it is in "So the Girl Marries" that he reveals his most personal beliefs on the familial and its relationship to a theory of racial uplift, predicated upon the "wedding" of life and art. Du Bois's theory that "all Art is propaganda and ever must be" literally came to life in the marriage of his daughter Yolande (who represented the quintessential modern black woman) to the poet-"laureate" Countee Cullen (the symbolic male embodiment of black artistic achievement). The couple's union signified a marriage between art and politics guided exclusively by the feminist nationalism of the "father" of the Talented Tenth.

W. E. B. Du Bois forged a critical relationship between art and politics, and he crafted through his art some of his most impassioned statements concerning the racial progress of black people in the United States. Du Bois would show himself to be a consummate *political* artist. No place does his creative power express itself more than in fiction. Let us turn now to Du Bois's first novel, written before the decade known as the Harlem Renaissance. It stands on par with the best black feminist novels of the period. As one of the earliest black novels to feature a dark-skinned, female protagonist, *The Quest of the Silver Fleece* represents a stunning achievement in the African American fictional tradition. No other black male writer of fiction has created a character like Zora Creswell. In the following analysis of the novel, I explore how Du Bois translated his feminist politics and ideas on racial progress into fictional form, and how he artfully wove African mythology with Western ideas of womanhood to create his vision of the (quint)essential black woman(ist) protagonist.

4

Novel for the "Darker Sisters"

The Quest of the Silver Fleece *and W. E. B. Du Bois's Vision of the (Quint)essential Black Woman(ist)*

> The world that wills to worship womankind studiously forgets its *darker sisters* [emphasis added].
>
> —W. E. B. Du Bois ([1920] 1999, 96)

> The book shows . . . an unprecedented respect, on the part of a male writer, for black women as fully human beings. It is the first novel in the black American literary canon in which a woman, black in color, stands at the center, not in a stereotypical role, but as an autonomous, positive character in a position of leadership.
>
> —Nellie McKay (1985, 245)

> At the heart of the novel is Zora, the beautiful, untamed black girl. . . .
>
> —David Levering Lewis (1993, 445)

After five years of writing and revision, W. E. B. Du Bois published his first novel at the age of forty-two. When *The Quest of the Silver Fleece* appeared in 1911, he was already nationally known—so much so "that clubs bearing his name had sprung up" across the country. His noted biographer David Levering Lewis writes, "Most members of the Du Bois clubs, like much of the general public, would have been surprised to learn that the austere editor who wrote empirical studies of the race, championed Latin and philosophy in the college curriculum, and disdained the evangelism of the black church was really 'a poet and a dreamer' " (1993, 443).

Though Du Bois spoke modestly about the novel, Lewis has pointed out that, "it would have been entirely out of character for [him] not to have had large hopes for [the novel], not to have wanted it to be seen as more than an economic treatise embellished by dialogue" (444). The novel received little critical attention and few copies were sold. Lewis notes, "Perhaps the fact was sufficiently well known that reviewers of *The Quest* felt no need to mention that Du Bois had joined the ranks of possibly the country's most exclusive twentieth-century profession—the African-American novelist" (445). Interestingly, no novel by a black novelist had been published for three years prior to *The Quest*.

As a first-time novelist, Du Bois may not have achieved notoriety for literary genius, but his creative impulses in the novel deserved serious commentary. "Poet" and "dreamer" aptly fit the author of *The Quest*. The novel unfolds through mythic symbolism and metaphor. Characters, places, and things stand for its creator's dreams of political progress of his people. According to Arnold Rampersad, Du Bois claimed three goals for himself in a short foreword to *The Quest*: "to tell it well, to tell it beautifully, and to tell the truth. In finishing his novel, however, he vouched for success in only the last category. Whatever the artistic shortcomings of the book—and he conceded that they existed—Du Bois could say, 'I have been honest.' At the heart of the novel is an uncompromising hatred of racism and economic exploitation, and a determination to expose both evils in the greatest detail as they affect the lives of black Americans in all walks of life" (1989, 7–8). Considering the novelist's aims, its literary merit must be understood within a political context. "In depicting the black world in *The Quest of the Silver Fleece*," Rampersad states, "Du Bois orchestrates two themes with a virtuosity almost unprecedented among black novelists and social commentators. The first concerns intraracial color prejudice. Depicting this prejudice among blacks, he defies the black novelists' tradition of favoring light-skinned heroines. . . . The second significant theme concerns the place of women" (1989, 8–9).

As two of the major themes in *The Quest*, the issue of intraracial prejudice and the issue of black woman's place in leadership underscore the revolutionary nature of Du Bois's vision of black womanhood. As both a dark-skinned female and the protagonist of the novel, Zora Creswell represents the author's dream of racial purity, an idea that may be traced back to his racial theories espoused in "The Conservation of the Races" (1897). The literal and figurative *blackness* of Zora indisputably connects her to an ancestral home in Africa, where, as Du Bois proclaims in the poem "The Song of Smoke"(1907), "blackness was ancient ere whiteness began" (qtd. in Rampersad, 1985, 65). All that Zora personifies racially is symbolically linked to her development as a woman. Nellie McKay suggests that "images of women provide one important index to Du Bois's general political and philosophical insights and to his personal convictions concerning women's place in life and art" (1985, 287). In *Biography of a Race, 1869–1919*, Lewis asserts that images of black women Du Bois admired in history, his personal life, and the fiction he wrote became the feminist models for Zora's characterization. They, including Du Bois himself, "merge into the luminous Zora, symbol of the childhood of the race, corruption in slavery, white-world skills and black-world intuitive wisdom and humanity, *and of the truly developed woman* [emphasis added]" (Lewis 1993, 450). Certainly a precursor to "The Damnation of Women" (1920)—Du Bois's most incisive critique of sexism, of patriarchy, and of the appalling condition of black women in the early twentieth century—as a woman-identified novel the feminist impulse of *The Quest* resides in the notion that freedom will come for all people when black women are free. Defending the novel, Lewis (quoting directly from "The Damnation of Women") maintains that Du Bois believed "the race question" was inextricably tied to the question of women's liberation:

> *The Quest* reflected the force and sincerity of Du Bois's feminism, his credo that the degree of society's enlightenment and of the empowerment of disadvantaged classes and races was ultimately measured by its willingness to emancipate women—above all, black women. What he would later affirm with pistol-shot accuracy was found on virtually every page of the novel: that the race question was "at bottom simply a matter of the ownership of women; white men want the right to own and use all women, colored and white, and they resent any intrusion of colored men into this domain." (1993, 449–50)

Zora Creswell: Du Bois's Vision of a *Black* Black Female Protagonist

Zora Creswell's dark skin is integrally connected to the Africanist ideas Du Bois held about womanhood, and to his vision of race and gender liberation. Conceptually, Zora's blackness accomplishes several key tasks in the novel. First, it performs as a racial trope signifying Du Bois's conviction about the power of art to effect social change. Second, at the beginning of the novel, the dark female body we view rising from the swamp (a pivotal symbol of mysterious, supernatural power in the novel) enables Du Bois to recast African mythic notions of the black feminine, modeling them on and in the body of Zora. Moreover, he employs black skin to create an archetypical image for black American women's liberation experience. These ideological elements cohere to form a complex, multidimensional, and revolutionary conception of black womanhood.

To create a black woman as the liberator of her race was not a new idea for Du Bois's time. It had been done. As noted in the previous chapter, eight years before *The Quest*, Frances Harper had already conceived the notion of a "feminist" *woman* race leader (albeit light-skinned) in *Iola Leroy or Shadows Uplifted*, as Hazel Carby maintains in her introduction to the novel ([1893] 1987, ix–xxvi). McKay emphatically praises Du Bois for what she aptly characterizes as a representation comparable to that of today's black women writers. Few scholars of W. E. B. Du Bois's literary works have dealt with the issue of the dark-skinned black woman in his writings. His use of sociological constructs in the creation of fictive ones in *The Quest* continually undergirds its intentional, propagandistic nature. In writing the novel, Du Bois aimed to politicize black women's skin color. McKay insists, "One of the outstanding characteristics of the women in Du Bois' fiction is his insistence on describing their colors." She makes the claim that "[t]he 'black' heroine was born in [his] novel [*The Quest*], marking a major breakthrough in the overthrow of the stereotypical use of near-white versus black people in positive and negative ways in early black fiction" (1985, 239). Moreover, McKay argues that "clarity of vision" is what Du Bois gave the women he created. For her its presence foreshadows feminist representations rendered by current African-American women authors: "[I]t is the gift of clarity of vision that Du Bois gives to his imagined women which most separates his images of black women from those of his contemporaries, and even from writers who come much later in the Afro-American literary canon. Creative writers, until contemporary black women writers, have seemed unable to conceive of black women other than as wives, mothers, or sirens, and thus never as intellectual beings, who exert subtle and overt influence on their communities and beyond" (249). Zora Creswell functions in direct reaction to what in Du Bois's mind had become the domination of the light-skinned heroine in black fiction.

Rampersad ([1976] 1990, 117) has suggested that Frank Norris's *Octopus* (1901) and *The Pit* (1903) act as epic models for *The Quest*, and it is possible that Frances Harper's *Iola Leroy* served as its model for a feminist representation of the black woman as race leader. Whether Du Bois drew directly upon the novel's heroine for his portrayal of Zora is not known, but a comparison of the two shows significant similarities. Both Harper and Du Bois were outspoken advocates of higher education for blacks. Both emphasize the importance of intellectual growth in the development of their heroines. Addressing this point, Hazel Carby remarks, "[N]owhere is Harper's pedagogic intent clearer than in her representation of the importance of black intellectuals to the development of the race as a whole. Harper's representation of a black intellectual elite clearly prefigures the idea of the

'Talented Tenth' that W. E. B. Du Bois developed in a 1903 essay by that name" ([1893] 1987, xx).

As intellectual black women committed to racial liberationist ideas, Iola and Zora must leave the South and develop in the North before they can return to fulfill their mission. Each struggles against forces of patriarchy and sexist oppression of white and black men as she comes into conflict with her emerging sense of self-autonomy. Neither woman views marriage as her ultimate goal in life nor possesses any interest in traditional domestic roles of women. Iola and Zora are independent thinkers and hold definite ideas about racial progress focused on self-determination. At the end of each novel, both men and women, white and black, come to acknowledge the extraordinary intelligence and ability of each black woman protagonist.

Du Bois's vision of black female empowerment differs from Harper's, however, though both authors used the novel as a political platform to advocate "racial uplift" and equality for black women. Whereas, as Carby claims, "[t]he immediate audience for Harper's novel was black Sunday school students" and "[d]idacticism is a dominant characteristic of [the novel]" ([1893] 1987, xvi–xx), the audience for whom Du Bois wrote *The Quest* had to be one composed of individuals unlike the provincially moralistic black folks he critiqued in "Criteria of Negro Art" (1926). Not only did Harper and Du Bois have different audiences in mind whey they wrote these two novels, but their visions of womanhood also differed. Iola Leroy is a black woman grounded in the reality of the natural world. Zora Creswell, on the other hand, remains connected to dreams and visions of another more mysterious, *super*natural world.

As a visionary dreamer, Zora symbolizes the archetypal black feminine. As such, she represents his earliest working out of a theory of black feminist nationalism rooted in an African "anima" (the black feminine soul/spirit). Du Bois would later articulate this concept more clearly in "The Damnation of Women." In the vision of black womanhood he formulates, Du Bois places the "darker sisters" at the center of civilization's beginning so that they cannot be forgotten by a world that *wills* the worship of womankind:

> [T]he world must heed these [darker sisters], *from the primal black All Mother of men down through the ghostly throng of mighty womanhood, who walked in the mysterious dawn of Asia and Africa* [my emphasis]; from Neith, the primal mother of all, whose feet rest on hell, and whose almighty hands uphold the heavens; all religion, from beauty to beast, lies on her eager breasts; her body bears the stars, while her shoulders are necklaced by the dragon; from *black* [emphasis added] Neith down to

> That starr'd Ethiop queen who strove
> to set her beauty's praise above
> the sea-nymphs. . . .
> (Huggins 1986, 953–54)

The "primal black All-Mother" Du Bois imagines inspires awe and reverence. She embodies power and dreadful beauty as the African symbol of womanhood. Neith is mother to "that starr'd Ethiop queen . . . *dusky* Cleopatras, *dark* Candaces, and *darker*, fiercer Zinghas, to our own day and our own land,—in gentle Phillis [Wheatley]; Harriet [Tubman], the crude Moses; the sibyl, Sojourner Truth; and the martyr, Louise De Mortie" (Huggins 1986, 954). The last three women named were Du Bois's contemporaries and served as models of black feminist nationalism.

Du Bois refers to the female progeny of Neith as "the ghostly throng of *mighty* womanhood." The phrase "ghostly throng" becomes his metaphor for a collective female spirituality characterizing the power of women. Upon further examination, what Du Bois seeks to convey in the word "ghostly" is a signifier of *soul*, the source of female "might." Zora Creswell exists as a "Soul" woman, a Neithian symbol of black female power and creativity. As *Soul-woman*, her woman-identified attributes are inscribed in mystery and the supernatural. In *The Quest*, Zora evolves from "elfin" child to Neithian liberator. The evolution begins in the world of nature. Nature appears as a wooded swamp, home to the supernatural. The swamp functions as the Du Boisian trope for Africa, hence the thematic development of Ethiopianism as recurring mythmaker and shaper of Zora's "precivilized" soul. The swamp, located on the Creswell plantation, is a more "natural" home to Zora than the dilapidated cabin in which she and her mother, Elspeth, live. A source of mystery, magic, fantasy, and the visionary, the swamp nurtures the young girl's dreams and enables her to see visions, to glimpse her future greatness.

William Stanley Braithwaite, writing in *The Crisis* the first critique of *The Quest*, a critique that appeared in the same year of the novel's publication, comments on the "otherworldly" nature of Zora: "There is no more subtler portraiture of womanhood," he says, "than that *apparition* [emphasis added] that rose out of the swamp, *a child of nature and dreams, who made her soul an altar of sacrifice and a messenger of life*" (1985, 39). Through the image of the swamp Du Bois employs Ethiopianism as the major thematic device to redefine black womanhood. This, first and foremost, exists as the overarching, propagandistic purpose of the novel. Arlene Elder, interpreting the significance of the Ethiopian tradition in *The Quest*, reads both swamp and plantation as symbols "of two opposing world views. . . . The swamp represents all that is free, wild, joyful, and loving. The plantation, on the other hand, stands for all that is self-serving and exploitative" (1985, 201). But Elder sees neither as fixed in oppositions of good and evil. For example, while Elder points out that Zora's mother (whose function in the novel will be addressed later) embodies evil, at the same time she suggests that Elspeth stands allegorically for the power of creativity. The swamp itself is both a place of mysterious beauty and a world of horror. However, according to Elder, Zora is Du Bois's most representative symbol of the swamp's higher qualities (202). Compared to other romantic novels dealing with the impact of slavery on black people, such as those produced by the Plantation school, *The Quest* operates as the antithesis of the proslavery genre. Fiction of this type generally depicted the "peculiar institution" as composed of loving masters and contented slaves. Countering this treatment, Du Bois weaves fantasy and realism together to produce a romance situated in the political struggle of black people to achieve economic, social, and political freedom (McKay 1985, 245). His novel seeks to codify the qualities he believed exemplified the quintessential modern black woman. As such, from its beginning, Zora Creswell is self-possessed, intellectually superior, physically grounded in a "natural" African aesthetic, and spiritually centered. She is Du Bois's idealized vision of black womanhood. According to Rampersad, "As an early supporter of feminist causes, Du Bois wrote with sympathy of the attempts of women to assert the value of their separate sensibility and experience in the affairs of the nation. His admiration for the character and capacity of black women is stamped on his fiction; in all his novels, the black woman is the intellectual and spiritual superior of the male and the real hope of the race" ([1976] 1990, 1331–32).

From "Elf-Girl" to "Soul-Woman": Zora as Black Liberationist

As Zora matures from "elf-girl" (Du Bois [1911] 1989, 15) to "Soul-woman," she "ma[kes] her soul an altar of sacrifice and messenger of life" (Braithwaite 1985, 39) in the liberation of black people. Intellectually, physically, and spiritually she remains linked to the swamp—a reservoir of dreams, visions, and fantasy. In the opening chapter ("Dreams"), Zora ("child of nature and dreams") revealed herself as more ghostly "apparition" than human being. The effects of her supernatural powers were first experienced by Bles Alwyn, a young black boy who encountered Zora on his way to the plantation's school for black children. He became her "journey" companion and future love interest. Hearing a strange, seductive music emanating from the woods, he was drawn to it by some unidentifiable force. He saw an old shanty of a "cabin crouched ragged and black at the edge of black waters" (Du Bois

[1911] 1989, 14). At that moment its door swung open, "and a flood of light illumined the wood. Amid this mighty halo, as on clouds of flame, a girl was dancing. She was black, and lithe, and tall, and willowy. Her garments twined and flew around the delicate moulding of her dark, young, half-naked limbs. A heavy mass of hair clung motionless to her wide forehead. Her arms twirled and flickered, and body and soul seemed quivering and whirring in the poetry of her motion" (14–15).

Out of the night the dark-skinned, statuesque Zora appears in a flame light. Her darkness, sensuality, and physical appearance—even her "heavy mass of hair"—define the beauty of this *black* girl. Du Bois intends her image to be sensuously arresting, a model of black female beauty. A new ideal of black womanhood, body and soul, is set forth. From Zora's childhood on, Du Bois builds on this description through repetition and enumeration. He repositions black female sensuality from racial marginalization to the center of attention in the novel. Zora's "black" beauty contests Eurocentric standards of beauty by which African American women have been historically judged, and Du Bois reformulates black female sensuality to complement and add visual power to Zora's physical presence.

Moreover, Du Bois employs physical description that suggests the fantastic. Bles's first meeting with this "child of nature" itself takes on an aura of fantasy. Observing Zora "[a]s she danced and sang[,] [he] heard her voice as before, fluttering like a bird's in the full sweetness of her utter music. It was no tune nor melody, it was just formless, boundless music." Unable to differentiate dream from reality, "[t]he boy forgot himself and all the world besides. All his darkness was sudden light; dazzled he crept forward, bewildered, fascinated, until with one last wild whirl the *elf-girl* [my emphasis] paused." In the swamp, Zora personifies creative impulse in an unmediated form. The sensual, seductive dance and mysterious song she sang expand the surreal quality of her image. Her physical form bridges the space between the real and the imagined. Very much flesh and blood, Zora is no illusion—"[t]he crimson light fell full upon the warm and velvet bronze of her face—her midnight eyes were aglow, her full purple lips apart, her half hid bosom panting . . ." (15). Zora's being rejects logic, rationality, and linear thought for that of a psychic animism rooted in mythic Africa, suggested by the swamp. Once Zora's actual existence is confirmed by sight, Bles begins to comprehend her way of being. Yet, from this moment to the conclusion of the novel, "Zora's Way" (355–62) will baffle and disturb him.

The physical and psychic representation of Zora operates in direct relation to and continual engagement with the swamp and its mysterious darkness. First of all, Zora—a young girl when the narrative begins—is initially "sighted" in the darkness of night. "With dancing mischief in her eyes . . . with impish glee, laughing low music," Zora comments on Bles's fear of the darkness the night they meet. She says to him,

> "You was a-feared."
> "Well, I reckon you'd be a-feared if you was caught out in the black dark all alone."
> "Pooh!" she scoffed and hugged her knees. "Pooh! I'se stayed out all alone heaps o' nights. . . . who's a-feared of the dark? *I love night.*" (16–17)

The night serves as the source of her dreams. They instruct and guide Zora according to nature. She privileges what she learns over the education Bles seeks from the white teachers who run the plantation school. Du Bois's ideas about the education of blacks in the South, during the novel's narrative time span (from the late nineteenth through the opening decade of the twentieth century), inform how Zora reacts to Bles's goal to be a student at "Old Miss' [Smith's] school" (18). "Old Miss" is Sarah Smith, its white founder and director. Bles explains to Zora that he has come from Georgia to attend the school. Her reaction issues forth without reservation: "I hate it! . . . Yon way's nicest . . . *the swamp* [emphasis added]" (18). When he asks her what lies beyond the swamp, Zora's response leaves him in a state of wonder:

> She crouched beside him and whispered in eager, tense tones: "Dreams!"
> He looked at her, puzzled.
> "Dreams?" vaguely—"dreams? Why, dreams ain't—nothing."
> "Oh, yes they is!" she insisted, her eyes flaming in misty radiance as she sat staring beyond the shadows of the swamp. "Yes they is! There ain't nothing but dreams—that is, nothing much.
> "And over yonder behind the swamps is great fields full of dreams, piled high and burning; and right amongst them the sun, when he's tired o' night, whispers and drops red things, 'cept when devils make 'em black." (19).

Bles not only does not understand Zora's dream theory, but his grounding in material reality keeps him from "seeing," for envisioning a different kind of life. His inability to reconceptualize reality, to transform it, ultimately leaves him visionless, though he will be continually validated intellectually by his white teachers as he develops from boyhood to manhood. Zora's education, in contrast, begins in nature. Du Bois shows her more closely related to nonhuman figures and signs (which cannot be comprehended by the uninitiated) than to anyone unwilling to move beyond conventional definitions of existence. And Zora "plays" on Bles's fear of the supernatural, illustrating the superiority of dreams as the most effective teacher of wisdom. The description of the "great fields full of dreams" appears incredible to Bles. The territory of the unconscious, the site of imaginative and creative transformation, is where, for Zora, experience reconstructs and reorders itself in disparate, mysterious ways: "I goes there [to the "great fields full of dreams"] sometimes. I creeps in 'mongst the dreams; they hangs there like big flowers, dripping dew and sugar and blood—red, red blood. And there's little fairies there that hop about and sing, and devils—great, ugly devils that grabs at you and roasts and eats you if they gits you; but they don't git me. Some devils is big and white, like ha'nts; some is long and shiny, like creepy, slippery snakes; and some is little and broad and black, and they yells" (19–20). Dreams are the principal enabler for Zora's intellectual maturation. That she reveals to Bles the function of dreams in her life demonstrates her feeling of innate connection to him. Though he lacks the intuitive power Zora possesses, she appears to be just as drawn to him as he to her. In fact, in Zora's way of thinking the two have always been connected. At the end of the first chapter, Zora says to Bles, "We'se known us all our lives, and—before, ain't we?" He agrees and responds, "And we'll be friends always won't we?" (18).

From their chance meeting to the end of the novel, they struggle to remain connected in spite of capitalist, racist exploitation and sexist oppression, which threaten to drive them apart. How Du Bois handles Zora's experiences after chapter 1 illustrates his insight into the ways race, sex, and poverty act as interlocking forces of oppression. They determine the nature of her relationship with Bles, with other men (white and black), and with other women (black and white). *The Quest* is a novel about the effects of racism, sexism, and classism on womanhood generally and black female experience in particular. Northeastern University Press marketed the novel's most recent edition (1989) as an "epic of cotton," focused on Bles Alwyn's development as its hero. It says the novel "dramatizes the economic conflict between cotton growers and Northern capitalists. . . . *[It] also deals with the coming of age of Bles Alwyn . . . and is as much an allegorical romance as a political novel* [emphasis added]."[1] The publisher privileges Bles Alwyn's "coming of age" over Zora's. The plot description it gives obscures the pivotal function Zora serves in the text. Arnold Rampersad states that the feminist identification of women as the superior of men in the leadership of the race is a major feature of *The Quest of the Silver Fleece*. (Indeed, Du Bois depicts women—black and white—as the superior sex in terms not only of morality but also of intellect and leadership.) "While Bles Alwyn is a principled and intelligent young man . . . *Zora Creswell emerges finally as his intellectual and spiritual superior* [my emphasis]. It is not empty chivalry but the recognition of her true superiority that makes Bles, in the final scene of the book, kneel before Zora and declare himself 'not worthy' of her" (Rampersad [1911] 1989, 9).

Much of the scholarship by men has asserted a male-centered interpretation of the novel's plot as a sociopolitical "love story." For example, Richard Kostelanetz states that Du Bois had mastered a range of rhetorical strategies from the formal essay and the political treatise to poetry. However, Kostelanetz views *The Quest* as "an off-and-on romance" composed of a series of related subplots; and he characterizes Zora as little more than a "romantic figure with no surname more precise than 'child of the swamp' " (1985, 174).

Many chapters in *The Quest* show Zora to be central in its construction of thematic unity. Five carry her name in their titles, not including chapter 1. Chapter 5, entitled "Zora," continues to shape a portrait of a black girl outside "civilized" notions of the feminine. Du Bois creates this picture through descriptive repetition that contributes to the imagery surrounding Zora and shows her to be a woman of royal Neithian descent: "Zora, child of the swamp, was a heathen hoyden of twelve wayward, untrained years. Slight, straight, strong, full-blooded, she had dreamed her life away in wilful wandering through her dark and sombre kingdom until she was one with it in all its moods; mischievous, secretive, brooding; full of great and awful visions, steeped body and soul in wood-lore" (Du Bois [1911] 1989, 44). Zora is also a master of the tall tale. In fact, as revealed in chapter 4, the dreams she recounts to Bles demonstrate the boundlessness of her imagination. Her storytelling power, "steeped body and soul in wood-lore," keeps Bles coming back to the swamp to hear more. "Zora" offers a more detailed examination of the twelve-year-old girl's visionary power, which exists, she says " 'cause [her] mammy [Elspeth] is a witch" (44). This power informs her attitude toward white people, and learning, and her views regarding work (or the lack thereof).

During the first year of Zora and Bles's friendship, "her wayward teasing and the almost painful thrill of her tale-telling nettled him and drove him away" (45). When the two met again after many months, Zora had changed. Though she had not, like Bles, spent nearly a year at Miss Smith's school, her unbridled energy and mischievous nature had become more tempered and directed: "She had dropped the impish mischief of her way, and up from beneath it rose a wistful, visionary tenderness; a mighty half-confessed, half-concealed, striving for unknown things" (45–46). Bles develops from his exposure to formal education, but Zora's development comes from a turning within herself that is sparked by an emerging desire to understand the unexplained.

Even as a young girl Zora possesses insight into people, and visionary power aids her in reading their motives—"I can see right through people" (46), she says. But manifested in her attitude toward white people is a critique of white supremacy. When Bles tells her that she must learn to read, Zora says:

> "What for?"
> "So that you can read books and know lots of things."
> "Don't white folks make books?"
> "Yes—most of the books."
> "Pooh! I knows more than they do now—a heap more."
> "In some ways you do; but they know things that give them power and wealth and make them rule." (46)

But her retort comes in the form of an indictment of the white ruling class that clarifies her perception of its control over the production of knowledge: "No, no. They don't really rule; they just thinks they rule. They just got things,—heavy, dead things" (46). In Zora's analysis of race, what makes blacks different from whites is "spirit." "We black folks," she says, "is got the *spirit*. We'se lighter and cunninger; we fly right through them; we go and come again just as we wants to. Black folks is wonderful" (46). As a young black nationalist in the making, she herself embodies the qualities she names. As propagandistic spokeswoman for Du Bois here, Zora stands in emblematic relation to the novel's political agenda—the racial and economic liberation of black people in the South.

"I'se thought it all before . . .": Zora's "Primal Battle with the Word"

Even though Bles concedes there are things beyond white people's knowledge, he challenges Zora to become literate, arguing that she ought to know everything that whites know. She accepts his challenge with astounding results, beginning a "primal battle with the Word." She wins with speed and agility. Stories about great men, things, and places intrigue her. Yet, mysteriously, it appears that what she reads is already known to her. Zora says, "I knew it all . . . every bit. I'se thought it all before; only little things is different—and I like the little change things" (Du Bois [1911] 1989, 48). As Zora had introduced Bles to the imaginative world of dreams and tall tales, so he had introduced her to the world of words. But the next challenge remained: getting Zora to agree to attend the white-run school headed by Miss Smith. During a conversation between Bles and Zora about it and the money needed to study there, she expresses her attitude toward work. She dislikes it passionately, stating, "[Y]ou see, mammy's pappy was a king's son, and kings don't work. I don't work; mostly I dreams" (49). But because Zora values Bles's friendship and believes there to be a certain benefit to formal education, she expresses a willingness to work picking cotton with him to pay for their education. She works beside him, without complaint about the backbreaking nature of the work, even to the point where her hands bleed; and she nearly collapses from exhaustion.

Through Bles, Zora has been exposed to the value of work, and that becomes an important lesson for her later. Du Bois creates a role for Bles that complements Zora's natural abilities. He takes a leading position in her "worldly" education and introduces her to the story of Jason and the quest for the Golden Fleece (as his analogy for a plan he devises to help Zora meet the school tuition). Bles comes up with the idea for them to plant and sell cotton—to create their own "Silver Fleece." After he conceives the idea, Zora "sees" the swamp as the natural place to sow its seeds. The more she comes to have a sense of her destiny, the more Bles must release himself from the traditional role of patriarch and protector. Only at the end of the novel, when Zora assumes the position of leadership in liberation struggle, does Bles realize that he has to rid himself of his sexist notions of male identity. Yet one of the most poignant moments in the novel occurs when Bles takes his own meager earnings to buy a dress for Zora (who had no real knowledge of "proper" school wear), realizing that she had earned just enough money to pay for her first year of schooling: "He carried it to Zora in the wood. . . . Of course, it was long and wide; but he fetched needle and thread and scissors, too. It was a full month after school had begun when they, together back in the swamp, shadowed by the foliage, began to fashion the wonderful garment" (50). Early in the text, as Bles aids Zora in making the transition from nature to "civilization," he serves as a bridge to the next stage of her development.

Wearing the scarlet dress she and Bles had remade, Zora enters Miss Smith's school. It marks her step into a world where she must learn new ways of seeing and being. Rather quickly her precocious and "odd" nature is recognized and commented upon by Miss Smith and her teacher, Miss Taylor, who sees her as a threat to the progress Bles has made as the school's star pupil. Mary Taylor perceives him to be far superior to Zora, not because he is smarter but because she appears so different. To Miss Smith Mary says,

> "She is so far beneath him."
> [Miss Smith:] "How so?"
> "She is a bold, godless thing; I don't understand her."

> [Mary:] ". . . she is unnaturally forward."
> "Too bright," Miss Smith amplified.
> "Yes; she knows quite too much. You surely remember that *awful scarlet dress* [emphasis added]? Well, all her clothes have arrived, or remained, at a simplicity and vividness that is—well—immodest." (66)

For Mary Taylor, Zora is "a bold, godless thing," beyond her understanding. And her "unnatural forward" disposition, coupled with the fact that she is "too bright," poses more of a threat to Mary Taylor than to Bles Alwyn. The otherness of Zora in this white woman's imagination is compounded by the "simplicity and vividness" of her clothing (particularly the scarlet dress). Miss Taylor continues to be intrigued by Zora even until the day she finishes her training at the school. What frightens her most about this strange black girl, whose "classification in school was nearly as difficult as her classification in the world" (71), is Zora's beauty, intelligence, and rebellious nature. But more than anything, the young precocious black girl poses a threat to Mary Taylor because of her ability to see through falseness. While Mary refuses to relate to Zora across the boundaries of race and class, she admires her physical features: "She was beautiful as she stood there—strangely, almost uncannily, but startlingly beautiful with her rich dark skin, softly moulded features, and wonderful eyes" (74).

Zora continually outwits her teacher and refuses to conform to rules in which she sees no validity. When Mary gives her a lesson on the evil of lying, the astute pupil reveals that her teacher is herself a perpetrator of deception and lies, particularly in the way she masks her contempt for black people:

> "Is it wrong," asked Zora, "to make believe you like people when you don't, when you'se afeared of them and thinks they may rub off and dirty you?"
> [Miss Taylor:] "Why—why—yes, if you—if you, deceive."
> "Then you lies sometimes, don't you." (72)

In another conversation Mary Taylor questions Zora about her future and the kind of work she will take up. Suggesting that she would make a good cook or maid, Zora responds that she hates cooking and does not know what a maid does. Mary, explaining that a maid takes care of people, gets a positive response from Zora: "Helps folks that they love? I'd like that." However, when Mary tells her it harldy matters whether or not she cares for those she serves and that the pay received should be the primary motivation, Zora rejects the notion of "help[ing] folks" for pay. "Living," she says, "should come free, like—like sunshine" (73). One should serve freely those one loves. Du Bois places this belief, one completely incomprehensible to Mary Taylor, at the core of Zora's dreams for the liberation of her people.

At the end of her formal education at Miss Smith's school, she emerges a more "refined" thinker, though her connection to the swamp remains a continual source of inspiration and her imaginative power has been maintained. In fact, the swampland, where Zora had suggested to Bles earlier that they plant, has miraculously brought forth the "Silver Fleece." In the process of their working, sharing, and nurturing the cotton, however, Zora begins to grow distant from Bles: "She was drifting away from him in some intangible way to an upper world of dress and language and deportment, and the new thought was pain to him" (128). But there are also other signs of Zora's maturation that unsettle Bles, who has grown to possess deep feelings for her. In the various trials that they faced in the cotton enterprise, to Bles Zora had changed. She was to be seen as neither a child "nor sister nor friend, but as the One Woman" (153).

Du Bois's Radical Critique: Black Male Sexist Idealization of Black Womanhood and Female Sexuality

On one level, Du Bois constructs images of Zora and Bles in mythic proportions, as idealized versions of black womanhood and manhood. Yet, on another, calling into question masculinist ideas of black womanhood, Du Bois represents its judgmental standpoint in the critique Bles advances about Zora's lifestyle. Bles challenges the moral foundation of Zora's life, which, by his own standard, is less than perfect. Her life, as he had known for the greater part of his youth, is wrapped in the mysteries of the swamp. Even so, Bles attempts to draw a perimeter around what she should represent. Acknowledging her sensuality, he frames it in traditional male notions of woman as object of desire. He says to Zora at one point while contemplating her "feminine" attributes, "Your lips—your full and purple lips—were made alone for kissing, not for words." She retorts, "They'll do for both" (Du Bois [1911] 1989, 166). Her response makes it clear that, though she loves Bles, she refuses to be objectified or silenced for love. The nature of their love changes because Bles refuses to accept Zora's past. From the young woman's early childhood on, the cabin she and her mother inhabit has been used as a site for the orgiastic, drunken escapades of white men—with Elspeth as its overseer. Bles's reaction to this information determines how Zora will thereafter respond to him, to other men and women (both white and black), and to society's perception of her sexuality as a black woman.

Du Bois raises the issue of black female sexuality in connection with questions of race, religion, color symbolism, and sexual stereotypes of purity. Early in the novel, Bles shows Zora a picture of the Virgin Mary holding a lily. Having had no prior exposure to Christianity, Zora's curiosity is aroused. Upon her request to know more about this woman, Bles explains who the Virgin is and that the lily is a symbol of purity. Zora, struck by the whiteness of the Madonna, remarks, "How white she is; she's as white as the lily, Bles; but—I'm sorry she's white—Bles, what's purity—just whiteness (98)"? Zora's question forms the basis for Du Bois's continual critique of "whiteness" as a sign of racial and moral superiority. Where the un-Christianized Zora readily interrogates "white" supremacy, Bles, who accepts it unwittingly, defends the racist and sexist ideology of color symbolism that has become attached to it as dogma: "[I]t [purity as identified by whiteness] means being good—just *as good as a woman knows how*" [emphasis added] (98).

During the couple's discussion of female purity and goodness, Zora never states directly to Bles what it is that troubles her about the concepts. Rather, she implicitly seeks his validation of her purity by repeating his statement in the form of a question. Emphasizing "good" (as opposed to "better," its comparative form), Zora inquires: "Not better—not better than she [woman] knows, but just as good, in—lying and stealing and—and *everything* [emphasis added]?" (98). Zora's notions of lying and stealing are different from society's notions of moral behavior. Bles answers the question in the affirmative, leading Zora to exclaim, "I'm—pure" (99). Logically then, she is pure, *possessing no knowledge of "better."* Bles, at that time, having no evidence of her life history that would suggest anything different, agrees: "Of course you are" (99). Through Zora, Du Bois challenges traditional notions of sexual purity and female "goodness," particularly as they have been [mis]applied to black women. Her questioning of the meaning of sexual purity is part of the novel's critique of the virgin/whore myth. Du Bois portrays Zora as the antithesis of the racist and sexist stereotypes of black womanhood, but he never allows the reader to lose sight of her sensuality.

Black female sexuality in *The Quest* functions in two interrelated ways. On the one hand, it defies sexual "otherness." On the other, it underscores the sexual vulnerability of black women under the control of white male exploitation and abuse. While Zora resists being confined to Bles's version of the virgin/whore, Elspeth succumbs to white men's racist objectification and sexually perverse treatment of her. Her cabin on the Creswell plantation functions as a house of prostitution frequented by white men. Apparently, Zora (a girl of thirteen when the novel begins), had been brought into the "service" of these men by her mother. Though a symbol of the evil that racism works on the lives of black women, Elspeth, "a conjure woman," is capable of using her power for good ends. For example, she gives the cotton seeds to Zora and Bles, and the seeds become the "Silver Fleece." Yet Du Bois remains insistent upon emphasizing the horror of Elpeth's distorted image, describing her in hideous terms as: "an old woman—short, broad, black and wrinkled, with fangs and pendulous lips and red, wicked eyes" (20).

Traditionally in black communities, the matriarch has stood as a symbol of familial continuity and wisdom. Elspeth has become the ultimate symbol of perversion of the black feminine in the West. As a conjure woman in the diasporic tradition of African religious mythology, Elspeth possesses magical powers of fertility and creativity. But this power is "othered." In the white supremacist imagination, she stands in for the evil itself. Thus, Elspeth's primeval African qualities have been subverted and dehumanized, and she is equated with the swamp as a malevolent force. Her demonization severely undermines the maternal relationship she has with Zora. Not only that, but it allows for other young black girls to be violated by white men in the cabin where Elspeth lives. Until her death, she exercises a kind of psychic control over the young Zora that keeps her in a state of shifting emotions about their relationship. She fears, loves, and hates her mother. Before Zora breaks free of the mother's stranglulation hold, Elspeth comes to embody the battle Zora has to wage against the forces that oppose her beyond the swamp: "The world was against her [Zora], and again she saw the fingers of Elspeth—the long black claw-like talons that clutched and dragged her down—down" (187).

Du Bois creates an unresolved tension between mother and daughter, one always informed by their status as sexually violated black females. Zora's fear of Elspeth lay in the real possibility that she could have become her, falling prey as her mother had to the racist myths of black womanhood. As a helpless young girl, Zora had to continually struggle to resist the impulse to give over to this base condition. Even after her death, the nightmarish vision of Elspeth still comes to Zora in her dreams: "For yonder where the black earth of the swamp heaved in a formless mound she felt the black arms of Elspeth rising from the sod—gigantic, mighty. They stole toward her with stealthy hands and claw-like talons. They clutched at her skirts. She froze and could not move. Down, down she slipped toward the black slime of the swamp, and the air about was horror—down, down, till the chilly waters stung her knees; and then with one grip she seized the oak, while the great hand of Elspeth twisted and tore her soul" (371). Ultimately, to survive and to escape further victimization, Zora has to sever her ties to this distorted, misshapen form of black womanhood Elspeth represents—the only maternal figure she has known.

Though Elspeth is not redeemed in the novel, she is not without historical context. She represents the myth of the "mammy-whore" as both surrogate and "madam" in the life of Harry Creswell. When he was a child,

Elspeth served him as "mammy" on the Creswell plantation. Confessing to Mary Taylor (who symbolized "a good woman" in his mind) about the nature of his relationship to Elspeth, he says,

> You have been to Elspeth's cabin; it is an evil place, and has meant evil for this community, and for me. Elspeth was my mother's favorite servant and my own mammy. My mother died when I was ten and left me to her tender mercies. She let me have my way and encouraged the bad in me. It's a wonder I escaped total ruin. Her cabin became a rendezvous for drinking and carousing. I told my father, but he, in lazy indifference, did nothing. I ceased my visits. Still she tried every lure and set false stories going among the Negroes, even when I sought to rescue Zora. I tell you this because I know you have heard evil rumors. I have not been a good man—Mary; but I love you, and you can make me good. (206–7)

Harry Creswell's narrative about the corruption of the white male at the hands of the "evil," sexually permissive black woman defies credibility. His attraction and later marriage to Mary Taylor is little more than a means to secure favor from her brother, a Northern cotton speculator. Creswell characterizes himself as the victim of a plot concocted by Elspeth to ruin him. While aspects of his story may be true, he no doubt fabricates others. One questions Elpeth's power to corrupt him sexually, as one ought to question his attempt to "rescue" Zora. In reality, it is precisely his intense hate for Zora that causes Mary Taylor to question his relationship to her. Creswell, we discover later, has fathered a child by one of the black women, Bertie, whom Elspeth kept at the cabin.

The cabin and all that goes on there stand for evil. Ultimately, it will be the sexual evil perpetrated against Elspeth, Zora, and the other women (black and white) who cross the path of the Creswell men (father and son) that will return to undo them. After Elspeth's death, Zora obtains the power to send away all the women who had been "kept" at the cabin. But before Zora comes to understand how the sexual abuse of these women had turned them against one another, she (still under the sexist moral inculcation of Bles) condemned to hell "bad" black women. About one of them who had given birth to a "blue-eyed and golden-haired" child, Zora says: "Her mother [Bertie] is bad. She is gone. I sent her. She and the others like her . . . to Hell" (205). Zora's distinction between "good" and "bad" women is made clear only after she herself experiences public condemnation by Harry Creswell, heir to the Creswell plantation.

Unscrupulously racist and sexist, Harry Creswell had often been found at Elspeth's cabin, seeking sexual pleasure. Perhaps it is his own feelings of internalized guilt and hatred for Zora that lead him to humiliate her in the presence of Bles, Mary Taylor, and others. Intending to viciously malign Zora, he scoffs, "[T]he girl is notorious," implying that she is commonly known to be sexually promiscuous. Interestingly, the slanderous remark comes just after Bles and Zora have been seen embracing by Creswell and his party. Approaching the two, Creswell lashes out at them, condemning such behavior as prurient and distasteful. His angry reaction indicates to Mary Taylor that "her worst suspicions had been confirmed" (166)—that Creswell, whom she has come to love, himself has possibly been sexually involved with Zora. Until her sexual conduct comes under attack by Creswell, Bles had confirmed—indeed, reaffirmed—to her that she was "good" and pure. Creswell recruits Miss Taylor, who under the guise of concern for Bles leads the impressionable youth to confront Zora about her sexual conduct: "You—you told me—you were—pure" (169). She responds by painfully recounting her history of sexual abuse. Now Bles must confront the gap between his image of Zora as a virgin and the reality of her sexual violation. In Zora's mind Bles has the power to make her a virgin again. His definition of purity, validated through his worship of the Virgin Mary, has sexually purified ("whitened") Zora. Even after having been sexually abused as a child, Zora still maintained that she possessed sexual innocence, on the grounds that as a child she "knew" no better. Beyond reason, Bles retorts: "Knew! All women know! You should have *died*" (170).

As a young black man (at this point in the novel) without real power to challenge Zora's sexual abusers, Bles can, like Creswell, exert tremendous power over his female counterpart. In his mind, Zora should have chosen death rather than be defiled. For him the loss of "purity" signified the loss of status as a "good" woman, a loss he views as synonymous with loss of life. Zora defends herself on the grounds that "all *girls* [emphasis added] do not know. I was a child." Obviously, as the concubine of white men, Zora and other black girls kept at the cabin have no power to withhold their bodies. Naively, Zora believes that through the power of words, Bles can free her. All he has to do is say so, and she can reclaim her sexual innocence: "I began running away, and they hunted me through the swamps. And then—then I reckon I'd have gone back and been—as they all are—but *you* came, Bles—*you* came, and you—you were a new great thing in my life, and—and yet, I was afraid I was not worthy until you—said the words. I thought you knew, and I thought that—that purity was just *wanting* to be pure" (170). Taking Bles as her "savior," in gratitude for his having been the first male with whom she felt kinship and empowerment, Zora allows him to assume power over her. Initially, Bles "said the words" that validated the worth of a young impressionable, needy child. For Zora to reclaim the power of her own words, she must come to understand that her desire for sexual liberation is caught up in the illusion of freedom spoken in Bles's words. She comes to realize that they reinforce both racist and sexist notions of female "virtue" that will revictimize her. Refusing to see beyond the racism and sexism that inform Harry Creswell and Mary Taylor's misrepresentation of Zora, Bles ironically becomes an agent of racial and sexual oppression. Like Creswell, he blames her. But Zora learns a painful lesson in Bles's rejection. Neither he nor any other man will be her liberator.

As such, Du Bois shows how the nature of sexism plays itself out across race and class lines. He criticizes white and black male sexist practice without reducing his critical interrogation of racism. Yet he focuses sharply on Bles's rejection of Zora to expose the mechanics of black male sexism. As stated before, Bles is powerless to act against a white man in defense of Zora, and that compounds the problem. His masculinity is at stake. In his mind he, as the black cuckold, becomes the victim, not Zora: "Oh, he was a innocent—a blind baby—the joke and laughing-stock of the country around, with yokels grinning at him and pale-faced devils laughing aloud. The teachers knew; the girls knew; God knew; everybody but he knew—poor blind, deaf mole, stupid jackass that he was" (170). Bles, having determined his reputation now to be more tainted than hers in the public's eyes, shuts himself off from a compassionate reconsideration of Zora's sexual past. "[H]ow can I grow pure?" she asks him. His response is to exclaim "Never—never again" (171). McKay underscores the fact that Du Bois did not hesitate to interrogate black men's role in the oppression of black women. She places the portrayal of Bles in a historical context, observing: "Nor were black men always helpful and understanding in connection with the sexual exploitation of their women, as the actions of Bles illustrate. Women were often left to struggle through to their own salvation, alone or in the company of other women" (1985, 242).

Coupled with Bles's unrelenting rejection, Zora must contend with the fact that Harry Creswell virtually steals the cotton crop she and Bles have produced. He calls it payment for back rent on the cabin. The racist accusations of sexual promiscuity and the loss of respectability from the man she loves leave Zora seemingly on the verge of complete and utter despair. Up to this point in the novel, the only woman who speaks on her behalf is Miss Smith. The relationships Zora has with various women in *The Quest* reveal the extent to which racism and sexism work to undermine them. As previously argued, the gulf created between Zora and her mother exists because of white men's sexual objectification of black women. While the jealousy and hatred Mary Taylor harbors against Zora have much to do with her own personal insecurities, they are surely compounded by Mary's belief that Harry Creswell has had sexual relations with her. Among the Southern white women in the text, aside from Miss Smith, Mary is a particularly intelligent, though racist, woman. Yet she allows her abilities to be thwarted by men, first by her brother and then by Harry, whom she marries. In the course of their marriage, he discredits her intelligence, and his ruthless womanizing leaves Mary shattered. His flagrant sexual impropriety results in the death of their first child due to syphilis. By the end of the novel, Mary acknowledges to herself that his deceit had destroyed her ambition to excel. She admits that "[Zora] was the sort of woman she herself might have been if she had not married" (Du Bois [1911] 1989, 419).

Zora is fundamentally different from Mary in two ways. First, her ideas of femininity and sexuality (prior to Bles Alwyn's influence) contest the cult of domesticity. Second, she has a will to resist female oppression (sexually and racially). To assume the role of feminist insurgent and community organizer, Zora must reject a masculinist version of female "purity." The vision of revolutionary black womanhood in the text depends upon her ability to reconceptualize it in womanist terms. This becomes Zora's "quest" for the remainder of the novel. Counter to Bles's assertion that she can never regain her innocence, Zora begins a search for another kind of purity integral to discovering a great purpose in life, and to be found in a spiritual realm rather than a physical one. Du Bois clearly crafts the intellectual, physical, and spiritual evolution of Zora Creswell against Western notions of female beauty, virtue, and power.

Beyond Western Notions of Womanhood: Zora's Search for Autonomy as a *Self*-Identified Black Woman

For Du Bois, Zora's search is about self-autonomy, and it must be integrally linked to a liberatory idea of black female sexuality. It must also affirm mental and spiritual health. In this framework, self-knowledge becomes the critical tie between personal liberation for Zora and freedom for the people of her community in the South. To fulfill her destiny, she must confront the racism and sexism perpetrated by Harry Creswell, by Mary Taylor, and by the man she continues to care for deeply—Bles Alwyn. The question "How can I grow pure?" is the single most important one Zora asks herself in the novel. The answer will come only after a long, painful process of self-examination and reeducation regarding her place and social contribution *as a black woman*. But even before contemplating a new life course, she resolutely vows not to be consumed by despair: "A desperate resolve to find some way up toward the light, if not to it, formed itself within her.

She would not fall into the pit opening before her. Somehow, somewhere lay The Way. She must never fall lower; never be utterly despicable in the eyes of the man she had loved. *There was no dream of forgiveness, of purification, of re-kindled love; all these she placed sadly and gently into the dead past* [emphasis added]. But in awful earnestness, she turned toward the future; struggling blindly, groping in half formed plans for a way" (Du Bois [1911] 1989, 189).

"Somehow, somewhere lay The Way." In *The Quest*, "The Way" functions as a Du Boisian trope signifying a journey, a process toward self-empowerment. For Zora it initially means a letting go—of the need to be forgiven for sexual misconduct, to be "pure" or virginal as determined by men, to be loved romantically. "All these [Zora] placed [albeit with trepidation] in the dead past." The path Zora must travel to self-determination leads her away from her community, away from the South. But she carries with her the lessons learned from nature. Nature remains an enabler to the process Zora has begun to rediscover the importance of dreams and the imagination in solving social problems. Those imaginative dreams and visions will operate in conjunction with the development of a new level of intellectual power. Together imagination and intellect will prepare the budding visionary for the service she will render the downtrodden blacks (and whites) in her community.

From the South to the North: Zora's Intellectual *and* Physical Makeover (Consider the Politics of Black Women's Hair)

Furthering Zora's imaginative and intellectual maturation, as well as her physical movement from South to North and back again, are two white women: Miss Smith and Mrs. Vanderpool, a Northern aristocrat. While Mary Taylor finally concedes Zora's superior intellect and beauty, she never accepts her as an equal. On the other hand, Miss Smith, founder of the school for black children, takes a particular interest in Zora's welfare, introducing her protégée to Mrs. Vanderpool. Du Bois continually juxtaposes Mary's attitude toward Zora with that of these two white women. He characterizes Sarah Smith as a white woman who has a genuine interest in the humanity of black people. As her relationship to Zora develops, Miss Smith serves as a surrogate mother for her—giving advice, encouraging her intellectual progress, and exhorting her to search within herself for a sustaining power that is not male-identified. After Bles has cast Zora off, Sarah says to her, "[N]o man is quite worth a woman's soul; no love is worth a whole life" (Du Bois [1911] 1989, 182). Sarah Smith saves her from falling back into the hellish pit of sexual enslavement from which she had escaped.

To get Zora away from this environment, Miss Smith agrees to Mrs. Vanderpool's suggestion that Zora accompany her North to be her personal servant. Recognizing her extraordinary potential, the two women believe this journey will open up certain opportunities for Zora. Mrs. Vanderpool says to her upon the outset of their trip to New York, "I need you, Zora. . . . Yes, and you need me; we need each other. In the world lies opportunity, and I will help you" (225). As an old, liberal, wealthy white woman, Mrs. Vanderpool fashions herself as a savior to Zora. Yet in the course of their relationship, it is Zora who becomes the savior for her, a white woman without purpose in her life: "She had all the elements of power save the motive for doing anything in particular. For the first time, perhaps, *Zora gave her life a peculiar human interest* [emphasis added]" (247).

Under Mrs. Vanderpool's guidance, Zora makes tremendous intellectual and cultural strides. Chapter 23, "The Training of Zora," marks the beginning of the remarkable young woman's physical and intellectual growth. "The girl's language came to be more and more like Mrs. Vanderpool's; her dress and taste in adornment had been Mrs. Vanderpool's first care, and it led to a curious training in art and sense of beauty until *the lady now and then found herself learner before the quick suggestiveness of Zora's mind* [emphasis added]" (247). When Mary (Taylor) Creswell visits New York one month after Zora's departure from Alabama, she calls upon Mrs. Vanderpool and is astounded by the progress Zora has made. With her own liberal racism, Mrs. Vanderpool treats Zora "equally" as an unequal. "I wonder," she says to Mary, "what I shall make out of her? . . . Do you know, I believe I could mould her into a lady if she were not black" (248). Mary Creswell cannot hide her disdain for the deferential way Mrs. Vanderpool behaves toward Zora. Mary Creswell is even more critical of how impressed the elderly socialite seems by Zora's physical beauty. Treating her to a makeover, Mrs. Vanderpool responds amusingly to Mary Creswell's claim that the greatest obstacle to transforming Zora into a lady is her hair: "It has artistic possibilities. You should have seen my hair-dresser's face when I told her to do it up. . . . Yet it was done. *It lay in some great twisted cloud* [emphasis added] and in that black net gown of mine Zora was simply magnificent. Her form is perfect, her height is regal, her skin is satin, and my jewels [have] found a resting place at last. Jewels, you know, dear, were never meant for white folk" (248).

Du Bois constantly references Zora's physical features, concentrating on the beauty and particular nature of her hair. He calls it "[a] heavy mass" (14), "a misty mass of waveless hair" (52), and "that great dark mass of immovable infinitely curled hair . . . lay[ing] in thick twisted braids about her velvet forehead, like some shadowed halo" (123–24). "[T]hat hair" (248), as Mary Creswell refers to it, remains a focal point in Zora's physical presence. Du Bois's repeated emphasis on its "heavy," "misty," "dark," massive quality—as of "some great twisted cloud" or a shadowed halo—raises the qualities of black female hair to mythic proportions. In *The Quest*, black female hair functions as a political statement affirming "naturally" textured hair. Almost a decade after *The Quest* was published, in "The Damnation of Women," Du Bois would write about the beauty of his own mother's natural hair; and in this particular physical feature, Zora and his mother bear a striking similarity.

While Mrs. Vanderpool believes Zora's makeover complements the young woman's natural beauty, as a white woman of the ruling class her motive is to show off her "creation" to the white social elite of New York. Her treatment of Zora leaves Mary Creswell with grave misgivings: "It's wrong to treat her as you do. You make her an equal. Her room is one of the best and filled with books and bric-a-brac. She sometimes eats with you—is your companion, in fact" (248). Zora's relationship to Mrs. Vanderpool is a complex one. While in her employment, Zora not only takes on more sophisticated ways of speech and dress, but also becomes increasingly more intellectually challenging. Mary Creswell's description of the room Zora occupies indicates that Mrs. Vanderpool has promoted her intellectual pursuits: "She can talk much better than many of my friends . . . she's a sort of intellectual sauce that stirs my rapidly failing mental appetite" (249). Indeed, that which enables the young black intellectual to stimulate the mental palates of Mrs. Vanderpool and her friends comes from Zora's passion for book reading: "Hour after hour, day after day, she lay buried, deaf and dumb to all else. Her heart cried, up on the World's four corners of the Way, and to it came the Vision Splendid" (251). The "Vision Splendid" takes form in Zora's expansive reading of world culture, literature, and geography—from the Bible to the histories of Greece, Rome, Paris, London, and Scotland. "She walked on worlds, and worlds of worlds, and heard there in her little room the tread of armies, the paeans of victory, the breaking of hearts, and the music of the spheres" (252).

Zora's room becomes a universe of "world" knowledge. She learns about the history and the accomplishments of many celebrated persons, including "the black and blameless Ethiopians . . . and her own [Alexander] Dumas" (251–52). The reading list comprises nonblacks as well, such as Napoleon and Balzac. "The [t]raining of Zora" combines studying both Africa and the West. Similarly, it mirrors the physical transformation of the precocious young intellectual. The education of Zora reflects Du Bois's ideological and cultural synthesis of Africa and Europe. Embodying both, Zora represents a hybridization of blackness. She leaves the supernatural dreamworld of the swamp, the Du Boisian mythic symbol of Africa. She develops from an elfin child of the rural South into an articulate, sophisticated young woman in

New York City. The more "worldly" knowledge Zora obtains, the more it enables her to translate her dreams and visions. In reality, Mrs. Vanderpool (like Bles and Sarah Smith) helps Zora to understand how "training" in the swamp and formal education can be integrated. Comprehending this prepares Zora for her next stage of development on the "Way" to the task of public service. New York City is where her future as a black liberationist takes shape, and there also an all-important reconsideration of the spiritual aspect of her existence occurs.

"The Vision of Zora" and Her Spiritual Awakening

In "The Vision of Zora," the most revealing chapter in *The Quest*, Zora Creswell finds the "Way." She arrives at it through nothing short of a traditional religious conversion, which takes place in a small black church she had wandered into late one evening. The experience there proves different from any previous ones she has had:

> She found herself all at once intently listening [to the preacher]. She had been to church many times before, but under the sermons and ceremonies she had always sat coldly inert. In the South the cries, contortions, and religious frenzy left her mind untouched; she did not laugh or mock, she simply sat and watched and wondered. At the North, in the white churches, she enjoyed the beauty of wall, window, and hymn, liked the voice and surplice of the preacher; but his words had no reference to anything in which she was interested. Here suddenly came an earnest voice addressed, by singular chance, to her of all the world. (Du Bois [1911] 1989, 294)

Personalizing the preacher's sermon, Zora accepts its message of salvation through service to black folk and their deliverance from the scourge of white racism: "The good of others is our true good; work for others; not for *your* salvation, but the salvation of the world. . . . Unselfishness is sacrifice—Jesus was supreme sacrifice. . . . Forget yourselves and your petty wants, and behold your starving people. The wail of black millions sweeps the air—east and west they cry, Help! Help! . . . The cry of death is in the air; they murder, burn, and maim us! . . . When we cry they mock us; they ruin our women and debauch our children—What shall we do?" (295).

The message embodies that which her previous religious encounters had lacked—a capacity for social agency. Zora had found this missing from both black and white religion, both Southern and Northern. She becomes aware, through the sermon, of the plight of the black masses struggling under the weight of racist oppression. Likening the condition of black folk in the postbellum South to that of the ancient Hebrew people bound in Egypt, she realizes that it calls for revolutionary leadership, someone to act as a modern-day Moses: "Go down to Pharaoh [the plantation owner] and smite him in God's name. Go down to the South where we writhe. Strive—work—build—hew—lead—inspire! God calls. Will you hear? Come to Jesus. The harvest is waiting. Who will cry: 'Here am I, send me!' " (295).

Zora's conversion comes with the realization that she must accept her own calling. "Zora rose and walked up the aisle; she knelt before the altar and answered the call: 'Here am I—send me!' " (295). She will become the Moses of her people, a modern-day Harriet Tubman. In "The Damnation of Women," Du Bois refers to Harriet Tubman as "the crude Moses"; and much earlier Frederick Douglass had praised Tubman for numerous acts of heroism accomplished in leading black women and men to freedom (McFeely 1991, 263). Though more learned and cultured than Tubman, Zora embodies the same self-sacrificing spirit that pervaded Tubman. As her historical counterpart had done, Zora places her own oppression as a black woman within the larger context of black struggle. "There she found God after a searching that had seared her soul; but He had simply pointed the Way, and the way was human" (Du Bois [1911] 1989, 373). This new awareness was marked by "something that seemed to tell how out of the dream had stepped the dreamer into the realness of things; how suddenly the seeker saw; how to the wanderer, the Way was opened" (296). For this revelation to take place, Zora had to leave the South to discover that she was destined to return to it. She then resolves, "I'm going back South to work for my people" (297). The "Way" of social activism found in the North becomes "Zora's Way" (chapter 32's title) only upon her return to the South.

Once again, "Zora's Way" is visionary. She sees the community of black folk with "new eyes," as if for the first time: "These men and women of her childhood had hitherto walked by her like shadows; to-day they lived for her in flesh and blood. She saw hundreds and thousands of black men and women: crushed, half-spirited, and blind" (355). Her concern for the welfare of both the men and the women earns her "the title of white folk, calling her 'Miss' Zora" (356), though in the beginning the community's minister accuses her of evil doings for wanting to change the condition of the people. They find hope in Zora. Through her, they come together to realize their own economic empowerment, illustrated by the community's joint effort in clearing twenty acres of the swamp for planting. Zora then envisions a "land scheme" (403) leading to the purchase and redevelopment of the swamp, principally through cooperative farming. Her eventual goal—a Du Boisian vision of an ideal, black socialist commune—is to establish an independent, self-determined, black community that includes a school, cooperative store, hospital, cotton gin, and sawmill, among other things. Having a woman oversee this enterprise represents a crucial intervention for Du Bois, signifying his commitment to a womanist vision of black liberation. Zora achieves great success as "the Moses of her people." Overcoming the original resistance of the community's patriarch and religious head, the black preacher, she wins the respect of both the women and men; hence to them, too, she becomes "Miss Zora." The scope and breadth of her vision for community development leave the men in awe, almost unable to comprehend its magnitude. "It was a proposal a little too daring for them, a bit too far beyond their experience. One consideration alone kept them from shrinking away and that was Zora's influence. Not a man was there whom she had not helped and encouraged nor who had not *perfect faith in her* [emphasis added]; in her impetuous hope, her deep enthusiasm, and her strong will. Even her defects—the hard-held temper, the deeply rooted dislikes—caught their imagination" (405). Zora has laid the groundwork necessary for them to make what has to be a leap of faith. In spite of sexist preconceptions, men must "reimagine" her as their leader.

Toward a Relationship of Comradeship: Reimagining Zora

Just as Zora must leave the South to find her "Way," so Bles Alwyn, after discovering his own pathway to maturity, must return to his origins. Having matured considerably in his view of women, both intellectually and sexually, Bles is unprepared for his reunion with Zora. He cannot help but notice the change that three years (since last he had seen her) have wrought, physically and mentally: "[S]omething had gone; the innocence and wonder of the child, and in their place had grown up something to him incomprehensible and occult" (Du Bois [1911] 1989, 379). Both people have changed. What Zora seeks from Bles is not a romantic love relationship but one of comradeship in struggle. To her, his training as a lawyer contributes more to that cause than their union as lovers. He proposes marriage, but marriage is not in Zora's plans. She rejects his proposal, but she asks, "[S]ince we understand each other, can we not work together as good friends?" (399). In many ways Bles still does not understand her—just as he had not when they were children: "Somehow he could not understand. His mental attitude toward Zora had always been one of guidance, guardianship, and instruction. He had been judging and weighing her from on high, looking down upon her with thoughts of uplift and development. Always he had been holding her dark little hands to lead her out of the swamp of life, and always, when in senseless anger he had half forgotten and deserted her, this vision of elder brotherhood had still remained. Now this attitude was being revolutionized" (399–400). Bles's vision of himself as the "elder," patriarchal figure in Zora's life is now being "revolutionized" by her own vision. Du Bois invites the reader to compare the two—one conceived in a male fantasy of masculine protector, teacher, leader; the other working in a woman-centered reconceptualization of power, development, and redistribution of economic resources to benefit the masses.

Du Bois constructs a strategic role reversal in the reuniting of Bles and Zora, whereby she takes on the duties and responsibilities traditionally associated with patriarchy. Bles then becomes the novitiate: "He was asked [by Zora] to be co-worker—nay, in a sense to be a follower, for he was ignorant of much." Essentially, he must rethink his relationship to Zora based on her new status. The process of reidentifying himself proves to be a difficult one. Whether or not he can maintain her respect and, in his mind, be subordinate to her raises two important questions for him: "[H]e was not unwilling to be simply human, a learner and a follower, but would he as such ever command the love and respect of this new and inexplicable woman? Would not comradeship on the basis of the new friendship which she insisted on, be the death of love and thoughts of love?" (400). The first question, though its context is completely different, operates similarly to the one Zora had posed much earlier to Bles on the issue of respect, once he learned of her sexual "impurity." Ironically, Bles finds himself wondering whether Zora views him as less worthy of her respect and love—for one incapable of "command[ing]" them. "[T]he readjustment was hard; he grew to it gradually, inwardly revolting, *feeling always a great longing to take this woman and make her nestle in his arms as she used to* [emphasis added] . . . yet ever again holding himself back and bowing in silent respect to the dignity of her life" (400). Gradually he does learn that the respect Zora has commanded reflects an earned self-respect. For Du Bois, the issue of black female self-respect carries immense importance with regard to the dignity of black womanhood, denied because of racism and sexism. Nellie McKay maintains that Du Bois confronts the history of black women's sexual abuse by white men through Zora's experiences, without making her a tragic figure: "Few imaginative works of literature address this problem in a similar way. . . . Given the opportunity, she [Zora] rises above the negative circumstances of her early life to initiate the heroine, on her merits, into our literature" (1985, 245).

The resulting anxiety Bles feels because of the role reversal in his relationship to Zora remains minimal. Only when he seriously reconsiders the horrendous nature of a childhood of sexual violation does he realize the magnitude of the struggle to reach the position she now occupies. "In her direst need he had deserted her. He had left her to go to destruction and expected that she would. *By a superhuman miracle she had risen and seated herself above him* [emphasis added]. . . . He was asked to help; he would help. If it killed his old and new-born dream of love, well and good; it was his punishment" (Du Bois [1911] 1989, 400). Bles comes to realize that Zora no longer needs him in the way she had before. For their relationship to continue, it must be on her terms; and what Zora desires most from Bles is support for her cause. The passion Zora had felt for Bles has been replaced by a consuming love for her people. He knows that, and is willing to accept his place in her plan.

Throughout the novel, Bles continues to be the one individual to whom Zora is drawn. His place in her life remains pivotal in spite of his earlier failings. Zora never forgets how he had helped her escape the horror of the cabin for a new world of experience. Though fraught with contradictions, experience becomes a masterful teacher, enabling Zora to gain insight and understanding of the potential the swamp holds for her people. But what she has realized in her journey toward womanhood as a revolutionary black woman is that intellect, vision, and sexual identity cannot be defined in patriarchal terms. Bles Alwyn had provided the first lesson. Only after questioning the validity of his male-identified worldview could Bles rid himself of the sexist ideology that had once led him to judge and condemn Zora. Coming to the realization that racism, sexism, and sexual exploitation have been the primary factors confronting Zora as a defenseless young girl allows Bles to comprehend "the superhuman miracle" that has enabled her to achieve her leadership status. In reestablishing the grounds for Zora's and Bles's relationship, Du Bois once again raises the question of sexual purity, the catalyst for her quest.

Just as Zora refuses to allow herself to be destroyed by historical circumstances she has no control over, so Bles has to free himself from the white supremacist representation of black women he has internalized. As comrades and coworkers, together Zora and Bles lay the foundation for a new, transformative love between them. This ideological shift signals the turning point in their relationship, which at the close of the novel unites them in marriage. While the novel ends much like a conventional romance, its protagonists break with the tradition in significant ways. First, in Bles's confession of love for Zora, now secure and self-possessed, he disavows sexist notions of female sexuality, claiming that "[Zora] is more than pure" (433). Moreover, he continues to believe that he is unworthy of her love. Second, while it appears the couple will wed, Du Bois has Zora "taking the lead." She proposes marriage to Bles. More significant to Du Bois than the couple's union in marriage during the novel's closing scene is resolving the question Zora raises regarding the sexual character of black women. Bringing the narrative full circle, Du Bois asks the reader to examine once again the issue of black women's sexuality in the novel. He has made the center of Zora's intellectual, physical, and spiritual development a quest for self-recovery and respect—not through a recovery of sexual innocence but through a commitment to public service.

Reading *The Quest* as a Womanist Novel on Its Literary and Political Merit

Nellie McKay reads *The Quest of the Silver Fleece* as a major literary and political achievement for Du Bois. She argues that his daring treatment of the complex sexual history of black women in the novel reveals a thin veneer between fiction and reality. Du Bois employs Zora Creswell as the artistic embodiment of the aesthetic credo espoused in "Criteria of Negro Art." McKay notes, "The woman [Zora] who emerges from th[e] two-fold attack [sexual abuse and exploitation] on her personhood justifies Du Bois's insistence that insult and degradation, sexual and racial, did not destroy the soul of black womanhood in white America. *Women like Zora, as young girls, forced to submit to the wanton lusts of white overlords, rose above the humiliation to bring their 'fineness up through so devilish a fire'* [emphasis added]" (1985, 242).

In politicizing the representation of black womanhood in *The Quest*, Du Bois strategically demonstrates the significance of white women to the education of Zora, as enablers and antagonists. His womanist nationalism does not preclude women working together across racial boundaries. Sarah Smith and Mrs. Vanderpool, in varying degrees, act as enablers to the young insurgent. Thus, it is partly in the context of interracial female relationships that Zora's vision of black empowerment and community development evolves. Her commitment to the welfare of all women and girls, both black and white, never wavers. Of Zora's accomplishments in public service, none are more important than her establishment of a home for orphaned girls and children. If Du Bois modeled his black female hero's character on Harriet Tubman as "the crude Moses," he most certainly shaped her love of humanity after that of Louise De Mortie, the first black woman to found a home for orphans. Bringing Zora's vision full circle, Du Bois connects her concern for the welfare of black girls with her own parentless past. In fact, Emma, the biracial child of Bertie, is the main reason Zora establishes her home for girls. One of the first things Zora sees on returning to the South is Emma, now an adolescent, cavorting with a young white man. Recalling her own history of abuse, Zora looks upon him, and at that moment "the paramount mission of her life formed itself in her mind. She would protect this girl [Emma]; she would protect *all* black girls. She would make it possible for these poor beasts of burden to be decent in their toil. Out of protection of womanhood as the central thought, she must build ramparts against cruelty, poverty, and crime" (Du Bois [1911] 1989, 359).

The vision of black recovery in *The Quest* is womanist-identified. In Alice Walker's words, a liberatory vision of black freedom is about being "committed to [the] survival and wholeness for entire people, male *and* female" (1983, xi). Womanhood becomes "the central thought" of Zora, and women's needs contextualize her fight against the other evils of society. The other important task Zora undertakes regarding women has to do with health care. The small hospital she establishes serves as the main community health-care provider for all children across racial lines. As such, it also becomes the means through which women form their own community: "The grateful mothers [black and white] came out twice a week at least; at first with suspicious aloofness, but gradually melting under Zora's tact until they sat and talked with her and told their troubles and struggles. Zora realized how human they were, and how like their problems were to hers" (Du Bois [1911] 1989, 420). Even Mary (Creswell) Taylor calls her "a vigorous, self-sacrificing woman" (418). She is inspired when Zora refuses Bles's marriage proposal. In light of her own failed marriage, Mary admires the choice Zora makes of service over love: "[T]his seemed fitting. Zora was not meant for marrying; *she was a born leader* [emphasis added], wedded to a great cause; she had long outgrown the boy and girl affection. She was the sort of woman she herself might have been if she had not married" (418).

While women in *The Quest* connect on different levels of communication, the racism of powerful white men repeatedly operates to sever the bonds they make. Zora, however, refuses to allow it or the men's sexism to destroy the connection she forms with black and white women in the community. Of the women in the novel who consistently support her, Sarah Smith is her closest female ally; this is evident when Zora confronts the patriarch of the Creswell family to regain her land and cotton. Perhaps the most important battle Zora wages is the one fought against Colonel Creswell in a court of law. The colonel, behaving as his son had before, virtually robs Zora of two hundred acres of swampland and its cotton by invalidating the deed of ownership he had signed over to her. Acting on her own behalf, Zora alone successfully defends and wins her case against the colonel. The judge rules that the land, including the cotton, be returned to its rightful owner. Even after accomplishing much of the work she has set out to complete and after the "Quest of the Silver Fleece" has come to an end, for Zora the liberation struggle of the people continues: "Think of the servile black folk, the half awakened restless whites, the fat land waiting for the harvest, the masses panting to know—why, the battle is scarcely even begun" (430).

From Genre to Genre: Du Bois as Sociological, Womanist Fiction Writer

Du Bois's work as a sociologist on the condition of poor blacks had gained him national recognition before the publication of *The Quest*. For him fiction represented yet another discursive field for the deployment of his beliefs in racial uplift. He was firmly committed to a vision of art as a political tool. With regard to black liberation, its purpose was undeniably clear: "[A]ll Art is propaganda and ever must be, despite the wailing of the purists. I stand in utter shamelessness and say that *whatever art I have for writing has been used always for propaganda for gaining the right of black folk to love and enjoy. I do not care a damn for any art that is not used for propaganda* [emphasis added]. But I do care when propaganda is confined to one side while the other is stripped and silent" (Du Bois 1926, 296).

Du Bois wrote *The Quest of the Silver Fleece* with the express purpose of promoting the humanity of black people. Zora functions as the feminist messenger for the novel's vision of black liberation. In his closing pronouncements on the novel, David Levering Lewis suggests that "reverberating in future African-American fiction and scholarship is the conviction that the race will be saved by its Zoras, by the black woman charting the course to culture, dignity, family, and work" (1993, 450). Not only does Zora Creswell follow in the nineteenth-century feminist tradition of Frances Harper's Iola Leroy, but she also foreshadows Janie Starks, the Harlem Renaissance creation that another Zora (Neale Hurston) devised for a literary era Du Bois's own creative quest helped to prefigure.

II

Black Feminist "Sisters," "Brothers," and Fathers

Securing the Womanist Legacy

The People Have Need of Our *Hands*

What must we do . . .
As gender-progressive black fathers, brothers, and sons
In our communities to enable every male to engage
In the much-needed healing work of our self-recovery
Against the myth that our manhood and masculinity is rooted in machismo?
In the name of womanist liberation,
We—
Men who know the labor of our foremothers' ***hands***
And the work for gender justice by our womanist forefathers—
In our self-interest,
We must be traitors to manhood bound to the Patriarchal Father.
We must possess the power to name ourselves in recovered, reclaimed
pro-womanist Terms . . .
Of a new vision of black liberation,
Terms that speak about our humanity, our spirit, our love for each other
(My brother, your brother; my father, your father; my son, your son)
And our sisters, mothers, daughters (not queens or concubines).
Vulnerable, strong when we know we need to be (for the greater good),
Sweet for no reason but to give joy, soft as in pliable
(Who we are as men does not reside in pathetic phallic power)—
To call and respond with our hearts,
To give what we have of ourselves
(Our time, energy, labor, comradeship in the time of need),
To be always becoming (without fear of what we will become),
Inventing new frameworks for naming our deepest desires
(Without harm to another),
To feel ourselves free in the embrace of the arms of another—

(Woman, man, or child);
To embrace the fullness of life and living once and for all . . .
To be whole again—
This is our gift to the world;
In giving we will have achieved our manhood
(in terms we have called into being for ourselves)—
This will be the moment of our great revolution!
Let us prepare—Let us hear the voices of the woman warriors,
For they call us into service to serve the people with them—
(without regard to the level of the task).
"Come, come, come," ever so gently they beckon us.
"Stand beside us—serve the people."
"Stand beside us, like this—arm in arm"
(Ever so gently they guide us).
"We will show you how" (and we will trust them fearlessly).
Let us prepare to serve the people with the woman warriors.
The people await our ***hands***.
They are hungry . . . We act; we take the risks without question.

—Gary L. Lemons, inspired by the
feminist activism of M. Jacqui Alexander

5

On the Power of Contemporary Black Feminist Profession

Black Male "Professional" Autocritography

In "Don't Be Like Your Father," the introduction to *Scenes of Instruction*, Michael Awkward uses the rather esoteric word "autocritography" to name the work he accomplishes in his book. He notes that this term had earlier been employed by Henry L. Gates in a promotional blurb on the book cover of a collection of essays by Houston Baker. What drew Awkward to the word was Gates's use of it to stand for an "autobiography of a critical concept." Such a concept is also the thematic thread that connects parts 1 and 2 of the present book. Part 2, concentrates on contemporary manifestations of the Douglass/Du Boisian legacy of gender-progressive *professions* based upon the "autobiography of a critical concept."

The present chapter asserts that autobiographical writing by black men who claim womanist/feminist thinking as a "critical concept" to oppose male supremacy and sexist oppression is not only radical but also revolutionary. As a contemporary memoir of a black male's journey toward becoming a feminist-identified man, *Scenes of Instruction* works within a discursive tradition represented in the autobiographies of Frederick Douglass and W. E. B. Du Bois. Awkward continues the tradition. Over the years, grappling with the implications for teaching black feminist thought through memoir, I began using the phrase "autocritographical writing" to name the pedagogical practice grounded in the confessional style of bell hooks. For me, hooks's strategic employment of the confessional as an anchor for her critique of the social is precisely what autocritographical writing aims to do—particularly in the context of Awkward's thinking about it. He postulates:

> If autobiography is a genre in which contributors shape their self-representations in response to earlier texts, "autocritography" is a self-reflexive, self-consciously academic act that foregrounds aspects of the genre typically dissolved into authors' always strategic self-portraits. Autocritography, in other words, is an account

> of individual, social, and institutional conditions that help to produce a scholar and, hence, his or her professional concerns. Although the intensity of investigation of any of these conditions may vary widely, their self-consciously interactive presence distinguishes autocritography from other forms of autobiographical recall. (Awkward 1999, 7)

In comparing the relationship between autobiography and autocritography, Awkward suggests that the latter intentionally reveals itself as "a self-reflexive, self-consciously academic act." Moreover, it is at once the author's determination to combine the self-reflexive and the self-critical in the discursive process that distinctly defines this writing. "In other words," he asserts, it "is an account of individual, social, and institutional conditions that help to produce a scholar and his or her professional concerns."

This chapter further explores what I perceive to be an important connection between the autobiographies of Frederick Douglass, W. E. B. Du Bois, and the autocritographical writings of contemporary, black male feminists/womanists. It tries to set into place a critical space for the fomentation of a revolutionary, gender-progressive vision of black manhood and masculinity. As I assert in *Black Male Outsider,* the vision has already begun to take shape in the memoir writings of such pro-feminist writers as Mark Anthony Neal (*New Black Man,* 2005) and Kevin Powell (*Who's Gonna Take the Weight?* 2003), among others. Writing in the tradition of gender justice promoted by Douglass and Du Bois offers an amazing location to consider the transformational power and potential of gender-progressive thinking in the lives of black men. Today, as I maintain in the opening of this book, its revolutionary power resides in the potential for black male self-re(dis)covery and self-healing from the wounds of patriarchy.

Before any celebratory pronouncements can go forth about the emancipatory power of gender-progressive transformation in the lives of black men, much has to be uncovered related to the controversial nature of feminism in black communities and the patriarchal politics that govern heteronormative black male identity. What is at risk for a black man embracing womanism/feminism? As shown in chapter 1, from Frederick Douglass's decision to cast the deciding vote at the historic meeting of majority-white women at Seneca Falls in 1848 (signified as the beginning of the movement for woman suffrage) to the contemporary period, the very idea of black men and black women claiming feminist thought as a personal and/or political way of being remains a source of intense debate and controversy. In *Scenes of Instruction*, Awkward (well known as a black male feminist literary critic) addresses with candid self-reflection the risks involved in being feminist-identified as a black man (inside and outside the academy, among or separate from black women who self-identify as feminist and/or womanist). He remarks,

> I am not naïve enough to claim that my gender has not been an obstacle to my pursuit of feminist truths; indeed, I am quite aware of the incompatibilities between such truths and masculine self-interest. In my effort to produce an insightful black male autobiographical inquiry, I've chosen not to focus primarily on incidents that could be seen, even by the most skeptical of gatekeepers, as nascent signs of feminist consciousness. Rather, I linger primarily on moments that dramatize the tensions between male self-interest and a recognition of women's systemic oppression, I believe that only by exploring such tensions, by remaining both self-interested and cognizant of the myriad costs of misogyny, can the activity that Tom Digby terms "men doing feminism" contribute to that ever-expanding social, intellectual, and philosophical project. . . . Indeed, it requires a willingness to take risks. . . . *[G]iven the persistence of pejorative meanings attached to black male subjectivities, if a feminist discourse informed by an acute awareness of such perceptions is not a risky venture, its social and intellectual contributions will be, at best, negligible* [emphasis added]. (1999, 7–8)

In the passage quoted above, Awkward makes several observations about the autocritographical act his memoir represents that are critical to understanding the stakes generally for men "doing feminism" (as the title to Digby's book calls it), and especially for black men engaged in this work. Pointing to the always complicated gender politics inextricably attached to normative male identity rooted in male supremacy, he underscores the "incompatibilities" between gender-progressive men's "pursuit of feminist truths" and "masculine self-interest." What makes Awkward's self-reflexive and self-conscious address of the problematics of male feminist intellectual, social, and institutional labor potentially self-transforming and healing for black men is its acknowledgment of the history of black male vilification under white supremacist, heteronormative ideas of manhood. It is his "acute awareness" and (self-)conscious grappling with "the persistence of pejorative meanings attached to black male subjectivities" in the context of feminist subjectivity that frames *Scenes of Instruction* as a contemporary model for pro-woman(ist) black men's autocritographical work—individually, intellectually, and institutionally.

From Douglass and Du Bois to Awkward, Neal, and Powell, among others, black men writing for *self*-liberation have done so against pernicious myths and stereotypes of who we are as men and human beings. Documenting the commitment of gender-progressive black men speaking and writing about their everyday struggle against sexist notions of black manhood and masculinity represents the "critical concept" theorized in the chapters that follow. I wholeheartedly agree with Michael Awkward that feminist work is risky for all men. However, I maintain that for gender-progressive black men, the support for female equality is always complicated by systemic and institutionalized racism. Moreover, as proponents of a politics of gender justice our antisexist position is inherently called into question in a culture where male supremacy and white supremacy interlock to emasculate straight and gay black men. If, indeed, the gender, racial, and sexual risks for us as pro-feminist "brothers" (as heteronormative gender outsiders) is greater for us as "black" males (inside the racialized boundaries of heteropatriarchy), it is bound up in the perception that we are not only traitors to our manhood, but also considered traitors to our race. More than this, we are also considered traitors to heterosexuality (if we do not identify as straight). But, as Douglass and Du Bois clearly illustrate in their gender-progressive writings, the "profession" of a belief in female equality, woman suffrage, and equal rights for all women positioned them also as *black male outsiders*.

As articulated in the introduction, in historical and contemporary narratives of black men becoming committed allies in the struggle to end gender oppression the subject of black female oppression resonates profoundly. Like Douglass and Du Bois (as Awkward demonstrates), contemporary pro-feminist black men have located the development of their political consciousness in an experiential connection to the black mother. I have argued thus far that the historical and material condition of the black maternal (embodied in the figure of the mother herself) functions as a critical catalyst in the development of feminist consciousness in the black male narratives represented in this book. Reinforced by the power of contemporary black feminist women's search and discovery of their foremothers' narratives of self-empowerment, the narrative of my own journey toward an emancipatory familial connection with pro-woman(ist) black forefathers and "brothers" is a central feature of the confessional in my own memoir writing. My pedagogical practice as a professor of feminism is largely defined by my struggle to make sense of my mother's past as a survivor of domestic violence. Black feminist thought offers the analytic tools to mine the caverns of our trauma as part of a self-healing process. Part of that process involves admitting that notions of black machismo and heteronormative, sexist, homophobic, and internalized racist ideas of manhood and masculinity inside (and outside) black communities have conspired to obliterate the life-sustaining presence of a loving, caring image of black fatherhood.

Transgressing the Law of the (White) Father: Toward a Pro-woman(ist) Rereading of Black Fatherhood

> Whose child are you? What's your name? American history can be read as a long paternity suit, or series of suits. If the suit fits. . . .
>
> —John Edgar Wideman (1995, 82)

In *Fatheralong: A Meditation on Fathers and Sons, Race and Society*, John Edgar Wideman provides a collection of poignant autobiographical narratives about the complex relationship he and his father shared over a number of years. In the epigraph quoted above, Wideman reflects on the history of slavery and (inter)racial relations, and their impact upon issues regarding "black" paternity. Wideman asks, "Whose child are you? What's your name?" With these questions, he formulates a reading of fatherhood and race in the United States "as a long paternity suit," particularly as they figure in relation to black male identity. At once, the phrase "paternity suit" connotes both a set of clothing and legal proceedings.

Clearly, Wideman troubles the waters of a history that many black men would rather forget, but it is a past that is always with us—haunting us, refusing to die. His questions remain. In the history of black male identity in the United States, the questions above strike at the core of the psychic and emotional wounds many black men harbor deep within themselves. The question is not so much who our biological father may be, but whether the "founding (white) fathers" of this nation robbed black men and women of their humanity—of their inherent right *to be* human(e). In the brutal institution of slavery, black people learned to dehumanize one another, to hate one another and all that constituted *blackness* (under white patriarchal rule as the signifier of the subhuman). Ours, then, has been a long struggle to reconstitute ourselves as a people.

For many black men "the people" came to be synonymous with the struggle for black manhood against "the (White) Man" (the founding father). From this standpoint, Wideman's postulation is absolutely correct. Male identity in the United States can be read as "a long paternity suit, or series of suits" played out in the social, economic, political, cultural, sexual, *and* legal realms of representation. It has been black male contestation of the paternal law of the White Father and his rule through white supremacy that has propelled the black liberation movement from the origin of the abolitionist movement to the black power movement to the black (male) nationalists' calls for black patriarchal atonement in the 1990s. We have sued for our legal rights as black Americans to bring an end to segregation. We have successfully sued for the right to vote, equal employment, fair housing, and integrated schooling.

Yet we collectively, as black men, have done little to address the psychic and emotional wounds wrought by the history of white supremacist patriarchy and the myths and stereotypes of black manhood and masculinity that black men, *all* women, white men, and other men of color have internalized (inside and outside the United States) as a result of it. While many black men were inspired by the Million Man March in 1995, more than a decade later it has become clear that Louis Farrakhan's message of black male empowerment through the rhetoric of heteronormativized, (hetero)sexist patriarchy has failed to address what ails many black men lost in the mythic power of black machismo. It has not saved us. It has not enabled us to deal with the psychic and emotional wounds we bear.

The ironclad image of the "strong black man" is killing us. Stripped of our humanity, many of us have fallen prey to the very racist myths and stereotypes of black manhood and masculinity we fight against. In dehumanized, commodified, and media-exploitable images of the black male—as the gendered, racialized, classed, and sexualized Other—many of us have left ourselves in a place of our own undoing. But where do we go to deal with the painful fact that for most of us the (paternal) "suit" of black manhood, as currently idealized in images of the strong black patriarch, does not fit? Where do we go to re(dis)cover a black manhood and masculinity free from the suit of black patriarchal machismo, which was fashioned with the threads of misogyny, sexism, heterosexism, and homophobia? Where do we go to (re)dress its wounds? While John Edgar Wideman's questions probe the depths of the mangled wreckage racism represents in the history of the black American family, I consider a set of questions focused on where black men go to find locations for mental health, self-recovery, and self-healing from the wounds of white supremacy and patriarchy, inside and outside black communities. In the sphere of black familial relations, from the time of slavery onward, black males have had a long history of childhood self-loss associated with the disembodiment of black maternal and paternal symbols. Many of us have been particularly wounded by the presence and/or absence of a father figure.

Where Did George Go? Searching for the Little Boy Lost (in Black Men?)

The cover of *Newsweek* on August 30, 1993 showed the haunting face of a seven-year-old named George Martin. It is the face of a little black boy. His is a face of sadness, and the camera captures his mournful eyes. The bold headline on the cover reads: "A World Without Fathers: The Struggle to Save the Black Family."

I bought the issue of *Newsweek* magazine at a newsstand the week it came out. It took me thirteen years to open it and read the feature story connected to the image of George, a fatherless black boy. Looking at the picture of him, I think about my childhood as a black boy. At the age of seven, I could have easily been that little boy, except that my father was not absent from my life. Yet the image of his presence for so many years of my childhood made me wish for his absence.

One sunny Saturday morning in May 2006, I sat outside on the deck of my house in New Jersey and read every line of all the stories in that issue about black fatherhood and its impact upon black boys (as if its bearing upon black girls did not really count). Statistical reporting on the black family in 1993, according to *Newsweek*, suggested that the image of the black father was at best a shadowy one (marked by a prevailing absence related to his family). George Martin was only one of several black boys featured in the stories whose lives were being shaped by the absence of a father. Article after article and statistical chart after chart represented the economic, education, and employment factors that contextualized the high rate of family absentism among black fathers, and it became glaringly clear why George's story and the others had been so hard for me to read. Why had it taken me so many years to read a series of magazine stories about black fathers? Fear, shame about what they said about me/us? Not wanting to deal with the pain I saw in George's eyes, I had simply kept the magazine stored away—out of sight like the wound I had kept hidden about my father.

Today, George Martin (having grown up fatherless in a ghetto of Washington, DC) would be twenty-three years old. Where is he? What has become of him? Is he a father? "Statistics" would suggest that he has gone the way of many black males who grow up in the urban environments of black ghettos in the United States. Such places are infested with gang violence, drug trafficking, and, all too soon, the loss of life for many young black males. Many of them will barely reach the age of twenty-two before becoming a fatal victim of black-on-black (male) crime. The article quoted a telling comment by George's struggling young mother about discipline, her son, and the absence of a father figure in his life. "George minded my father. When my father was there, I would have no problem with him. *When my father went, that's when my son went* [emphasis added]" (Chideya and Gates 1993, 19).

What did George respond to in his mother's father that he "minded"—that made him think, made him listen, made him behave better in the father's presence? A longing addressed? Something different from what he received from his mother—a figure of masculine authority and/or a loving image of manhood with which to bond? Upon closer examination of the story, the writers Farai Chideya and David Gates report: "Valerie [his mother's name] says he's getting hard to discipline. He craves male companionship: his grandfather, who used to come over and watch wrestling with him, has eased out of their lives" (18). It is obvious that the (grand)father's physical absence may be directly related to the shift in George's behavior. He is acting out. I suspect Valerie's disciplinary problems with her son had to do with displaced aggression tied to feelings of anger toward the absent father figure. Implicit in the mother's statement on where her son "went" is that there was an emotional place where she could not go with him. In the boy's mind, the (grand)father's leaving represented a form of abandonment. Clearly, aggressive behavior was his way of mourning the loss of the father figure. But where did George go?

A Loving Place "to Be" in Self-Re(dis)covery: Black Men Embracing the Wisdom *and* Soul of Visionary Feminist Politics

> Visionary feminism is a wise and loving politics. It is rooted in the love of male and female being, refusing to privilege one over the other. The soul of feminist politics is the commitment to ending patriarchal domination of women and men, girls and boys. Love cannot exist in any relationship that is based on domination and coercion. *Males cannot love themselves in patriarchal culture if their very self-definition relies on submission to patriarchal rules* [emphasis added]. When men embrace feminist thinking and practice, which emphasizes the value of mutual growth and self-actualization in all relationships, their emotional well-being will be enhanced. A genuine feminist politics always brings us from bondage to freedom, from lovelessness to loving.
>
> —bell hooks (2004, 123–24)

Black men writing about being gender-progressive activists necessitates having to come to grips with childhood memories of familial dysfunctionality, sometimes demonstrated in the form of domestic violence perpetrated by their fathers. Many black males from an underclass background grew up in the presence of patriarchal abuse or in the absence of any father at all. The result is a sense of profound self-loss. In a culture of male supremacy interconnected with notions of white supremacist, capitalist consumption, black boys learn very early on in life that being *black*, *male*, and *poor* are the ingredients for certain failure. In such a culture, there exists no place for black males "to be" in self-recovery or to discover themselves outside the pain of such a deep loss. I know at first hand the sorrow of this pain, the feelings of self-lovelessness, the soulless self-hating. Coming to embrace the healing power of black feminist thought over the years, I have made a commitment to the life-sustaining politics of the human rights struggle at the core of womanism.

More and more, it has become increasingly clear to me that black males experiencing the wounding effects of patriarchy in a culture of white supremacy are (must be, have to be) in need of gender and racial healing. Racist representation of black male identity is perpetuated in capitalist commodification of (hetero)sexist, misogynist, homophobic images of the "thug," "gangsta" "pimp," "drug dealer," and "con artist." Like the "controlling images" of black women that Patricia Hill Collins incisively identifies in *Black Feminist Thought*, black men—regardless of sexual and/or class difference—labor under the myth of black machismo rooted in dehumanization. Not only does it represent all black men as hypermasculinist, heterosexist homophobes, but it defines us in monolithic terms that are heartless, void of love—foreclosing on the recognition of our humanity. As Awkward insists, there must be a self-referential space that not only interrogates male supremacist thinking but also its traps, especially for black males confronting patriarchy within a culture of white supremacy.

Decentering the black male self in a racial environment hostile and toxic to our mental, emotional, and spiritual well-being may, at first, seem like an act of self-annihilation. However, as Awkward and other black male proponents of gender-progressive thought argue, feminism is emancipatory for women *and* men. Neither Douglass nor Du Bois challenged the gender norms associated with heteromale subjectivity, but for contemporary gender-progressive black men such a task is necessary. Opposing heteromasculinist thinking about manhood calls into question black patriarchy and black male heterosexual privilege. For many heterosexual black men, this is the worst form of black male emasculinization. In a culture of white supremacist patriarchy, it *is* the denial of our manhood. But even as we black men battle racism, we must simultaneously reject our investment in male supremacist, heterosexism, and homophobic thinking. This is precisely what black male, heterogender transgression of the patriarchal father's law represents. Rather than effeminizing black men, black male feminism functions as a radical gesture of *de*-emasculinization that offers a vision of self-re(dis)covery for liberated manhood. Contemporary gender-progressive black men writing about the wounds of patriarchy have entered confessional territory that neither Douglass nor Du Bois ever imagined. In this uncharted space of narrative self-disclosure, black men advocating a politics of gender justice speak to the radical possibility of pro-woman(ist) transformation in our lives.

As stated in the opening pages of this book, a new generation of black men for gender justice has emerged, many of whom have read or studied with some of the most well known black feminists of the day. They speak in gender-progressive terms, calling for black male accountability on the issue of sexism. Today, many gender-progressive black men speaking and writing are university professors in solidarity with feminist women of color and antiracist, feminist white women and men. These black men have produced a formidable body of scholarship devoted to gender justice. Their politics are tied to a firm recognition that gender justice is linked to the struggle for human rights and must be equally grounded in the fight against homophobia in black communities. Can we afford to exile any one black person to the margin of struggle if he or she does not pass the litmus test of a masculinist, heterosexist, homophobic blackness? Womanist/feminist black men must fight for a black woman's right to autonomous womanhood as forcefully as they demand their right to be treated with human dignity as black men (of all sexual orientations).

At the same time, they must champion as aggressively the liberation of their black lesbian sisters and gay brothers, whose experience of white supremacy is no less insidiously felt than that of heterosexual black folk. In the historic document known as "A Black Feminist Statement: Combahee River Collective," black lesbian feminists powerfully speak at the intersection of race, gender, and sexuality to assert their alliance with a transformed vision of struggle against racial oppression: "Although we are feminists and lesbians, we feel solidarity with progressive Black men and do not advocate the fractionalization that white women who are separatists demand. *Our situation as Black people necessitates solidarity around the fact of race, which white women of course do not need to have with white men, unless it is their negative solidarity as racial oppressors. We struggle together with Black men against racism, while we also struggle with Black men about sexism* [emphasis added]" (Combahee River Collective 1983, 213).

All black men need to understand that antiracist strategies that uphold sexist, patriarchal, homophobic dictates of black male empowerment doom themselves to failure, for they ignore not only the historical centrality of black women in the movement for racial justice, but also their role in the movement for women's rights. For we black men who believe in the equality of women, ours is the certain knowledge that womanist/feminist black women have given us the tools to deconstruct the (patriarchal) master's house. With these tools, we rebuild communities dedicated to "the wholeness and survival of all people."

Again I Say, Patriarchal Atonement Just Won't Do

> [F]eminist thinkers were accurate when we stated that patriarchy in its most basic, unmediated form promotes fear and hatred of females. A man who is unabashedly and unequivocally committed to patriarchal masculinity will both fear and hate all that the culture deems feminine and womanly. However, most men have not consciously chosen patriarchy as the ideology they want to govern their lives, their beliefs, and acts. Patriarchal culture is the system they were born within and socialized to accept, yet in all areas of their lives most men have rebelled in small ways against the patriarchy, have resisted absolute allegiance to patriarchal thinking and practice. *Most men have clearly been willing to resist patriarchy when it interferes with individual desire, but have not been willing to embrace feminism as a movement that would challenge, change, and ultimately end patriarchy* [emphasis added].
>
> —bell hooks (2004, 108)

In *The Will to Change*, bell hooks asserts that patriarchal masculinity promotes fear and hatred of all things associated with the feminine, and by transference all things connected to women. However, I suggest that in light of renewed calls for patriarchal atonement (as issued by such figures as Louis Farrakhan, an architect of the Million Man March), for black men patriarchal thinking represents a source of black male empowerment. In a culture of white supremacy and male supremacy, it is true that patriarchal masculinity represents a critical source of power for black men as a strategic tool in the struggle against racism. But it is the new emergence of a collective male consciousness forged in patriarchal thinking in black communities that threatens not only the welfare of all black women and girls, but also the mental, emotional, and physical health of all black men and boys. Calls for patriarchal masculinity in black communities is reinforced by the support of conservative black religious leaders (mainly men) who claim they defend patriarchy on biblical grounds. In a form of spiritual blasphemy, they mask their own patriarchal dictatorship by making mean-spirited attacks on anyone who questions their androcentric vision. Blatantly clear in the coalescence of black masculinist nationalism and religious patriarchal dogma is the propensity for homophobic attacks lodged in heterosexism.

By openly admitting the wounding effects of patriarchy on our self-image, our relationships with women, *and* with other men, our confessions of being black and male in a culture of racism lead the way to an inner cleansing, initiating a process inner self-reclamation. In this space of reclaimed vulnerability, we are not emasculated as the patriarchal father would have us believe. Rather, we are empowered to define manhood and masculinity free from the (self-)dehumanizing power of male supremacist dogma predicated upon the subjugation of the feminine. Contemporary black men writing and speaking publicly their stories of self-reclamation (within the "herstory" of black gender progressivism) reaffirms the legacy of Frederick Douglass and W. E. B. Du Bois as unrelenting pro-woman advocates of gender justice.

6

"Brother"hood Called into Question

I am concerned about the issue of women's rights because I am striving to be a revolutionary, and without the eradication of sexism there will be no true and thorough going revolution. . . . At this moment in history, asserting a position which I feel is my revolutionary responsibility to put forward, I hear the echoes of our heritage urging me to be firm. I hear Frederick Douglass, who also spoke out strongly in support of women's rights. Douglass was vilified and shunned by former friends who could not understand his concern for the rights of women. *I hear Douglass being called an "hermaphrodite" and other terms which questioned his sexuality because of his stand on sexism. But in the spirit of Frederick Douglass, I do declare that I too should rather be called "hermaphrodite" and other names because of my support for women's rights* . . . [emphasis added].

—Kalamu Ya Salaam (2001, 114)

Black male liberationists must relearn their own history, by grounding themselves in the wisdom of their sisters. . . . The underdevelopment of Black America will end only when Black men begin to seriously challenge and uproot the patriarchal assumptions and institutions which still dominate Black civil and political society.

—Manning Marable (2001, 120, 146)

I, like most Black men I know, have spent much of my life living in fear: fear of White racism, fear of the circumstances that gave birth to me, fear of walking out my door wondering what humiliation will be mine today. *Fear of Black women—of their mouths, of their bodies, of their attitudes, of their hurts, of their fear of us Black men* [emphasis added].

—Kevin Powell (2003, 61)

If the hip-hop thug represents a threat to the sanctity of the image of the "Strong Black Man," then the black feminist movement represents not just a threat to that image, but one capable of forcefully asserting a critique of the sexism and misogyny practiced by the "Strong Man."

—Mark Anthony Neal (2005, 41–42)

> I believe that only by exploring [the tensions between male self-interest and a recognition of women's systemic oppression], by remaining both self-interested and cognizant of the myriad costs of misogyny . . . it *requires a willingness to take risks* [emphasis added].
>
> —Michael Awkward (1999, 8)

For black men—in a culture of white supremacist, (hetero)sexist, homophobic patriarchy—identifying as a "feminist brother" is risky business. This chapter focuses on the politics of antifeminist name-calling and the gender, racial, and sexualized fallout that surrounds pro-feminist/womanist black male identity. In the main, black male feminism does not even register in the minds of many black men *and* women. But as is widely known, feminism in black communities is most often ideologically constituted as traitorous complicity with white supremacist aims to undo the black male. Actually, the target—as many outspoken gender-progressive black women well know—is the *black feminist woman*. In the minds of many black males caught up in the power of patriarchal thinking, it is she who must be racially and sexually "othered." Black men in the tradition of Frederick Douglass and W. E. B. Du Bois have had to be willing to be "called out of their names," as outlaws to black heteromasculinity and manhood, in order for them to represent themselves as allies in the struggle to end the gender oppression of all females. In this way, we pro-feminist black men are not only viewed as traitors to our gender, but as betrayers of our race.

Like Kalamu Ya Salaam, I too "hear the echoes of our [pro-feminist] heritage urging me to be firm." And like Kalamu, I too have heard the pro-woman(ist) voice of Frederick Douglass (and W. E. B. Du Bois). I, like Kalamu, am willing to risk being called out of my name in the spirit of our womanist forefathers in support of women's rights, firmly believing that "women's rights are human rights." That means, as Kalamu Ya Salaam courageously asserts, even if being a pro-feminist black man means being called (or thought of as) a "hermaphrodite."

Black Male Feminist Confessions and Pro-Woman(ist) Autocritographical Acts

From the mid-nineteenth century through the twentieth and now into the twenty-first century, pro-woman(ist) black men have written autobiographically about the politics of supporting women's rights. For example, Bayard Rustin, a principal organizer of the historic March on Washington in 1965, was a voice for women's rights in the eras of the civil rights movement and the women's liberation movement in the 1970s, and remained one until his death in 1987. Others, like Derrick Bell (whose protest against the gender and racial discriminatory practice at Harvard Law School made national news), have placed their careers on the line for equal job opportunities for women of color. Writing about his decision to leave Harvard in *Confronting Authority: Reflections of an Ardent Protestor* (1994), Bell notes:

> My protest reflected my desire to support and further the continuing efforts of students to diversify the faculty. Most recently, those efforts had focused on Harvard's failure to appoint a black woman to the law faculty. I had few expectations that my protest would, by itself, cause Harvard to alter [its] elitist hiring standards. . . . *[H]owever, I hoped that my drastic action might both fortify students and perhaps even prompt a few faculty members to take a stand that would apply sufficient pressure to get Harvard to do for a woman of color in 1990 what they had done for me two decades earlier* [emphasis added]. (1994, 4)

I will always hold Professor Bell in high regard for the pro-black woman stand he took at Harvard. I personally witnessed his unwavering support for the hiring of women of color in institutions of higher learning. When invited in 1996 to participate in a public forum contesting my then home institution's refusal to continue the contract of a highly respected black woman professor, his willing participation demonstrated his long-standing commitment to race and gender justice.

A new generation of black men publicly self-identified as pro-feminist is charting a revolutionary path promoting progressive discourse on the subjects of gender and sexuality in black communities. In 1994, a small group of male students at Morehouse College organized Black Men for the Eradication of Sexism. Two years later, they staged the conference "To Be Black, Male, and Feminist/Womanist." In 1999, Devon Carbado edited *Black Men on Race, Gender, and Sexuality*, comprising a complex range of male perspectives. In 2001, Rudolph P. Byrd, with Beverly Guy-Sheftall as coeditor, published *Traps: African American Men on Gender and Sexuality*, which (re)presented pro feminist voices of black men from Frederick Douglass to W. E. B. Du Bois to some of the most noted and emerging pro-woman(ist) black men of our time. In new narratives of gender-progressive consciousness, there has emerged a genre of pro-feminist autobiography written by black men. Since the publication of Michael Awkward's memoir *Scenes of Instruction, a Memoir* (1999), several others have appeared. Kevin Powell wrote *Who's*

Gonna Take the Weight? Manhood, Race, and Power in America in 2003 and in 2005 Mark Anthony Neal published *New Black Man*. My own "pedagogical autobiography," *Black Male Outsider*, followed in 2008.

Writing about how one comes to identify as a pro-feminist man who is black is an exercise in gender and racial vulnerability. It necessitates a discursive stripping away of the mask of masculinity that too often conceals our humanity. The one thing I know with certainty that connects my narrative to that of Awkward, Powell, and Neal is that black feminist thought transformed our vision of manhood *and* masculinity. Both Kevin Powell and Mark Anthony Neal write autobiographically through the lens of hip-hop culture. Rather than simply writing hip-hop off as a performance of aberrant heteromasculinist misogyny, they probe its ethos and their gender-progressive, antisexist position in it. Critical of the gender and sexual politics that have come to be associated with hip-hop in a culture of gross materialism and capitalist greed, Powell and Neal decry the politics of black machismo. According to Neal, it is rooted in the image of the "strong black man." At its core lies a patriarchal worldview predicated upon the subjugation of women—and of black women in particular. Powell and Neal insist that the attitudes and behaviors that many of the "old heads" find reprehensible are simply bold-faced, spectacularized representations of their own more insidious, normalized sexist attitudes and misogynistic behaviors. Powell aims his critique of the cross-generational normalization of heteromasculinity at the reification of machismo: "Men are applauded for their machismo, their grit, their toughness. Show any level of sensitivity, shed a tear or two in public, display any feelings that have nothing to do with winning, and you are reduced to being a 'sucker,' a 'punk,' a 'pussy,' or a 'fag,' your sexuality thoroughly interrogated while your ego is being riddled with hollow-point innuendos. Those men with the power get to tell powerless men what manhood is, *modeled after themselves or whatever tall tales they have spun about themselves* [emphasis added]" (Powell 2003, 110).

Powell connects the fallacy of machismo with the trauma of abandonment by fathers of their sons. He compares his absent father with that of Tupac Shukur, and says of rap artists, "All offer a model of manhood based on absences, inconsistencies, allegiance to the movement, allegiance to the streets, allegiance to selfish and myopic priorities that were more important to them than the boys left behind to sift through the ruins of their battered and bruised lives" (94). The last pages of the book are filled with painful autobiographical remembrances of his own father's abandonment of him. Powell acknowledges his anger towards older black men:

> I will be completely candid here and say that I have carried around a great deal of resentment toward older Black men since

> my father disowned me when I was eight years old. Indeed, I have had little tolerance, little respect, and very little interest in what most of them have to say for themselves. It is the worst form of cowardice to bring a child into the world and then abandon that child either because you cannot cope or because you and the child's mother are not able to get along. How many Black boys and Black girls have had their emotional beings decimated by that father void? (Neal 2005, 24)

Mark Anthony Neal approaches heteronormative masculinity in a different way, but he also deconstructs the image of the "strong black man." He says that he himself had once desired to assume this role. He thought it stood for a man who possessed "a real love of black folk," cared for his family's economic welfare, was present in his home as a firm disciplinarian of his children, and illustrated the antithesis of the emasculated black man. But Neal came to see what this image rests upon:

> [D]espite [its] seemingly positive attributes [is] the figure of the 'Strong Black Man' [who] can be faulted for championing a stunted, conservative, one-dimensional, and stridently heterosexual vision of black masculinity that has little to do with the vibrant, virile, visceral masculinities that are lived in the real world. Black masculinities that are often masked—the DLs (on the down low homosexuals who live as heterosexuals) immediately come to mind. . . . Some of these so-called 'Strong Black Men' have at times been unrepentant in their sexism, misogyny, and homophobia. (28)

At once Neal strips away the image's veneer to reveal an inner man ideologically invested in heteronormative privileges of masculinity conceived in sexism, misogyny, and homophobia (with the latter masking the potential health danger of his DL tendencies for the heterosexual woman with whom he may be partnered). I cite Neal and Powell because they belong to the younger generation and speak from within the ethos of hip-hop. Neither tries to justify the virulent strains of sexism, misogyny, homophobia, and the normativization of violence that have come to be associated with it. Rather, they disclose the reality of the larger culture from which it emerged—one saturated with violence, racism, (hetero)sexism, and capitalist greed that has wreaked havoc on certain vulnerable segments of black communities. These communities are overwhelmingly urban and lower-class.

Neal maintains that his purpose in *New Black Man* is "to rescue [Louis] Farrakhan's 'New Black Man' from the claws of old-school black male patriarchy." Like Powell and a number of other black male pro-feminists—including myself—Neal remarks about the impact of the absent father in his life: "Because my father—a strong black man in his own right—often marked his worth to me as a father and as a man in the larger society with the number of hours he put in at work (trying to create some semblance of lower middle-class existence for his family), homie was a real ghost throughout much of my youth" (32).

What do the Black Sexism Debate (1979), the Million Man March on Washington (1995) and the "Black Male and Feminist/Womanist" conference at Morehouse College (1996) have in common with the women's rights discourse of Frederick Douglass and W. E. B. Du Bois? Perhaps a meeting place of gender-progressive possibility, a space of revolutionary reconnection that defies not only the limits of time and location but also the politics of separation. In the physical and discursive spaces above, I have imagined an infinitely expansive landscape of radical possibility that might arise from the union of renewed faith and hope in black solidarity, where heteromasculinist notions of black liberation come to an end, so that "a new and more possible meeting" might take place between black women and men—across the differences of gender and sexuality—unimpeded by patriarchal initiatives that recenter the dogma of black manhood as the driving force of self-determination in black communities. A black feminist vision of radical liberation rejects all ideas rooted in (hetero)sexism and homophobia, which have historically undergirded, promoted, and perpetuated a masculinist agenda that continues to keep black women (heterosexual and lesbian) and gay black men from claiming mutual subjecthood in the movement for black liberation.

Radical movement by black men will come when we collectively begin to denounce publicly the varying ways compulsory heterosexuality, sexism, misogyny, and homophobia undermine black political solidarity. Black men must collectively begin to imagine ourselves free from the manacles of male supremacist "dick"tum. It is a form of gender slavery that keeps us bound to heteronormative, black (male) power as the only viable expression of our manhood. We promote black male self-healing in the rejection of machismo.

In white supremacist culture rooted in capitalist consumption, certain racist myths and stereotypes of black masculinity hover around the black male body like vultures zeroing in for the kill. Under such a regime, colonized black men function as willing objects of commodification (demonized and/or glorified) in service to white fantasies of the black male Other. As Spike Lee brilliantly illustrates in *Bamboozled* (a biting satire on the legacy of black minstrelsy and white capitalist consumption of black culture), in the contemporary marketplace of American popular culture it sells. Images of the black male as Sambo, Uncle Tom, Step-and-fetch-it, and the infamous black buck/rapist have become racial symbols of white America's fear/fascination with black masculinity. As a source of unresolved fear/threat/desire in the white imagination, black men must be contained—socially, politically, sexually, and physically. Mapped onto the bodies of black men, the more fearfully aggressive representations of black masculinity function to keep in place a set of physical and ideological containment structures. They exist in the arena of sports, in the entertainment industry, and (perhaps most dramatically) in the construction of the prison industrial complex. A black man under white supremacist patriarchy is not just "any body"—he is "the" body of surveillance, always under suspicion. His body type, more than that of any "other" (ethnic) body in the country, fits the racial profile of culpability—the racialization at this historical moment of Arabic and South Asian men notwithstanding.

Explicit in the racial profiling of black males in the United States is the clear suggestion that if one is *black* and *male*, one is *always* suspect, which means that one must *always* be policed (more often than not through violent means of control). How do we deal with this and other forms of daily racialized dehumanization under white supremacy, even as heteromaleness affords nearly unregulated gender power for men in our communities? It cannot be in the ways many of us choose to respond—through the mask of what Michele Wallace called "black macho" and what Richard Majors and Janet Mancini Billson refer to as the "cool pose" (Majors and Billson 1992, 2). As Majors and Billson assert, machismo carries a high price for black males, undermining their emotional and physical well-being and influencing their treatment of women. Yet for so many of us, keeping up a masculine facade becomes a matter of life and death. Many young black males, in particular, would literally rather chance death than risk being called a "punk," or "faggot" (terms associated with colonized notions of emasculinization) or "bitch," a term of male effeminization through the denigration of females. But the sure reality is that under white supremacist, capitalist, homophobic patriarchy black men are suffering enormously—in body, mind, and spirit. Evidence indicates, as Majors and Billson note above, that compared to every other reported group in the nation, black males suffer a higher risk for heart disease, high blood pressure, and stress-related illnesses, as well as being more prone to diabetes, alcoholism, and prostate cancer.

Moreover, drug addiction continues to be the foremost source of self-medication for black male pain. Without question, racism is a toxic experience for all people of color, but using the subjugation of women to salve our feelings of wounded manhood can never be a substitute for the self-healing work we must perform. Allegiance to patriarchal dogma and sexist thinking as a means of "reclaiming our lost manhood" does nothing to strengthen our relationships with females in our lives. We cannot return to a motherland where once upon a time we were all kings and queens, despite the rhetoric of beneficent patriarchal nationalism that folks like Louis Farrakhan advocate.

How do we get to a place called "renewed faith and hope," to solid ground where "a new and more possible meeting"[1] between black women and men can happen? Like a compass pointing to freedom, black feminist thought lays out a potential pathway. Encompassing a history of black female struggle against the odds of racism and sexism, it leads the way in words of visionary possibility for black men and women working on each other's behalf and for all people's human rights. Black feminist thought speaks in terms of inclusion and wholeness, in remembrance of a time long ago when black women and men stood in solidarity against race and gender oppression.

Dismantling the Myth of "Black Macho"

When Michele Wallace published *Black Macho and the Myth of the Superwoman* in 1978, she created a firestorm in black communities across the nation that disrupted the familial politics of black gender solidarity. Her subject: a critique of black sexism. More than thirty years have passed since the book's publication. In the last decade, however, we have witnessed the emergence of a body of work by gender-progressive black men that has moved beyond the discursive walls of black masculinity Wallace breached.

In *Constructing the Black Masculine: Identity and Ideality in African American Men's Literature and Culture, 1775–1995* (2002), Maurice O. Wallace charts the steadily increasing appearance of works on black masculinity since the early 1980s. He says the first wave was 1984–94; the second wave was 1994 to the present. He notably mentions *Black Macho and the Myth of the Superwoman*, which he says has "sustained its elucidative currency beyond the first wave as the emergent formations of black feminist knowledge exemplified by *Black Macho* had come, by then, to diminish the prosaic sociology of the other nearly 'inconceivable' efforts to theorize the black masculine" (M. O. Wallace 2002, 3). Michele Wallace's slender volume proved to be highly influential in the gender politics in black communities upon its publication (by Dial Press). On the book's cover, pointing out what she believed to be an increasing contentious relationship between black men and women, Wallace boldly proclaimed, "[T]here is a profound distrust, if not hatred, between black men and black women that has been nursed along largely by white racism but also by an almost deliberate ignorance on the part of blacks about the sexual politics of their experience in this country" (M. Wallace 1972, front jacket cover).

The statement above represented a dramatic illustration of the book's even more demonstrative critique of black sexism. With *Black Macho*, Michele Wallace crossed the boundaries of gender *and* racial loyalty, and for years it exiled her to the margin of black liberation struggle. Michele was excoriated (by both males and females) for airing the dirty (gender) laundry of *black* men, but as Maurice O. Wallace notes, in most studies on "American" masculinity *race* (a salient feature in its formation) has been largely omitted: "[W]hile the high profile of race in the West has created out of the black male body a walking palimpsest of the fears and fascinations possessing our cultural imagination, the body of scholarship foregrounding race as a significant text or subtext of masculinity studies remains ironically and inexplicably modest. . . . Prior to the mid-nineties, not even a new wave of U.S. masculinity studies . . . seemed capable of imagining black men paradigmatically 'at the center' of its critical contemplations . . ." (2002, 2). His observation sounds similar to that made by black feminists regarding the absence of racial analysis in some white feminist critiques of the oppression of women. Citing a number of well-known black scholars and writers whose names have become associated with gender-progressive and feminist readings of black masculinity, he underscores the influence the Million Man March had on the production of scholarship focused on black men since 1995.

The new wave of gender-progressive texts on black masculinity produced in the 1990s and beyond not only work to demythologize it but to demystify its heteronormative formation(s). In 1994, Philip Brian Harper incisively articulated the nearly inextricable, but very problematic, link between African American identity and black masculinity. In *Are We Not Men? Masculine Anxiety and the Problem of African-American Identity*, Harper points to a pervasive cultural masculinization of blackness and says, "[T]he dominant view holds prideful self-respect as the very essence of healthy African-American identity[;] it also considers such identity to be fundamentally weakened wherever masculinity appears to be compromised. . . . Its primary effect is that all debates over and claims to 'authentic' African-American identity are largely animated by a profound anxiety about the status specifically of African-American *masculinity*. . . . *Are We Not Men?* ultimately questions the very definition of traditional masculinity, as well as its import to black identity" (P. B. Harper 1996, ix–x).

It is precisely the work toward the demystification of black masculinity that threatens to unravel the monolithic, self made image of black manhood we have historically coveted as far back as the institution of slavery. Marlon B. Ross says in *Manning the Race: Reforming Black Men in the Jim Crow*

Era: "I hope to further the objective of characterizing the particular diversities evident in conceptions of black manhood, theorizing and historicizing the cultural differences *within* this identity by bringing attention to struggles around socioeconomic class, immigrant and migrant status, education, region, religion, color, gender-role conformity, political affiliation, cross-racial attraction, and sexual orientation" (2004, 7).

Twenty-five years after the "black sexism debate" appeared in *The Black Scholar*—in the wake of a virulent resurgence of black nationalist, patriarchal rhetoric articulated in (hetero)sexist and homophobic sentiment reminiscent of black power movement "manhood" politics—today, pro-feminist black men are boldly writing about our patriarchal disaffection. Today, gender progressive black women and men doing anti-sexist work—even as we denounce white supremacy—advance the vision of black gender liberation. When Beverly Guy-Sheftall and Johnnetta B. Cole conceptualized a strategic space for "multilogue"—across generation, gender, class, sexual orientation, and religious boundaries—about the issue of sexism in black communities, they produced *Gender Talk: The Struggle for Women's Equality in African American Communities* (2003). In so doing, they opened up yet another liberatory space for conversations between black women and men that breaks silence with the notion of "airing our dirty (gender) laundry in public." It was an enormous project five years in the making, but in *Gender Talk* these two black women feminist brought together black females *and* males across vast frameworks of difference to engage and grapple with one of the most pressing issues facing black females and males today. The multilogues they made happen provided a needed sense of hope for those who participated in them, and Cole and Sheftall remind us how critically important the work of feminist transformation has been in the past and can be for the future of black self-determination.

When Pro-woman(ist) Spelman Sisters and Morehouse Brothers Break Silence about Sexual Violence

> We believe that our relationship with women must be based on the principle of equality. Our notions of sexuality are based on domination. We are taught as boys to be sexual conquerors of women whose bodies are objectified and declared to be the property of men to be bought, sold and traded. We reject relationships based on domination and the violence against women and prostitution they create. We seek to establish relationships with our sisters based on equality. . . . We believe that sexist oppression against women pervades every aspect of our communities and must be eradicated. The oppression of women is a difficult issue for our community to deal with partly because it is such

> a personal one. . . . We ultimately demand a complete and fundamental change that eradicates oppression based on sex, race, class, and sexual orientation, both within and without.
>
> —Black Men for the Eradication of Sexism ([1994] 2001, 200–201)

> Black men often think that they lack privilege, but that is in relation to the relative privilege of their white male peers. *Their privilege in relationship to black women is real and it is often the basis, particularly within elite black institutions, that black women are expected to serve the needs—politically, socially, emotionally and sexually—of black men* [emphasis added].
>
> —Mark Anthony Neal (2007, internet, 2)

In 1996, Black Men for the Eradication of Sexism invited me to participate in the conference it had organized on the subject of pro-feminist/womanist black men. Along with these Morehouse men and a small group of noted black women feminists and other antisexist black men, I attended a series of weekend sessions that reaffirmed the power of black women and men working together to combat sexism—against the rise of a new, black patriarchal nationalism. The conference focused upon the founding "manifesto" of BMES. With great resolve the statement proclaimed, "We believe that although we are oppressed because of our color, we are privileged because of our sex and must therefore take responsibility for ending that privilege" (Black Men for the Eradication of Sexism [1994] 2001). Not since Douglass and Du Bois had there come such a bold, courageous, antisexist proclamation from black men. Along with bell hooks, Rebecca Walker, Beverly Guy-Sheftall, Robert Allen, and Thandabantu Iverson, among others, I took a stand against the patriarchal imperatives that had become associated with the Million Man March.

I went to Morehouse inspired by the pro-feminist work of Frederick Douglass and W. E. B. Du Bois; I left even more committed to practicing antisexism in my private and public life. Moreover, my involvement with the young black men from Morehouse and women from Spelman that unprecedented weekend confirmed the notion that antisexist education must be a primary goal of black liberation in the twenty-first century. Young black men promoting feminist movement to end sexism is a revolutionary act. According to bell hooks in *The Will to Change*, it is this group of black males who offer hope for a future of black manhood and masculinity free from the dictates of patriarchal thinking. They "[w]ere born into a world where gender equality is more a norm. Unlike older generations of men, they do not have to be convinced that women are their equals. These are the young males who take women's studies classes, who are not afraid to identify themselves as advocates of feminism" (hooks 2004, 122)

Now, thirteen years after the historic gender-progressive conference at Morehouse College, BMES no longer exists. It ended when all of its members graduated from the institution. The mission statement (a profeminist/womanist manifesto) the organization left behind speaks to the willingness and conviction of a group of young gender-progressive black males to stand for what they believed. At the same time, I question the climate that surrounded the gender and sexual politics of the Morehouse men. I distinctly remember a marked absence of Morehouse administrators or faculty at the conference. There was neither an official welcome to the college nor any statement regarding its support of the event. In light of recent and past allegations of sexual violence and assault on the Morehouse campus, one may only begin to speculate why a group like BMES no longer exists. It is deeply troubling that the historic conference was organized the same year (1996) that some Morehouse students were tried for the alleged rape of a Spelman student, and that in 2006 Spelman students felt led to organize a protest march on Morehouse's campus in defense of themselves against sexual violence and assault.

Recently while viewing a ten-minute online documentary on sexual violence and assault against women (produced in 2006 by and about students at Spelman) called "Breaking Silences: Violence against Women on College Campuses," I was reminded how powerful Audre Lorde's words have been in the lives of women and men in feminist struggle against sexism, misogyny, and homophobia. One of two historically black women's colleges, Spelman is noted for its commitment to black female higher education. I am struck by the tenacity of the young black women in the film, who courageously address the subjects of sexual assault and rape with unbridled candor. What makes the film particularly heartening is that these women are speaking out about these subjects in the context of charges against male students at Morehouse College. Through the lens of what has surely become a tenuous relationship between these two historic "sister" and "brother" schools, it is clear that "brothers" at Morehouse have been issued a wake-up call. The "sisters" are defying the code of secrecy that has governed black gender *and* sexual relations for generations.

Poignant, incisive, and decisively unapologetic, the message of the short film is grounded in a mixture of personal narration, critical commentary, and activist practice. The women of Spelman are represented by some of the most outspoken black feminists on the scene today—including Johnnetta B. Cole and Beverly Daniel Tatum (the former and current presidents of Spelman, respectively), Beverly Guy-Sheftall, Pearl Cleage, and Mark Anthony Neal. The film includes clips from a 2006 Spelman "town hall meeting, antirape forum" and an organized march to the Morehouse campus (sponsored by the Spelman students' Feminist Majority Leadership Alliance [FMLA]); and it features the voices of female and male students, faculty, and administrators (almost all from Spelman). The documentary cites a Harvard study stating that one in twenty female students on college campuses was sexually assaulted in 2005–6.

I am inspired by the support of black males in the documentary. Several male students and a male faculty member, who participated in the march, speak in support of Spelman students. The black male professor, Mark King, asserts that his participation in the march served to put pressure on other black males to "step it up," given the fact that "men direct sexual violence against women daily." When asked by Laura Rahman (a senior who is the film's producer) whether the time was right to insist upon the inclusion of gender issues on today's black civil rights agenda, the noted pro-feminist professor and pop-cultural critic Mark Anthony Neal offered a starkly pessimistic observation. Referencing Daniel Patrick Moynihan's 1965 report on the black family, Neal (as many black feminists have) criticizes its call for a strong patriarchal presence in black communities. Denouncing patriarchal power, he maintains that "concrete and concerted efforts to reclaim black patriarchy" have, indeed, made it even more difficult than forty years ago (when Moynihan issued his report) to get a critique of patriarchy on the agenda of black civil rights. Neal's assessment is not off the mark. He reads the times as they are especially related to the rhetoric of patriarchal atonement associated with the Million Man March. In his article, "Black Men Are Also Raping Black Women," Neal (a professor at Duke University, where charges of rape by a black woman against white male students made national news) states, "[W]ithin black institutions that still value patriarchy and the 'stability' it supposedly engenders, black women (and a few men) are often admonished for publicly criticizing and holding black men accountable for behavior that is clearly detrimental to our communities and our shared humanities" (Neal 2007, 2). Like Neal, I believe it is black male investment in patriarchal thinking that maintains black silence about our sexist and homophobic ailments.

As lamentable as the gender and sexual dynamics between Spelman and Morehouse are, the reality is that sexual violence and the assault of black females in black communities is not new. Black men and women have chosen silence over justice when it comes to the sexual violation of black females by black males. When it comes to light, often in high-profile cases, few can deny its devastating effects on black women and men, particularly on elite black college campuses. In one film clip, stating that her "world had come to an end," Johnnetta B. Cole recalls her dismay in 1996 when she (as president) heard the news of the alleged gang rape of a Spelman student by students at Morehouse. In another clip, the current president of Spelman, Beverly Daniel Tatum, announces the establishment of a presidential task force with Morehouse on gender, sexual assault, and campus safety. But as I have mentioned, no administrative representative from Morehouse actually appears in the film. According to Neal's article, "Members of the Morehouse College student senate . . . introduced a bill condemning the Spelman College protest, arguing that said protest 'created a hostile environment' and 'encouraged bad press and character defamation to Morehouse College and its student body.' . . . In the final section of the bill, the Morehouse College student senate requested 'a public apology from the Advisor(s) to FMLA . . . and student leadership of FMLA and all other organizers of the demonstration for its unruly nature' " (2007, 2).

In "Breaking Silence," Beverly Guy-Sheftall, the founding director of the Women's Resource Center at Spelman, offers a stunning critique of black male hegemony when she responds to those who attacked the student march on Morehouse on the grounds that its organizers did not follow protocol. Guy-Sheftall asserts that black people in struggle against white supremacy never asked white people for permission to protest racism. Why then, she questions, must black women obtain black men's permission to march in protest against the sexual assault and rape of black women by black men? The noted black feminist writer and critic Pearl Cleage rehearses the gender politics of the civil rights movement, commenting that "our brothers were not open to looking at questions of sexism . . . not open to looking at questions of domestic violence and rape." Quoting Dr. Martin Luther King (an architect of the movement), Cleage underscores the human rights principle at the core of his vision for the struggle for black rights. She asserts, "Oppression of one is oppression of all" (qtd. in "Breaking Silence").

For me, the most telling and at the same time the most deeply moving feature of this heroic documentary is the collective voice of young black women speaking out in solidarity about the dehumanization that sexual violence and assault involves. They speak as activists, some of whom had themselves been victimized. The production and release of this film is a powerful statement about the power of feminist sisterhood and brotherhood across gender and generational difference. It is a witness to the healing power embodied in the action of breaking silence about the devastating impact of sexual violence and assault in black communities.

Sexual Violence in the "House" and the Potentially Deadly Power of Homophobic Brotherhood

> The classic conception of the Morehouse Man is of these distinguished men who are the black version of the all-American man—the leaders of

> the world, the cream of the crop—and I'm not sure how homosexuality fits into that. When people look at the All-American man, they don't see a homosexual there. When you see an all-American man, you see a family, you see a wife.
>
> —A recent Morehouse graduate (qtd. in Neal 2007)

While silence has been broken about sexual violence and assault against black women on black college campuses, there has been little public outcry about these subjects related to the experience of black male victims. Morehouse College is neither the exception nor the rule in how students and administrators deal with gender and sexual difference. However, because of its high media profile, it stands out among other HBCUs (historically black colleges and universities). In 2003, Morehouse made news when there was a brutal assault by one its students on another. On November 3 of that year a student was repeatedly bashed on the head and other parts of his body with a baseball bat by another student in a dorm shower stall. The perpetrator accused the student of making a pass at him. Charged with aggravated assault and battery, the accuser in defense of his actions stated in court, "I was scared . . . I was embarrassed because I was naked and he was looking at me." According to the victim who recounted the near-fatal scene, his attacker (before leaving the shower and returning with the bat) had shouted, "I hate Morehouse and I hate all these faggots!"

The student who committed this heinous act was expelled from the school and was later found guilty and "sentenced to a pair of 10-year sentences, to be served concurrently for aggravated assault and battery" (Lee 2007). While the battered student denied that he is gay, the case created a firestorm of criticism around the treatment of gay men at Morehouse and other HBCUs. According to Lee, "The [Morehouse] incident may have shocked some at the nation's only all-male, predominantly African American college, but it was no surprise to gay students there. For them, taunting and the threat of physical violence are part of everyday life. . . . They would discover [after the incident] that not even such a brutal assault could open the eyes of the vast majority of students, faculty, and administrators." Lee's investigation found that few students, faculty, or administrators at Morehouse challenged its institutionalized homophobia. The president of the college, Walter Massey, did convene a Task Force on Tolerance and Diversity and voiced his support for its recommendations. And as Lee notes, "The campus held student forums and invited guest speakers for special lectures. The dorms began holding mandatory training sessions dealing with harassment, anger management, diversity, and homophobia." But according to gay students at the college, the campus climate and opinions of heterosexual students and faculty remained largely hostile to gay men, despite the president's stated desire for "a safe and supportive environment for all students—straight and gay." Considering the fundamentalist background of Morehouse and some of the other HBCUs, it is not surprising that the level of hostility against gay men is so high.

The reality is that on many of these campuses the lives of gay men are constantly threatened. Lee quotes black male students who feel the attack on the student was warranted. One student said, "A lot of people believe that [the student] deserved to get beaten up if he was looking in the shower stall . . . but everyone thinks the bat was a little extreme." Another stated, "It was like the biggest joke on campus coming true. . . . We would always say we'd take a bat to someone's head if somebody did something like that to me, and everybody would laugh. It was obvious that it was being said in jest, but that there was a lot of disdain for gay people in general under the surface" (Lee 2007).

Much of homophobia of black male students surrounding the student attack is rooted in the fear of the black male gaze. It was solely the victim's gaze (regardless of intention) upon the body of another black male that produced such a violent (irrational) response. The fact that the body of the black male perpetrator was viewed by another (black male) without the benefit(?) of clothing speaks volumes about the sheer magnitude of issues surrounding the politics of the black male body. Any perception of (physical?) weakness and/or vulnerability is, in the minds of many black men, fraught with danger—particularly for the black male onlooker. I argue that his sexual orientation is bound up in the gaze (whether the onlooker is gay or not). To be gazed upon as a black man—to be *looked at* directly by another black male—is a dangerous act for both men. Perhaps, in that moment, when we gaze upon each other's body (particularly when unclothed), what we see is the history of our dehumanization. Is it a fear bound up with internalized, racist perceptions of the black male body—of manhood status bereft of phallic power (despite actual penis size), of black male privilege denied in a culture of white supremacist patriarchy, where one's power as a man is tied to one's manly ability to subjugate women (and other men who are *viewed* as not manly enough)? For all the myriad reasons why many black men find the body-to-body gaze of another black man threatening, many black men continue to be blinded by a *mis*perception of each other's humanity.

In the end, it makes little difference if the gaze is from a gay or straight black man, when the look that is returned is a look that kills—filled with contempt and self-hatred. When the Morehouse student exclaimed, "I hate Morehouse and I hate all these faggots" (prompted, he says, by the look of his classmate upon his naked body), perhaps what he held in contempt was the image of the "classic conception of the *Morehouse Man* [emphasis added]" and its relation to pressures of manhood perfection encoded in "the black version of the all-American man." The black male student quoted here is quite well aware that in the black male vision of reclaimed patriarchy as "leaders of the world, the cream of the crop," no real/true representation of Morehouse Man could exist outside the imperatives of heteronormative patriarchy. Thus, being a Morehouse Man (the all-American man) and being gay are set as mutually exclusive identities. On the one hand, this student says he is not "sure how homosexuality fits into that [the all-American man]." On the other, he says, "[W]hen you see an all-American man, you don't see a black person there either." In truth, his observation on the politics of gender, sexuality, and race in a culture of patriarchy and white supremacy is a brilliant one. In the image of the heterosexist and homophobic image of the "all-American man" this student references as the ideal for the Morehouse Man, there exists no real place for a gay or straight *black* man. Perhaps, it was the false chasm of gender, sexuality, and sexual irreconcilability created in the all-American Morehouse Man(hood) identity that the homophobic student attacker could not negotiate. In desperation, could he have misdirected a preexisting fear and anxiety of all-American Morehouse Man(hood) failure to the gaze of another Morehouse man? In the tragic story of two Morehouse men, one survived as a severely battered victim of misplaced, homophobic aggression; the other was found guilty of aggravated assault and battery and received two ten-year concurrent sentences ending his dream of becoming the "all-American man."

For black men of all ages in a culture of patriarchy rooted in heterosexism and white supremacy, who we are as "black men" (whether gay or straight) can never fit the dream of an "all-American man(hood)." Being "called out of one's name" or beaten in black communities for not fitting the script of heteronormativity speaks to the egregious ways heterosexism and homophobia are condoned in the name of patriarchal order. Pro-woman(ist) thinking "queers" blackness in ways that all who embrace it become racial and gender suspects, not only opening themselves up to be "called out of their names," but also potentially exposing themselves to the threat of violence.

7

A Vision of Pro-woman(ist) Masculinity for a "NewBlackMan(hood)"

[M]anliness (in particular, being a husband or father) is associated with dominance over women and children. As *a result, men's domestic use of violence against women and children is a common way of exerting male authority* [emphasis added]. . . . [A]ny redefinition of fatherhood must address the degree to which manliness and violence are intertwined, and either justified or shunned in the domestic context.

—Aaronette White (2006, 45, 46)

I wanted to be a traitor to patriarchy. In one sense I began to see that to be a traitor to a sort of narrow form of masculinity was to be loyal to the greater forms of humanity.

—Michael Eric Dyson (qtd. in Cole and Guy-Sheftall 2003, 49)

Embracing feminism would require us to address problems stemming from patriarchal relationships between Black men and women—problems such as violence in the home . . . and unwarranted demands to express racial loyalty by passively accepting sexist attitudes and behavior.

—Luke Charles Harris (1999, 384)

There needs to be more feminist work that specifically addresses males. They need feminist blueprints for change. . . . As advocates of feminism who seek to end sexism and sexist oppression, we must be willing to hear men speak their pain. Only when we courageously face male pain without turning away will we model for men the emotional awareness healing requires.

—bell hooks (2004, 140, 142)

The Power of Black Feminist Thought Transforming the Lives of Black Men

"NewBlackMan" is the terminology that the self-identified black male feminist Mark Anthony Neal employs in his memoir (of the same title) to describe a man of African descent who defines his ideas of black manhood in gender-progressive terms. According to Rudolph Byrd, "feminist," "womanist," and "antisexist" are terms compatible with the tradition of High John the Conquerer ("[i]nspired by a trickster figure in African American folklore also known as Jack who is the human analogue of Brer Rabbit"). Byrd asserts that the tradition of John identifies "[a] mode of masculinity for Black men who are committed to the abolition of emasculating forms of masculinity; a mode of masculinity for Black men who are committed to the abolition of racism, sexism, homophobia, and other ideological traps" (Byrd 2001, 2).

The epigraphs above speak to contemporary issues involving the meaning of fatherhood, manhood, and masculinity in black communities. They embody voices of black women and men who advocate feminism as an ideology of healing for men in our communities who are suffering from the wounds of patriarchy—either as victims or as perpetrators of it. It is clear that male power in a culture of male supremacy is linked to the performance of violence, particularly within the sphere of the domestic. It is also clear in the voices of contemporary pro-feminist men who say that the desire to be "a traitor to patriarchy," as Michael Eric Dyson reveals, is a sure path to the recovery of our humanity as black men. Therein lies the gender healing so many of us desperately need. When we turn our ears to men speaking about the wounds of patriarchy, according to bell hooks in *The Will to Change*, we construct a blueprint for change. This chapter sets out to enable the drafting process for a new vision of black manhood, masculinity, and fatherhood outside the bounds of patriarchy. Through voices of pro-feminist black men sharing their paths to feminist consciousness as traitors to the patriarchal father in pro-woman(ist) frameworks created by feminist black women, we witness the emergence of a NewBlackMan. bell hooks remains one of the leading female voices advocating feminism as a site of radical intervention for male healing. She has devoted one book to black men and the power of feminist self-transformation (*We Real Cool: Black Men and Masculinity*, 2004) and another to the wounding effects of patriarchy in the lives of men (*The Will to Change*, 2004). Johnnetta B. Cole and Beverly Guy-Sheftall affirm pro-feminist black males in *Gender Talk*. Aaronnette White's groundbreaking essay "African American Feminist Fathers' Narratives of Parenting" (2006) documents narratives of gender-progressive black fatherhood. I feature excerpts in this chapter from White's interviews with fathers who consciously associate their ideas of parenting with feminist values. Combined with the pro-woman(ist) thinking of black males in *Gender Talk*, this chapter provides a foundation for theorizing the personal and political benefits of feminism in the lives of black men.

Consistent with (auto)biographical narratives from the history of black male gender progressivism, today its articulation remains located in the confessional mode. Largely through memoir writing and confessional narrative, pro-feminist black men are revealing the painful ways patriarchy wounded them, particularly within the context of domestic violence perpetrated by the father. *Gender Talk* enlarged black dialogic space for emancipatory talk about gender relations in our communities by defying the intraracial dictum against "airing our dirty (gender) laundry in public." An enormous project that was five years in the making, *Gender Talk* brought together different black females *and* males to engage and grapple with one of the most pressing issues facing black people today in the United States. The multilogue Cole and Guy-Sheftall helped to create provided a needed sense of hope for those who participated in it. The work of *Gender Talk* reminds us how critically important feminist transformation can be in the lives of black men.

Cole and Guy-Sheftall make a stunning observation about the narrative background of the feminist-identified black men they interviewed for the book: "We were struck by the number of men whose views about gender had been shaped by their witnessing violence within their families" (2003, 51). I assert that at the epistemological core of black male feminism lies a breach, a symbolic (albeit violent) disentanglement with patriarchy initiated by the scene(s) of domestic violence perpetrated by the father figure (whether physically absent or present in the family's "home"). Such violence provokes in the son a *dis*-identification with his father and a reidentification with the figure of the mother as the victim of patriarchy the son must save (not sleep with, as imagined in the Western theory of the oedipal complex).

In patriarchal struggle, the son to survive the trauma of violence in the house of the "father" must *re*form himself in the image of a man who stands up in defense of the subjugated "mother." In rejecting the father's image, the son begins the journey toward becoming a womanist—having fought off the (hetero)normativization of patriarchal masculinity. He *becomes* the "NewBlackMan" (the name given him by Neal's black woman feminist mentor, Alexis De Veaux, whom he fondly calls "Mama Soul"). Interesting enough, in Neal's pro-feminist autobiographical narrative, *New Black Man* (2005), he represents his relationship with De Veaux in familial terms; she becomes the feminist mother to him (her "Soul Baby") (Neal 2005, xvi).

Of the males interviewed in *Gender Talk* who narrate a childhood experience of domestic violence perpetrated by their fathers, some describe their biological mothers as "feminists." While the mothers would not necessarily identify themselves as such, these men credited them as the source of their gender progressivism. Like Neal, Michael Awkward, and Kevin Powell—who have all written pro-feminist memoirs—I, too, have acknowledged the profound influence of black women feminists in my pro-woman(ist) evolution. I, like Neal, needed a model of manhood that opposed patriarchy, that supported women's rights and equality, and that stood up against male supremacist ideology. Reading contemporary autobiographical narratives of black men describing the power of feminist transformation, I have become more appreciative of the racial *and* gender risks involved in transgressing the boundaries of patriarchy.

Narratives of Male Self-Liberation

In *Gender Talk*, Guy-Sheftall and Cole interview black men who self-identify as feminists or publicly acknowledge the transformative influence womanist/feminist thought has had on their political worldview and personal-identity politics. In these interviews, cited in their chapter 2, entitled "Having Their Say: Conversations with Brothers and Sisters," the men reveal how feminist thinking entered and changed their experience as black males. Sharing ways patriarchal gender norms were dealt with in the context of varying familial constructs while growing up, the gender-progressive men interviewed spoke to influences of the maternal and paternal in the rejection of patriarchal and masculinist notions of manhood. Family upbringing proved a critical site for the germination of progressive ideas of gender, particularly those contesting the patriarchal role of the abusive and violently dominating father.

Several of the men, including myself, addressed their childhood experience of domestic violence as a critically significant factor in the process of self-transformation. A "brother" whose progressive ideas of female equality I have long admired, Thandabantu Iverson, reveals that as an eleven-year-old child his mother, an abuse survivor, imparted to him a vision of gender justice he would take into adulthood: ". . . I want you to remember one thing. That every woman in your life will be someone's sister, someone's daughter. And I want you to learn how to live so that you will not treat any woman the way I have been treated" (Cole and Guy-Sheftall 2003, 37).

As I state in the interview and have written elsewhere, I am " 'a survivor of domestic violence': it has taken 'all the courage that I can muster to begin to speak about that in my life. To actually say that I have survived conditions which have destroyed many men of African descent' " (Cole and Guy-Sheftall 2003, 50). In my life, black feminist thought functions as a theory of self-recovery/transformation for men like myself who were traumatized by domestic violence as children. As a black man committed to gender justice, I have rejected patriarchy and done so as a means to living a life free from the bondage of male supremacist ideology. When revisiting my initial longing for pro-feminist father figures who embodied a disdain and abhorrence for female oppression, I reread Du Bois's essay "The Damnation of Women" to reassure myself with regard to the feminist commitment I have made to ending patriarchal subjugation of women. By all accounts, neither Douglass nor Du Bois ever witnessed actual physical abuse at the hands of his father (the father was absent during the childhood of each man); nevertheless, as I have argued, each man was, indeed, a product of domestic violence (directly related to the father's mistreatment of the mother). To say that all men who as children witness the abuse of their mothers grow up to reject patriarchy and ideas of male supremacy and become feminists is by all means a hasty generalization. On the other hand, it is a provocative idea worth investigation as one seeks to understand how pro-feminist conversion works in men.

While not interviewed in *Gender Talk*, Michael Awkward employs his memoir, *Scenes of Instruction*, as a discursive defense for the feminist claims he makes. A continual theme in the memoir is the attempt by Awkward to come to grips with the experience of his mother as an abused woman/mother (largely at the hands of his violently abusive father, who for most of Awkward's life remained absent). Despite a childhood of family abuse experienced by some pro-woman(ist) black men, there are those among them who have defied the self-fulfilling, patriarchal prophecy of the domestic violence perpetrator. Rudoph Byrd, the coeditor of *Traps* with Beverly Guy-Sheftall, recounts the childhood episode in which he intervened to stop the abuse of his mother:

> [I]n that instance I really declared war on my father and on that kind of behavior. And I maintained that position with my father until I was nineteen or twenty. We reconciled about a year before he died. But I was very clear from that moment on that this was not acceptable and that I would not tolerate this in my family, and that I would not treat other women that way. . . . When my father raised his hand and struck my mother's face the world as I knew it changed completely. It was in this moment that my commitment to gender equality crystalized. Such a commitment placed me, inevitably, in opposition to my father who held, like many men of his generation, deeply flawed and patriarchal views of family and society. (Cole and Guy-Sheftall 2003, 44, 49)

Haki Madhubuti also traces the impulse of his political commitment to black liberation to the liberatory moment he as a young boy intervened on behalf of his mother. "I came from a very violent home. At twelve years old, I pulled my stepfather off my mother as he was about to beat her into some unknown world" (Cole and Guy-Sheftall 2003, 51).

Unlike Rudolph or Haki, as a child frozen with fear I never physically intervened during my father's violent assaults on my mother. That is where the core of the trauma lies. I was always paralyzed with fear—afraid that it would make him even more violent, afraid that he would turn on me, afraid that the neighbors would hear and call the police . . . afraid that I would become like him. Like Rudolph, whose introductory essay to the volume *Traps* is a stunning tour de force on the transformative power of a womanist/feminist orientation in the lives of black men, I too loved my father, and by the end of his life he had conquered many of the demons that drove him during those years of abuse in the houses where we lived over the years.

While several men interviewed in *Gender Talk* spoke candidly about directly witnessing the abusive family behavior of their fathers, others like Douglass and Du Bois experienced living with a father's absence and the manifestation of family violence brought on by his mother's frustration related to it. For example, Kevin Powell, whom I first met as a student at Eugene Lang College in New York City, has written openly about the journey from his own violent demonstration of internalized sexism and misogyny. For Powell, the figure of a father, while absent from his life for more than two decades, loomed large in the contempt he once held for women:

> When I was eight, my father flatly told my mother, via a pay phone, that he felt she had lied, that I was not his child, and that he would never give her money for me again. The once remotely tangible image of maleness in my life was gone for good. Both my mother and I were devastated, albeit for different reasons. I longed for my father's affections. And my mother longed to be married. Silently I began to blame my mother for my father's disappearance. Reacting to my increasingly bad behavior, my mother turned resentful and her beatings [of me] became more frequent, more charged. I grew to hate her and all females, for I felt it was women who made men act as we do. (Powell 2003, 57)

As he writes in "Confessions of a Recovering Misogynist" (originally published in *Ms.*), rejecting the traps of machismo, male supremacist attitudes, and behavior is about daily practice and inner healing related to wounds of his mother: "My relationship with my mother is better than it has ever been, though there are days when speaking with her turns me back into that little boy cowering beneath the belt and tongue of a woman deeply wounded by my father, by poverty, by her childhood, by the sexism that has dominated her life" (Powell 2003, 65).

Powell admits that for many black men writing about the complicated relationship of being black and male, in a culture of white supremacy and sexism is that therapy can be a viable option. I have long supported the idea of black feminist thought as a form of healing therapy for black men recovering as misogynists and/or perpetrators of sexism. I myself have sought the aid of a therapist to confront the trauma of being a childhood survivor of domestic violence. Resisting the shame and fear of what "being in therapy" suggests for many black folk, I have a deep appreciation for Powell's candidness about the struggle to overcome his misogynistic ways. As he admits, coming clean about his purposeful mistreatment of females has allowed inner healing to take place. He says about therapy and recovery process:

> . . . I am at least proud of the fact I have not reverted back to violence against women—and don't ever plan to, which is why I regularly go to therapy, why I listen to and absorb the stories of women, and why I talk about sexism with any men, young and old, who are down to rethink the definitions we've accepted so uncritically. Few of us men actually believe there is a problem, or we are quick to point fingers at women, instead of acknowledging that *healing is a necessary and ongoing process, that women* and *men need to be a part of this process, and that we all must be willing to engage in this dialogue and work if sexism is to ever disappear* [emphasis added]. (Powell 2003, 66)

The reality is that in a culture of white supremacist capitalist patriarchy, as bell hooks has phrased it, the drama of slavery is repeatedly played out in blatant, capitalist commodification of black misogyny and sexual objectification of black male and female bodies. The reification of hypersexualized representations of black machismo and the glorification of gang violence in popular culture suggests that the white market value of black sexism and misogyny has returned the black body to the auction block of slavery. Black male and female complicity in our dehumanization in the marketplaces of white supremacy and male supremacy further suggests that a form of collective mourning is necessary. Like Powell, I bemoan the fact that there are few black men in my life, young and old, with whom I can talk or feel allied in "brotherly" solidarity about the dehumanizing impact of sexism, not only in our communities but directly in the lives of so many us who perpetuate misogyny masked in the form of black heteromale power.

The interviews with pro-feminist black men in *Gender Talk* and my participation in two public forums, under the title "multilogues," sponsored by the Ford Foundation and hosted by the book's editors, enabled me to feel the long-desired sense of community with "sister" and "brother" feminist/womanist activists. While I do not know Robin Kelly personally, reading his interview provoked in me a moment of catharsis, a moment of unfettered identification. Kelly is also a survivor of childhood domestic violence. Kidnapped by his father, he (at nine years old) and his sister were held "against [their] will in prison and presented . . . a completely dysfunctional notion of black masculinity because it involved violence from the first moment" (Cole and Guy-Sheftall 2003, 57). For six years, Kelly and his sister would experience the emotional trauma of family abuse, physically separated from their mother. Learning about their mother's successful attempt to recover them, the reader comes to understand the feminist worldview she imparted to her children. Kelly explains that even in the midst of impoverished living conditions in a Harlem tenement, she gave them a vision of humanity and feminist insight through something he referred to as her "third eye": "[S]he would not allow us to live as victims. Instead, we were a family of caretakers who inherited this earth. We were expected to help any living creature in need, even if that meant giving up our last piece of bread. . . . She simply wanted us to live through our third eyes, to see life as possibility. *She wanted us to imagine a world free of patriarchy, a world where gender and sexual relations could be reconstructed* [emphasis added]. . . . She wanted us to visualize a more expansive, fluid, 'cosmopolitan' definition of blackness" (Cole and Guy-Sheftall 2003, 56). While he likened his father to "a monster," considering his injuriously misguided notions of fatherhood, it was the holistic, womanist vision of black life his mother would teach her children that would validate his "[f]eeling as if he was raised to be a feminist by his mother" (57).

In truth, while some of the eight pro-feminist men interviewed, including myself, grew up in families where domestic violence was a feature of their childhood, there were others whose upbringing demonstrated the power of a father possessing open-minded views about gender. According to Guy-Sheftall and Cole, they "described relatively progressive fathers who taught them that their status as men did not require that they harbor sexist attitudes about women or behave in 'unmanly' ways" (2003, 38). Among these men was Zaron Burnett, a writer and the husband of noted feminist author Pearl Cleage. He thinks of his father as having been "very nonoppressive. He was very masculine in the traditional sense. . . . There was no presumption that women did this or men did that. There were jobs to do and everybody had to do them" (Cole and Guy-Sheftall 2003, 38). Of his mother, he says, "[She] wouldn't claim to be a feminist but by all definitions she is one" (40–41). The well-known pro-feminist historian Manning Marable attributes his progressive gender sensibility to his mother, but he underscores the gender-progressive ideas of his father: "My dad's view was that my mom should achieve the highest goals she wanted. . . . [H]e really believed that Mom's career should go forward. [At fifty, she obtained a PhD] Dad was very supportive through it all. He was not a feminist. . . . I never really thought before about the Marables being protofeminist, but it now occurs to me that you wouldn't see a more politically progressive, intellectually progressive group of folk" (Cole and Guy-Sheftall 2003, 54–55). While Burnett and Manning point to the forward-thinking gender ideas of their father, both (like nearly all the men interviewed) spoke of the influence not only of "feminist" mothers but also of black feminist women they would come to encounter as adults—among them Audre Lorde, Johnnetta Cole, bell hooks, and Angela Davis.

Whether they had been influenced by gender-progressive mothers, fathers, and/or noted black women feminists, what stands out in the interviews for me is the men's critical position against sexual oppression. As Guy-Sheftall and Cole note, "[On the one hand, some] shared with us their personal struggles around gender and their commitment to challenging attitudes about normative masculinity and homophobia in African American communities. . . . Others expressed how their own homophobia 'imprisoned' them and that the process of challenging their homophobia enabled them to understand the links between heterosexism, misogyny, patriarchy, and painful experiences they had as children" (2003, 55). Two of the most meaningful accounts of self-transformation regarding the issue of homophobia offered by these men were Thandabantu Iverson's account of his encounter as a graduate student with work by Audre Lorde and Rudolph Byrd's narration of a homophobic experience as a black gay student in college.

Iverson's fear of gay sexuality manifested itself in a way that made him feel ashamed to even purchase, let alone read, a book by Audre Lorde. He finally bought one of her books in a bookstore despite the fear that his sexuality would be questioned. While he does not say so directly in the interview, the book he purchased was Lorde's *Sister Outsider*. It was the essay about her relationship to her son, "Man Child: A Black Lesbian Feminist's Response," that brought him to tears in an intense moment of self-revelation. "I could not read beyond where she talked about how she was trying to raise her son to be a non-oppressive male. And it all came together and I was awash in tears. Something happened to me in that room. Since that, I have begun to try to think differently and live my life differently. *It moved me from a point of simply seeing these different kinds of discrimination or oppression as separate things and began to make me understand that our realities as African American people are complex* [emphasis added]" (Cole and Guy-Sheftall 2003, 55). What Iverson understood in reading Lorde represents a major tenet of black feminist thought: the notion that race, gender, class, and sexual oppression are interconnected. Perhaps one of the most radical ideas Iverson encountered was that of a lesbian mother of a black son. I have known Thandabantu for many years. He is a pro-feminist "brother" whose gender progressive politics are informed by a serious commitment to antihomophobic work. While in college as a gay black man coming into an understanding of his sexuality (itself a contestation of heteronormative ideas of masculinity), Byrd began to comprehend that female subjugation was linked to monolithic notions of blackness: "I could relate to the oppression of women and the oppression that I was beginning to feel as a gay man. I understood where this stuff was from. Because of how they're socialized, men want to prove two things—that they are not girls and they are not faggots. . . . [I]t was my experience with homophobia and the rejection of my blackness that caused me to empathize with women. . . . [T]hat early experience with my father and my experience in college were pivotal in my understanding of the connections between the oppression of women and homosexuals" (Cole and Guy-Sheftall 2003, 51). The critical connection Byrd makes between his experience of being gay and being a black outsider enables him to identify with female oppression. While gay identity is not in and of itself a prerequisite for an empathetic understanding of oppression based on gender, in Byrd's case the childhood experience of domestic violence and his marginalization as a *black* gay man laid the groundwork for the progressive ideas on gender justice he came to embrace.

Can a black man lay claim to pro-feminist thought while holding on to homophobic and heterosexist ideas of manhood (or womanhood)? For those men interviewed in *Gender Talk* who self-identified as pro-feminist and/or womanist, such a claim would prove unequivocally false. Like Thandabantu Iverson, when I came to understand black feminists' assertion that oppression is about the interconnection of domination, my sense of my place in the world as a black man changed. Black feminist thought enabled me to understand that my destiny as a human being is linked to all people who are oppressed, and that all forms of oppression must be eradicated for my full humanity to be achieved. What I have come to understand as a black father committed to female equality is that this belief is completely compatible with my spiritual beliefs, which in turn are grounded in an affirmation of loving nurturance toward my children. Not only is it the core of my faith, but the root of the antipatriarchal views of fatherhood I hold.

Black Men Embracing Feminist Models of Parenting

> [F]eminist fathering models allow men to recast masculinity in flexible ways that strengthen their ability to nurture their children without reasserting male authority. . . . [E]merging studies on families who adopt feminist parenting models challenge preconceived notions about fatherhood and masculinity in ways that benefit children, parents, and society at large.
>
> —Aaronette White (2006, 44, 47)

Sometimes when reflecting on my profession as pro-woman(ist) man over the years, I acknowledge to myself that the most beneficial lessons on manhood I learned growing up did not come from men. I learned the attributes of a liberated manhood and masculinity from black women feminists. Growing up as a survivor of domestic violence, I could not have lived with the notion of myself as a man consciously inflicting pain upon women—physically and/or emotionally. The idea of myself one day being a father was completely foreign.

Perhaps, deep within, before being introduced to feminism as a graduate student at New York University nearly twenty years ago, I believed that the abuser my father had been (for a decade before his spiritual conversion) still lurked inside me. Full of self-loathing, a captive of low self-esteem, a prisoner of prolonged periods of concealed depression, I masked my anger toward my father and my mother. I was angry with my father because I believed he had robbed me of a healthy childhood—had created a little black boy full of fear that he would grow up to be an example of failed, distorted manhood. When I married my wife at twenty-eight, emotionally I was still that fearful, wounded little black boy who had failed to protect his mother. The realization of my anger toward my mother did not come until, battling depression, I entered a Christian-based twelve-step recovery program a number of years ago. While engaged in the 4th-Step (a process of "soul-searching inventory"), I came to a startling self-revelation: for years I had repressed anger toward my mother.

Guided by two black women whom I call "sisters"—my sponsor Joann Oliver and the feminist Aaronette White, I came to understand that I felt a deep-seated anger toward my mother over what I took to be a betrayal. She had refused to leave my father during the abusive years. More than that, she had told my brother and me years later that enduring the abuse was for our welfare—that she sacrificed her life for our good. And in reality, her staying did reap some good. The abuse stopped after I graduated from high school and went off to college. As mentioned, soon thereafter, my father got "saved" in the Pentecostal church, and some years later he became a respected minister in our community. However, as my brother and I have talked with each other many times, we experienced the trauma of domestic violence as a lasting imprint on our identity as men, husbands, and fathers. While working through the 4th-Step with Joann, Aaronette asked me to write a confessional essay dealing with domestic violence as a pro-feminist and dealing with my feelings toward my father *and* mother. Writing it as a confessional narrative was, indeed, cathartic. I shared it with my wife and subsequently with my mother, who had no idea that witnessing my father's abuse of her had been so wounding to her sons. Though she does not fully understand its extent, having to a certain degree glossed over the force of the trauma inflicted upon us, neither my brother nor I allow her to understate its horrific impact. The narrative recording of that part of my life is a testament to the healing power of black feminist thought.

Complementing the spiritual search for wholeness I began years ago (having become a minister nearly a decade ago, after having embraced feminism as a strategy for male self-recovery), I have taken Aaronette's definition of it to heart (shared with me in one of our "sister/brother" conversations): "Feminism is a spiritual response to how one should treat women, other men, and children." Typed on a narrow band of white paper, taped to the top of my computer monitor, it constantly reminds me that being a minister and a pro-woman(ist) are rooted in the same spiritual source, the Divine Creator from whom the sacredness of all humanity flows. Rejecting patriarchy and embracing womanist feminism signified the beginning of my inner healing. I was free to become a loving partner to my wife of nearly three decades. Together we parent three children—two adult sons (one biological, the other having come to us through legal custody) and an adolescent daughter. Together my wife and I have parented them the best that we know how, spiritually and ethically. I have not become my father, the father of those awful years when I clung to fear more than life.

Feminist fathering is more than a notion. My sons and daughter know me to be a different kind of man—one who loves art, literature, music, and dance infinitely more than any sports event; one who believes that all people deserve respect, regardless of gender and/or sexual difference(s); one who adamantly opposes an infringement upon a woman's right to choose; and one who abhors all forms of representations that support an ideology of abusive male power and/or supremacy. Transgressive models of pro-feminist black fathering embodying a vision of parenting that attends to the minds, bodies, and spirits of children remain to be documented. However, Aaronette White's study of pro-feminist black fathers stands at the cutting edge of such research. In her groundbreaking essay "African American Feminist Fathers' Narratives of Parenting," White brings the practice(s) of gender-progressive black fathers into analytical focus. White asserts, "[S]cant information is available on responsible African American fathers who radically redefine fatherhood without adopting patriarchal models of the family. Therefore, this study asks, How do Black feminist fathers' parenting beliefs and practices challenge patriarchal models, and *what factors foster feminist parenting among them* [emphasis added]?" (2006, 44).

Like White, I focus on the influence of feminism in the transformational process of gender-progressive black men's thinking about fatherhood. However, while I specifically make the claim that black male experience of domestic violence in childhood is a contributing factor to the rejection of patriarchy by some gender-progressive black men, White makes a broader investigation of how an antipatriarchal standpoint impacts their ideas of parenting. Although, as she herself admits, the number of participants in her study is small, "limit[ing its] generalizability . . . the value of this project is the in-depth analysis that it provides for subsequent studies exploring the range of positive African American fathering models" (47). As I have stated earlier, my study is not meant to suggest that all black male pro-feminists are the products of dysfunctional family backgrounds. Rather, like White, I have chosen to examine commonalities in the narratives of black men for whom feminism became a critical personal and political location for their defiance of patriarchy. White's essay composes a rich tapestry of autobiographical narratives on the racial, gender, class, and sexual politics of black feminist fatherhood, articulated across lines of sexual difference. While the majority of the men interviewed were heterosexual, it is not represented as the "normal" sexual orientation of the participants.

Rather than include a point-by-point review of her study, let me mention the overarching commonalities White identifies as characterizing black male feminist parenting:

- nurturance and emotional intimacy with children
- politically conscious parenting
- nonviolent discipline
- supportive social arrangements
- open attitudes concerning who can parent a child

The fourteen men interviewed for the study provide a striking profile of gender-progressive fatherhood. While the majority of the men identified as heterosexual, they are all committed to a vision of fatherhood that defies not only patriarchy but also heterosexist and homophobic attitudes about fathering. All of them believed in child development that resists the fear of emotional intimacy. "Feminist concepts of fatherhood remove the stigma that defines men as 'too soft,' 'feminine,' and 'hen-pecked' when they care for the physical, emotional, intellectual, and spiritual development of a child" (48), says White. White is clear in her study that the men she interviews are atypical both in what they believe about parenting and in the socioeconomic and educational status they occupy. Moreover, she notes that these factors and others—such as the institutional structures of racism, employment opportunities, and gender and cultural conditioning also related to parenting—affect black men's notions of fatherhood. To understand the significance of pro-feminist black male attitudes about fathering, according to White, one must also take into account the dominant culture's construction of the black father: "African American fathers," she says, "are often described by policy makers and popular media according to what they lack, rather than what they possess" (47).

Even though the number of men documented in the study that White devised is small (as they are in my own study), the efficaciousness of black male feminism/womanism remains vital as a strategy of black male transformation and vision—impacting women, men, and children inside and outside black communities. Though some may take black pro-feminist male identity to be faddish, trendy, or even emasculating, for the fourteen self-identified black "feminist," "pro-feminist," or "antisexist" fathers White interviewed being gender progressive is a serious personal and political matter. She says, "[B]y resisting hegemonic masculinity and its tendency to define manhood in opposition to womanhood and homosexuality, feminist African American fathers challenge the idea that fathering has to be different, separate, and unique from mothering. The feminist vision of 'degendered parenthood' and increasing empirical evidence suggests that men and women are equally capable of performing and sharing most childcare activities" (55).

While the research on "degendered parenthood" may be accurate on female and male capability of "performing and sharing most childcare activities," I have some reservations about men's feminist fathering of daughters, and my wife does also. For nine years, my wife taught as a professor at a university out of state for one semester of each year. We had to share parenting roles in creative ways to cope with our periodic, physical separation and its effect on our daughter during her preteen and teenage years. My wife has always reminded me that there are certain things I simply cannot provide our daughter, outside my presence as a nurturing father. It is clear to me that her role, as a black mother/woman in the development of our daughter, is very different from mine. I absolutely agree with my wife that there are life lessons and experiences about being a black woman that I cannot provide our daughter.

In the first years when my wife was away teaching, the two male children (both now adults) stayed home with me. Our daughter split time with the two of us during those years. For five of the eight years involved, my mother lived with us, becoming an indispensable help in the children's daily life, particularly in that of our daughter. During the academic year 2005–6, my wife had to be away for an entire year. While our sons were, for the most, self-sufficient as college students, after weighing the benefits of our daughter living with one or the other parent—we (with our daughter's thoughts on the matter) determined that it would be in her best interest to live with her mother for the year. Although the children had adjusted to the possibility of such an arrangement over the years and even though our daughter would have preferred to stay with me to remain with her friends and school, she wanted to be with her mother more. In terms of practical matters of daily need, I think my wife would agree that our children benefited from their mother and father reversing the role-playing of traditional parenting. Without a doubt, as the narratives of White's participants illustrate, "supportive social arrangements" (in the form of extended family assistance with child care enabled) helped my wife and me to deal with the complexity of our employment situation.

Over the years, what I have learned as a black man promoting gender-progressive thought related to political self-proclamations about feminism is that talk is one thing, and acting upon it is another. This is precisely what represents the conundrum of male feminism for me: not the question of whether men can be feminist, but whether we possess the *will* to act upon what we espouse. Teaching antiracism in majority white classrooms over the years, I am often asked by white students who yearn to become antiracist activists what is required of them. I say to them that they must possess the will to act upon what they espouse. This is also what we pro-feminist men must do in our private and public lives. In this way, we continually put to the test the validity of the claims we make on feminism. This is how I have come to interpret the statement that the personal is political—or that the political must be personal. In other words, what I say and do as a man advocating female equality must illustrate itself in my private life—where my wife and children see me when I am not wearing the professorial mantle of the feminist pedagogue.

What exactly does White mean by the phrase "politically conscious parenting"? Framing it in relation to the participants' antiheterosexist beliefs, she says, "All participants in my study actively raise their kids to oppose racist, sexist, and heterosexist beliefs and practices" (2006, 56). However, she also notes that "very little is known about the ways African Americans parent in order to counter the effects of sexism and heterosexism on their children. Black feminist fathers' narratives provide sorely needed insight" (56). In contemporary gender progressive narratives by black men I have read, there exists a clear and unapologetic critique of heterosexism and homophobia—even if the "brother" professes to be heterosexual. In "The

Challenge and Possibility for Black Males to Embrace Feminism," Luke Charles Harris makes it clear that "[a] feminist perspective affords us the opportunity to identify and take account of the ways in which race, class, gender, and sexual orientation intersect to shape the problems and interests of our entire community" (1999, 383). The intersectionality of domination, as black feminist legal scholar Kimberle Crenshaw has theorized, defines the critical project of black feminism. A crucial aspect of being black, male, and committed to a politics of gender justice is not only interrogating heterosexual privilege but also defying it—even the "brother" who claims he is heterosexual. Devon Carbado speaks in the epilogue to *Black Men on Race, Gender, and Sexuality* about how heterosexual privilege functions in everyday life, and he notes, "My hope . . . is not to represent 'every heterosexual man,' but to intervene in the normalization of heterosexual privilege in everyday life, and to challenge the pervasive tendency of heterosexuals to see homophobia as something that puts others at a disadvantage and not something that actually advantages them" (Carbado 1999, 439).

Many heterosexual black men, as Carbado suggests, think that being black and gay only disadvantages black males in a white supremacist heteronormative culture. They link homosexuality in our communities to the racist castration and emaculinization that is ensconced in the history of black male identity in the United States. Carbado writes, "I am certainly not suggesting that straight Black men are more homophobic than straight men of other races. But it is the case that heterosexual privilege is one of the few privileges that straight Black men *know* they have—not being a 'sissy, punk, faggot' " (1999, 431). In the prologue, I insist that black men who profess to be feminist must be "willing to be called out of our name" (in the name of feminism)—to bear the sign of a man who is not a man according to patriarchal and homophobic ideas of manhood. Because we are black as well, we must also bear being called traitors to our race. After almost twenty years of public identification as an advocate of female equality and women's rights, I take having my sexual orientation, masculinity, and manhood called into question as par for the course. As I write in my own narrative of pro-feminist confession, even as a male child I never fit the mold of heteronormative masculinity.

In the interviews White conducted with black feminist fathers who did not identify as heterosexual, all the participants endorsed parenting arrangements outside a heterosexual framework, as she notes. Gay and bisexual fathers exhibited model parenting skills in a context of extended family support. According to White, "At the heart of their narratives [i.e., of both gay and heterosexual fathers] is the call to expand the idea of what represents a legitimate family and how responsibility for childcare must be dissociated from both gender and heterosexuality in radical ways" (2006, 64). I was particularly drawn to one of the participant's narratives. In it he talks about parenting as a young gay black man. A full-time college student and community youth organizer, he speaks about the challenge of being a "father" to his young niece and nephew after the death of their mother (his sister). Citing the value of extended family support (he had the help of his grandmother), he says, "Children need to be taken care of, so, if it falls on you, you should seek a system of support from whoever is in your immediate circle. . . . I'm strict, but my ideas of discipline are by no means physical. Also, in my parenting, I want my niece and nephew to know me as a person, not just as their provider" (White 2006, 64). Choosing to be a parent, with extended family intervention, he assumes parental responsibility for nurturing and financially supporting his sister's children, insisting that they come "to know [him] as a person" (who is open about his sexual orientation).

I have written extensively about my familial relationships with my father, mother, wife, and children. For me, the greatest challenge in being a feminist father has been inculcating into my children values of human dignity that defy heterosexism and homophobia. While they have observed me teaching in the classroom and preaching in church on more than one occasion, it remains an ongoing challenge for them to resist heterosexist and homophobic attitudes of church folk, friends, and the larger culture. As parents who hold our faith sacred, my wife and I have taught our children a belief in love and respect for all people—without respect to gender, sexuality, race, or class differences. We both hold them accountable for treating all people with dignity, above all else. Citing several narratives in her study where participants demonstrate a commitment to antihomophobic parenting, Aaronette White underscores the notion that heterosexist attitudes discredit all forms of sexual difference and demonstrations of masculinity outside the bounds of patriarchy.

As stated, the aspect of White's study that reinforces the objective of my project is her assertion that feminist fathering is antithetical to violent discipline. According to her research, "The use of corporal punishment (e.g., spanking, slapping, hitting) in American homes, particularly African American homes, is not unusual, yet all of the feminist African American men in this study shun its use" (White 2006, 59). One of the participants notes, "Children can learn how to nurture from their parents by seeing their parents nurture and respect each other . . . and men can be nurturers and disciplinarians. However, I believe discipline should take nonviolent forms." Another states, "A man must learn to be physically and emotionally available to his children and his mate and they should not be afraid to tell him when he's wrong. My children have permission to 'call me out on my stuff' " (60). While both my wife and I were reared in homes where notions of physical disciplinary measures were the norm, with our children we have disagreed on the issue of physical force in punishment. Like the participant cited above who associates it with violence, I have resisted the employment of corporal punishment with our children precisely because it reminds me of the physical violence I witnessed as a child in my home. When my father physically abused my mother, the level of his rage seemed boundless.

While not believing that one is biologically or naturally predisposed to violence, I have always feared that my spanking, slapping, and/or hitting my children would prove that I had, indeed, become the abuser my father was during those violent years of his life in our home. In truth, the trauma of those years, at times, has left me not only at odds with my wife, but also left me nearly paralyzed in dealing with any form of discipline with our children. Nevertheless, over the years, both she and I have become more skilled in dialoguing about the most effective means of discipline with our children—in nonviolent ways. While I have never believed corporal punishment of children can be considered a form of healthy nurturance for children, I have—like my father, raised my voice in anger toward my children in moments of frustration. My wife periodically cautions me about its tone and volume. At times like this, wondering if I will ever be free of the ghosts of the violent past that haunt me, I know clearly that being a pro-feminist man is a process. As Joann, my "sponsor," has said to me many times, "Sometimes change comes quickly, other times slowly."

On one level, the pro-feminist fathers in White's study, like the gender-progressive men interviewed in Guy-Sheftall and Cole's pathbreaking book, reveal the complex issues operating in the formulation of black male feminism. On another level, the narratives of these feminist fathers and "brothers" offer autobiographical evidence of the efficacy of struggle against heterosexist notions of black masculinity. Moreover, the memoirs of black men like Mark Anthony Neal and Kevin Powell follow in the path of gender justice that Michael Awkward courageously cleared in his autocritography. In coming to know the historical and contemporary lives of a select group of black fathers and "brothers" bravely denouncing patriarchy, I am even more committed to the struggle against a new and more specious rhetoric of black machismo popularized today. As stated in the opening pages of this book, in the heartfelt narratives of pro-woman(ist) black men I found a place/space to write out my own narrative of critical self-development, one full of hope about the transforming possibilities of feminism/womanism connected to theorizing a NewBlackMan(hood).

8

Hands-on Practice

Everyday Challenges of Pro-Woman(ist)/Feminist Fatherhood

> It is not true that men are unwilling to change. It is true that many men are afraid to change. It is true that masses of men have not even begun to look at the ways that patriarchy keeps them from knowing themselves, from being in touch with their feelings, from loving. To know love, men must be able to let go the will to dominate. They must be able to choose life over death. They must be willing to change.
>
> —bell hooks (2004, xvii)

In *Black Male Outsider*, I wrote about being a "professor" of feminism in the college classroom and my profession as an ordained "elder" (a minister in a black Pentecostal denomination). Growing up with a fundamentalist religious background, and having internalized the best *and* worst of it, I understood little about ways patriarchy functioned in the church to police difference and dissent, while reinforcing a gender hierarchy (with men in charge of things that really mattered). In really painful ways my experience of feminism as an education for critical self-development caused me to reject the religious dogma I had been spoon-fed for most of my life. On the one hand, the teachings I received as a boy in church about the preeminence of love and faith as the core tenets in the salvation of humanity have stayed with me. On the other, religious dogma rooted in (hetero)sexist patriarchy continually challenged my evolving feminist consciousness—particularly regarding its sexist ideas of women's roles in the church, its perpetuation of heteronormativity and homophobia, and its class politics rooted in the message of prosperity. My life as a black male "fundamentalist" preacher and gender-progressive, pro-feminist man has always been about complicated, seemingly irreconcilable contradictions. Longing to be free from religious dogma that reduced the humanity of women and men to a long list of patriarchal dos and don'ts, in 2001 I left the church of my childhood after thirty-five years. Since then, my struggle has been to eradicate the contradiction between the pro-woman(ist) discourse I "preach" outside the ivory tower and the autocritographical writing I promote inside it.

Over the years, reading, writing about, and teaching black feminist thought has compelled me to share publicly the unspeakable shame and guilt I associated with my experience as a childhood survivor of domestic violence. As a social theory conceptualized by black women for personal and political empowerment, black feminist thought provided me the necessary critical tools in this book to analyze the gendered and racialized effects of domestic violence in the lives of black men in the past and present. As the concluding statement in this book about the self-transforming and healing power of pro-woman(ist) autocritography, this chapter reaffirms the power of black feminist thought for black male self-recovery from the internalized wounds of patriarchy.

Pro-woman(ist) Profession, Autocritography, and the Will to Change

As a "black male outsider" growing up in the South during the 1960s, I was not fully conscious of the (normalized) ways white supremacy, patriarchy, and classism simultaneously functioned to (mis)shape my identity and view of the world. In Hot Springs, Arkansas, my hometown, whites ruled. "Whiteness," personified in white male (and female) privilege, possessed the power to define black manhood and black womanhood in gendered and economic ways that relegated all that was associated with "blackness" to the status of "less than," "unequal," "inferior." Doubtless, my parents' economic status as low-wage black service workers, struggling to make ends meet for many years, informed my father's problems with alcohol abuse and his abuse of my mother. However, as explained in the introduction, having internalized domestic violence in my family as a way of life was something I would not fully comprehend until I was an adult. For many years, not acknowledging the traumatic ways that my childhood experience of it damaged my sense of self, I was silent about my mother's plight as a victim of domestic abuse. To me, it was inextricably connected to her status as a black working-class woman under the thumb of my patriarchal father and white supremacy.

Growing up in a working-class family in the South during the first decade of racial integration, I simultaneously learned lessons of male supremacy and white supremacy. But being black, whether female or male, in a culture of white hegemony was always linked to patriarchal power, which meant that to be white *and* male represented the highest form of authority. As far back as I can remember as a child, this idea had been seared into my consciousness. Interestingly enough, while I knew religion, gender, and class were racialized in my hometown, it had never occurred to me that Hot Springs actually had no recognizable black middle class. Except for black folk who were teachers and principals in our town's segregated school system and pastors of our largest black Baptist and Methodist churches, almost all the blacks worked in the town's service industry. No wonder we revered our black teachers, principals, and preachers. They were our community leaders. They lived among the people. They could not separate themselves from working-class and poor black folk even if they wanted to—the town's long-standing segregated housing pattern simply forbade it. In my hometown, like that of many across the South during the time, blacks well understood the parameters of their economic and social place. Movement beyond its boundary had its costs. In Hot Springs, a resort town known as the place "where the world bathed," its bathhouses, luxury hotels, and restaurants operated on the backs of black service workers. Maids, porters, bathhouse attendants, and waiters were employed all over town, but their lower-class standing restricted black economic, social, and political movement.

As noted in other autobiographical texts I have written, my mother was a domestic worker, a housekeeper, and a cook in the homes of elite whites for many years. My father worked for many years as a machine operator for the city's water treatment facility. We had it better than a whole lot of other black people in town. I remember my mother telling me once that at one time there had been a black male doctor in town, the husband of the black elementary school principal. I never got the opportunity to verify this, as a visit to a doctor's office was not something I ever experienced growing up. To my knowledge, we had no medical-care coverage. Television functioned as the primary tool for my education about the myth of white superiority, heteronormative gender identity, and working-class and poor black folk. As a child, my earliest notions of class materialized through images of middle-class and elite white people on my family's big black-and-white TV (strategically positioned in the living room of every house where my family ever lived). Considering the fact that my parents could not afford a color TV, I think the literal and figurative absence of color that restricted representations of race and class to images of "black and white" on our black-and-white TV furthered reified the idea(l) of the norm in Hot Springs. While there existed no stereotypical train tracks dividing whites from blacks in my hometown, the visual racial codes were clear to all. Whites stayed with whites; blacks stayed with blacks.

In the late 1960s, however, with the end of segregation and the beginning of integrated schooling, I quickly learned in overwhelmingly white classrooms that the more I valued middle-class white identity (the signifier of both race *and* class superiority), the more success I would achieve as a black student. As early as I can remember in my impressionable black-boy mind, to be "classy" was to possess something that white people valued. Mainly for that reason, as a young child I came to associate nice things with "whiteness," white people, and upper-class standing. I think my parents did too, though they never openly said so.

Yet racial consciousness founded upon white middle-class ideas of respectability was very apparent in my parents' insistence that my brother and I should dress in our best (Sunday) shirts, pants, and shoes when we went to school—particularly when we began attending school with white students (after segregated schooling ended in 1968). Joking about my parents' seeming obsession with "upper-class" appearance, I tell the story of buying a pair of blue jeans for the first time at the age of nineteen (after having left home for college). My parents' class attitudes were no different from that of many other black parents who came from poor or working-class backgrounds. The idea was and continues to be that black people to be successful have to let white people with class privilege know we can look as good as (or better than) they. Passed on from one generation to the next, from slavery on, this is a racial lesson about class that many black folk (poor, working-class, middle-class, upper-class, and elite) have never forgotten, even if we would rather not admit it.

Growing up in a town where blacks constituted the service class in an economy controlled by whites, I continued to believe that *all* white people possessed economic privilege. Were there working-class and poor whites in my hometown? If there were, they were invisible. Maybe, like so many blacks in town, they were passing as middle-class. Perhaps they (if they did exist) shared the shame associated with being poor that some black families like mine worked to hide. I do remember, however, at one point during my second year at our newly built integrated high school, a white family lived next door to us. In 1969, my parents bought a small home in a previously all-white, lower-middle-class neighborhood. As things would go (and have gone in the history of racial housing patterns in the United States), those whites who remained in the neighborhood eventually moved away.

April, the Cruelest Month of the Year in My Father's House

> April is the cruelest month, breeding
> Lilacs out of the dead land, mixing
> Memory and desire, stirring
> Dull roots with spring rain.
>
> —T. S. Eliot, "The Waste Land"
> (in Friar and Brinnin 1951, 179)

I have argued that in historical and contemporary autobiographical narratives of pro-woman(ist) black men, childhood experiences of domestic violence (perpetrated by a father figure) act as a catalyst for their rejection of patriarchy and patriarchal fatherhood. These narratives renew and transform the dialogue about the possibility of feminist healing in the lives of men. One of the memories I kept secret for years as an adult male was my father's abuse of my mother when I was a child. Next to that very painful memory is the pain I felt watching my father die.

When I was a little boy, I tried to remain out of my father's way to avoid his anger. At home, his presence constituted a painful reminder of the last time rage had exploded (most often against my mother). During the years when domestic violence ruled our home like a merciless warlord, I learned what being a father was *not* supposed to be.

In June 1997, my father died of lung cancer. He was diagnosed the preceding March, and given six months to live. In April of that year, I went back to my parent's home in Arkansas to spend the month with him. Interrupting a sabbatical leave from the university in New York where I taught, I thought the time with him would be good for both of us. I hoped to write about our time together—to write about our feeling for each other, about our relationship as father and son, about being black men in the world. The writing never happened. Instead, who we were together and alone that April was mediated by the unspoken reality of his slow and certain journey toward death. Two month before I arrived, my parents had received the dreadful news of the diagnosis with adamant denial, grounded in their unshakable faith in divine healing. To me the devastating effects of his illness suggested otherwise, and every day of that exceptionally beautiful month I stayed with them. April in Hot Springs (a town known for its natural beauty) is always beautiful.

However, the April I returned to my hometown proved to be a cold and cruel month in my father's house. The inevitability of my father's death was never acknowledged in conversation with either one of my parents during that month, yet death was always lurking behind eyes filled with sadness, and the words he spoke to me and mine to him censored what we really wanted to say to each other in the days toward the end. In light of his increasing antagonism toward me, which began almost the first day I arrived, one might have imagined that I represented death's messenger. Thought he never said so, he evidently thought I had come home to watch him die. Every gesture of help I offered, he rejected. Nothing I did was right. He interpreted my presence as an attempt to rob him of his power as the patriarch of his home, never letting me forget that he was in charge. Three days after arriving, I packed my bags in preparation to leave. Three days was all it took for me to feel like the helpless little boy I had been thirty years earlier. Even though I had a wife and children (proof that I had grown up), the passage of time would not validate my manhood.

All of the nightmares of the past had returned. In the house where domestic violence had been a constant feature of our family life, I feared that this time his anger would destroy me, not my mother. But he had changed (or had he?). He had been "saved" (the Pentecostal term for spiritual conversion) for years—over twenty years earlier, after I left home for college. Miraculously, it did bring an end to his abuse of my mother as well as to his excessive drinking and smoking. After turning to the church, he never struck her again. But the month of April I spent with my father was like reliving the violence of the childhood I had never forgotten. I began to hear the screams and cries for him to stop, to see the blood, to feel the utter helplessness and fear with every blow, every punch he directed toward her face. I wished he were dead then. Neither I nor my brother had possessed the power to stop him. Now all those feelings had returned. During that month of April, feelings of fear, hatred, abandonment, and the absence of his love haunted me. Even in my attempts to be sympathetic, given the physical and emotional trauma my father was experiencing because of the disease, I could not let go of the memory of the man he had been. The image and experience of him as an abuser kept returning. The more he verbally struck out at me or ignored me, the more my memory of the violent past informed our interactions nearly everyday of the month I lived with my father.

The month ended as it had begun, with my father and me at odds. The writing I had hoped to do with him about our experiences as black men did not happen that April or afterward. There will be things I will always love about my father—his love of people and the downtrodden; his belief in justice; his laughter; his love of knowledge, building things, planting flowers and vegetables; and the love he possessed for his faith. After his death, I began to understand how much I am like him. In coming to acknowledge the similarities between us, I began making peace with him. Have I been able to let go the heart-wrenching pain of patriarchal fatherhood I experienced that April? In truth, after a decade and more, I am still working through feelings connected to it. Yet, from that tragic time, I came to acknowledge the depth of the profoundly wounding effects of domestic violence in my childhood. The feminist critique of patriarchy and of patriarchal fatherhood has enabled me to release the shame and guilt associated with it. I am no longer bound by secrecy and silence. As a survivor of domestic violence, I found in black feminist thought a strategic place to voice my rejection of patriarchal identity. Growing up witnessing my mother's abuse at the hands of my father taught me the most valuable lesson that I have learned as an adult male: that manhood is not measured by mistreatment, subjugation, objectification, exploitation, or oppression of women and girls because they are female. Commitment to this belief on a daily basis is key to my recovery process.

Leaving My "Father's House" for the Last Time

After my father's death in June 1997, I stayed in my parent's home for the remainder of that summer. My mother, brother, and I agreed (with my partner's consent) that my mother should come live with us in the Northeast. Our mother had never lived alone. She (without a mother since the age of nine) had gone from the home of her father to make a home with the man who would become our father. With a new pastor taking over the reins of our father's church and no one else living with our mother, we were certain that loneliness would have soon taken her life. After sorting through the accumulation of nearly thirty years of living in this one house and mostly giving things away to family, church members, and friends, I packed a small portion of what remained into a U-Haul, hitched it to my father's red van, and with my mother headed northward to my home. I remember that last day, going from one empty room to the next, checking to see if we had left anything. There was just emptiness. It was like the first day we moved in when I was fifteen and my brother was nine. Closing the front door, locking it securely, would be for the last time. I would never enter my father's house again. Two years later, it burned to the ground, having been struck by lightning.

While dialogue between my brother and me about being childhood survivors of domestic violence has drawn us closer, conversations with our mother on the subject have rarely taken place. Over the years, she has clearly romanticized her life with my father and chosen not to revisit those painful years. "After all, he got *saved*," she says. And they did spend many happy years together before his death. But his salvation did not save me (or my brother). After years of life-threatening, self-destructive depression, I am still haunted by feelings of self-worthlessness. While I write about the black Pentecostal Church as a foundational spiritual anchor and "sanctuary" (a place to hide growing up in the face of the marginalizing experience of black masculinity), it too contributed to my inner feelings of spiritual unworthiness and gender otherness. In my experience as a card-carrying Pentecostal preacher, few "holiness" ministers I know supported feminist values. In a denomination where women serve only supporting roles to men, they clearly know their place in a long history of patriarchal order and hierarchy. Challenging this system is a struggle few men *or* women I know in the church have been willing to engage.

Growing up as a Pentecostal, I remember always being at odds with the church's patriarchal/sexist views. Women seldom complained, however, having devised ways to circumvent the ruling male power structure. While the church doctrine has always opposed homosexuality on biblical grounds, its recent public stand against same-sex marriage has been such a chilling condemnation of it that it belies the teaching of Christian love and compassion. In retrospect, my becoming an elder in the church only exacerbated preexisting feelings of discontent—old thoughts of not fitting in, of being out of place even in the certification of male power it awarded me. Sometime after being ordained, I experienced an increasingly painful split between my feminist pedagogy "professed" in the college classroom and my doctrinal conservatism "preached" in church, and I felt like a hypocrite. I had conceptualized a form of confessional-memoir writing pedagogy that compelled students to break their silence about experiences of oppression in their lives. It challenged them to take an ethical stand against racism, sexism, classism, *and* homophobia. However, as I became bolder in my claims regarding the transformative power of black feminism in the context of a majority-white-female classroom, I was becoming even more silent about its possibilities for radical change in the lives of black women and men in my local church.

As more time passed, I began to feel more and more complicit in the patriarchal practices of the church. In my local church, I never spoke of it beyond a small group of like-minded, progressive congregants. My silence felt like compromise. More than this, I felt like a traitor to my students and myself. Often sharing my frustration about the personal price of silence with students in my classes, I am reminded of conversations with my wife about the fear we felt when inviting them (and colleagues) to our church. We desired to share the richness of its spiritual and cultural dimensions. Yet we were always concerned about something being said from the pulpit that would offend students. Would they question my credibility as a feminist advocate in a church that openly endorsed sexism and homophobia? While nothing offensive was ever said or done during times when students came, I hoped we would one day garner the courage to leave the church.

Eventually, I came to believe that openly voicing my differences with the leadership of my local church would make little difference. I finally realized that for all my love of its ritual and traditions, the church was not going to change. Having reached the limits of my endurance, convicted by my own teaching and preaching, I gained the courage to cancel my membership. So at the end of the summer of 2004, with much anguish and inner turmoil, I finally ended a long on-and-off relationship/membership with the church of my youth. From the experience, I learned that practicing what one teaches/preaches is about personal and social accountability. The respect of my students meant much to me, particularly because I impress upon students the importance of social accountability inside and outside the classroom. We measure our commitment to the struggle for social justice by the strength of our will to stand up for human rights. I tell students that the love of struggle against injustice must be tested to ground our faith in the righteousness of the work we do toward advancing the welfare of all people.

I think of my work in the classroom as an extension of the work I did in the church—that is, *to minister* to the welfare of people suffering from the ills of oppression. I am not a psychologist, nor am I formally trained as a therapist. Yet I have combined my academic training with work in addiction recovery to enable students to comprehend—in mind, body, and spirit—the necessity of love in the struggle against all forms of injustice, love for freedom and love for the people. Not always disclosing to students at the beginning of a course that I am a minister, invariably, one or more of them will claim that it was apparent to them from the start. I have little trouble letting them know that black feminist pedagogy is integrally linked to the history of black folk religion.

On Forgiveness and Reconciliation: A New Beginning

On a muggy night in May 2006, closing out the day in the midst of routine matters, shuffling over things atop my bedroom dresser, I came upon a picture taken in 1991 of my father standing casually with my son (then six), wife, and mother in Washington Square Park in Greenwich Village. I scrutinized the image of my father in the photograph—it was not that of the father from those terrifying years of my childhood. He was a "God-fearing" man of the cloth. A devoted grandfather of three (at the time my son, his first, and my brother's two small children). He wore the title with pride.

Observing him that day and on other occasions fussing over my young son Gabriel, I often wondered whether my father—a kinder, gentler man—sought to relive his relationship with me through him. He adored my son, giving him the nickname "Mo Mo." Its origin is unknown to me. I never heard him raise his voice toward his firstborn grandson, his namesake. He loved the name "Gabriel," and when he became pastor of his church, he renamed it the "Angel Gabriel Christian Center." In truth, Gabriel was not my father's birth name. It was his given name for his first communion in the Catholic Church. That his firstborn grandson was carrying on his name probably made him feel even more connected to a child very much like him—outgoing, rambunctious, not at all timid. As a child, I was just the opposite of my son and father—introverted, shy, and very timid (according to one of his sisters). Did I ever resent the bond my father and my son (as a little boy) shared? My father died when Gabriel was twelve. Nothing about his grandfather's demeanor would ever have suggested to him that years before his birth, he had been a father whose sons growing up experienced him as an alcohol-abusing perpetrator of domestic violence (at least from the time I was six years old, my earliest memory of it). I will always be grateful for his spiritual conversion when I was nineteen. It miraculously changed him. But even more dramatically, it changed life in our family. Though I was away at college when it actually happened, I directly benefited from what my mother firmly believes was the result of the "years of prayers" that followed upon her own soul-saving experience while I was a junior in high school.

So the end of my father's wicked ways brought domestic peace for my mother and brother (six years younger than I). Mother would become the "first lady" of the church Dad pastored. He would become a revered minister in the community among blacks and whites. Today, the street on which "Angel Gabriel" sits was renamed "Lemons" in honor of my father. Why has it been so difficult for me as a grown man, having survived the trauma of childhood domestic violence and having become the biological father of two and the surrogate of another, to forgive my father for the sins he committed against his family? Or for feelings in the deepest darkest place in myself of abandonment and loss? Even after he found God, his heavenly father—the One who absolved him of all his sins—my earthly father never once apologized for the horrific, gut-wrenching hell to which he consigned my brother and me in our home. He never once mentioned it—as if the ten years of violent physical and psychological abuse never happened. I was not willing to forgive *or* forget. Every violent outbreak, every fist against my mother's face, every hand around her neck, all the ugly words spoken to subjugate, to silence, to obliterate her presence—I feel them even as I write these words. Each blow knocked me deeper into myself—into the darkness of secrecy, hidden wounds, concealed pain, repressed anger. How can I forgive when I cannot forget? I have come to know in rejecting the law of the patriarchal father (measuring the value of manhood in the misogynist subjugation of all that is feminine) that I did not become my father—the father of those hellish years filled with continual nightmares of a mother's bloody death. I fight against the heteromasculinist, homophobic demons within me to identify as a gender-progressive man. Pro-woman(ist) male identity requires that I love gender justice and the right of women to intellectual, economic, physical, and spiritual self-governance more than I do the possession of male power rooted in patriarchal allegiance.

Identifying as a black man who promotes a politics of gender justice also requires that I acknowledge male privilege and culpability in the ongoing systemic subjugation and objectification of all women. After twenty-five years of marriage, my wife often chides me about touting my allegiance to feminism, particularly when I cut her off or talk over her when she speaks, condescend to her on women's issues, claim to know how women "really" feel about being female, or exercise what she calls "typical male behavior." At times like these, I feel rattled and unsure of myself. "Why bother?" I sometimes say to myself when she puts me in check. I am always acting like a (patriarchal) man, which according to Stephen Heath in *Men in Feminism*, means that "no matter how 'sincere,' 'sympathetic' or whatever, we are always also in a male position which brings with it all the implications of domination and appropriation, everything precisely that is being challenged, that has to be altered" (1987, 1).

Yet feminism as a strategy of male self-re(dis)covery has helped me to understand the manhood demons that drove him to become inhuman. More importantly, I have learned that my humanity depends, not upon forgiveness of a system of maleness that seeks to destroy *all* men who buy into it, but upon the act of forgiving my father as a patriarchal victim who before the end of his life accepted the power of love over the death of his own humanity. In contrast to the fundamentalist dogmas of my religious upbringing founded upon male, heterosexist, homophobic power, womanism represented a healing path through which my myth-laden vision of the Creator as the embodiment of the patriarchal father has been dismantled, law by law.

Games Daughters Play and the Challenges of Feminist Fatherhood

Putting into practice ideas of feminist fatherhood garners different reactions from my wife and children. While my partner supports me, she says that too often I jump to defend the rights of women without a fundamental consideration of her desires, which may or may not coincide with my *male*-identified notions of feminism. During moments of personal insecurity, I throw up both hands in frustration, thinking the idea of male feminism is an impossibility. At times like these, I remember what is personally at stake for me. Regardless how incredulous it may appear sometimes—to my partner (the closest woman to me) or even myself—I remember why becoming a gender-progressive black man has been so important to me. Through feminist critique of patriarchy and sexism, I possess the critical tools to fight the sexist within me(n) in a culture of male supremacist domination.

Together, my wife and I struggle to educate our children about the fundamental right of all people to be free—free from discrimination, hatred, and violence for who they are. This belief is deeply rooted in the emancipatory faith we practice. Having become a pro-feminist teacher and preacher, I have learned that a love of justice must be forged in a spirit of forgiveness. It is not that all wrongs—institutionally and/or systematically created—should be simply forgiven in the name of some naive notion that good will triumph over evil. Rather, it is a belief in forgiveness grounded in the most rigorous, heartfelt struggle to eradicate all forms of patriarchal domination. Over time, I have come to realize that my father (who left home when he was only thirteen years old)—the son of a father who also abused his mother—was also a victim of patriarchy. Having internalized its ideology of male supremacy, he brought it into his marriage to my mother.

As gender-progressive parents, my partner and I hold our children accountable for ways their everyday behavior and attitudes may perpetuate certain sexist, racist, and homophobic ideas of female and male identity. My daughter (in her teens) has a strong sense of my gender-justice politics. Yet her sense of herself as a black female comes directly from her mother. She has instilled in her a feminist identity that is racially and culturally specific. Being a pro-feminist father in relation to my wife and daughter means knowing my limits regarding the female spaces they create and share in ways that I cannot. I have to be okay with that. While never having formally sat down with my daughter to recite my feminist beliefs, I have shared some of them with her on a few awkward occasions.

For example, I remember that some years ago, during one afternoon after school, I asked our daughter (then eight years old) how things had gone that day. She told me about a game she and other girls had played during recess. The game required they pretend to pick cotton for their "rich boss." Rather disturbed, I asked whose idea the game was. She responded saying it was her best friend's idea. Her best friend, "M," was white, and she was the one who played the part of the "rich boss." Even more disturbed at this point, I asked my daughter if she knew the game had anything to with slavery. She said no. As calmly as possible, I began her first lesson in American slavery—that a make-believe game in which she pretended to be a slave picking cotton was not good for her. I explained that she was a descendent of slaves—that had she lived less than two hundred years ago in this country, she might very well have been a slave. Speaking as directly as possible, without showing any disdain or anger, I talked about the implications of being *black* and *female* in a racist and sexist culture. Though she nodded in response, I was not exactly sure she understood my point. As much as I wanted to, I did not forbid her friendship with "M."

A week later, when her best friend from class invited our daughter to her home, I seized the opportunity to discuss the matter with her parents. When we arrived at the front door, "M" grabbed my daughter in tight embrace. After the two girls went whizzing up the stairs to play, I recounted the incident to "M's" parents. Her mother stood completely silent as her father innocently related that "M's" idea for the game must have originated in her "love for reading about slavery." He obviously saw no harm in the game—it was all make-believe. With as much composure as possible, I unequivocally informed both parents that though "M" had little knowledge of the game's implications for my daughter, as her parents it was critically important that they understand them and share them with their daughter. Whether they ever discussed the matter with "M," I never discovered. All I can say is that "M" and our daughter remained friends through the end of the school year. In any case, I left her parents' home still angry. Why were they so calm about the whole thing, so unabashedly innocent (ignorant)—as if I had completely overreacted? I have witnessed this form of white innocence before.

That day, I vividly recalled Jane Lazarre's definition of the "whiteness of whiteness": "that terrible and inexcusable ignorance of racism which denies history and reality" (Lazarre 1996, xv). No matter how innocent "M's" parents perceived the "game" of slavery to have been that our daughters participated in, I still hold us as parents *and* the girls accountable for knowing the dehumanizing history of slavery in the United States and its contemporary, painful reality for people of color and whites as well. To forget it or act, play, or pretend it no longer makes any difference is to perpetuate a form of willful blindness that keeps us all in denial about the evil of white supremacy—even in the innocent imagination of a little white girl.

A-shirts and "Wife-Beaters": Fashioning Domestic Violence in a Culture of Misogyny

Our sons (one of whom is biologically related to my wife and me as a nephew) have long been aware of the principles of female equality and women's rights their mother and I advocate. Over the years, they (as well as my daughter) have sat in on my feminist classes and have weighed in on the race and gender dialogues/debates their mother and I carry on at home. What happens in public is another story, however.

While sitting at a table in the food court of a crowded mall on a sweltering Saturday afternoon, catching a quick bite with a minister friend from church, his teenage son, my son/nephew, and my daughter (who was nine at the time)—I overheard my friend's son and my son talking about "wife-beaters." When I told them I was interested in knowing more about the topic of their discussion, I received a quick, humorous response: "Wife-beaters are white A-shirts. You can get three packs for $20," my friend's son volunteered. "Why are they called wife-beaters?" I inquired. In a state of disbelief, I heard my friend's son say, "The reason the A-shirts are called 'wife-beaters' is that on TV (on shows like *Cops*, for example) the men the cops usually arrest for beating up wives have on A-shirts. Almost always the men are Italian, black, or Latino."

I had no idea that A-shirts had come to be associated with men who batter women. Disturbing to me was the fact that the misogynistic stereotype reinforced the myth that men of color are more abusive in their relationships with women than white men. Waiting until his son finished explaining to me what the term meant, in a tone reflecting as much disgust for it as I the minister verified what was said.

While my daughter sat silently eating her food, my appetite for a burger and fries was replaced by a new hunger to know what these young men personally thought about the term. I anxiously asked with a raised voice, tinged with anger, "Do you guys use the term?" "Yes," they nonchalantly replied. Numb with disbelief, especially by my son's response, I asked him in a deadly serious tone (that silently said, "You better come correct with your answer") how he could use the term so cavalierly. Why weren't he and his friend as offended by the term as we fathers were?

"Think about it," I said. "A black man wearing an A-shirt, regardless of his reasons for wearing it, is stereotypically associated with domestic violence. That really, really upsets me. As young black males, you both should be aware of ways language is racialized in this country. Racist myths about men of color would have us believe that we are inherently violent and abusive toward women." While my friend's son's reaction to what I said was rather glib and off-the-cuff, as if I had made much more out of the whole thing than was necessary, my son's reaction was of more immediate concern to me. Why had his reaction been so passive? Having lived with us for the past five years, I had hoped he would have been more outspoken. In his last year of high school at the time, he had become more socially and politically involved in issues relating to black people. He was a founding member of an activist group at his high school called MOBCA, Messengers of Black Cultural Awareness. Given his commitment to progressive racial politics, his uncritical response had completely thrown me. Not letting the moment go, I seized the opportunity to do some hard-core consciousness-raising work on the critical need for black males to understand the relationship between racial profiling, internalized racism, and domestic violence as a means to "keep women in their place." Hearing my voice tremble with rage, I emphatically stated: "Don't you know that right now, somewhere a woman is being brutally beaten to death by a man? I can't believe you can sit here and act as if this doesn't mean anything to you." My friend said, "We're desensitized by violence; this is a good example how language shows it."

While criticizing racial stereotyping of men of color was clearly, I thought, an important thing for me to do, it was even more pressing that as young black males they be critically aware of the interrelation between internalized racism and the internalization of female oppression or the normalization of domestic violence. Not wanting them to think that I was coming down on every man of color who wears an A-shirt, I reiterated my point about the power of language, racist stereotyping, and the perpetuation of male violence against women in a culture of male supremacy. (I myself am a black male who will occasionally wear an A-shirt [shirtless] in the summer, as an inexpensive means to stay cool). As we gathered our things to leave the food court, I wondered if our words as concerned fathers had made an impact upon our sons. Telling us they would meet us later at another destination in the mall, they walked away; I focused on the A-shirt my son was wearing, and wondered whether he would reflect upon the social implications of this seemingly neutral article of clothing before he wore it again.

Thinking later about our discussion, I knew my reaction emerged from a place deep inside me—as "a survivor of domestic violence." Years ago, I had no words for what took place in the house I grew up in. Breaking silence, writing out these words publicly today, represents years of personal struggle against remembering what the words actually mean.

The Dutch Door Incident: What Happens When Sons See Fathers Cry?

I do not approach the question of what happens when sons see fathers cry with a definitive answer, for the emotional lives of fathers and sons is a complex one bound up in heteronormative ideas of masculinity, manhood, and patriarchal fatherhood. Two years ago, my biological son had to confront a myth of machismo deeply ingrained in every male, regardless of race, class, gender, and sexuality: "Real men don't cry." On a sweltering summer's afternoon, my nineteen-year-old son witnessed an emotional outburst in me that left him feeling completely embarrassed about my behavior as a father. I had cried in front of his roommate. It just happened—unplanned, unrehearsed. It revolved around a matter my son actually knew nothing about, which is why to this day he still may not understand the motive for my intense emotional reaction. A close, "sister" feminist friend, upon moving out of her historic Harlem brownstone bound for another country, had left me several personal items she had acquired over the years. One was a massive desk from her study that I had admired for years. It sat below the memorial quilt crafted to honor Audre Lorde upon her passing. The other items she passed on to me had remained in the house as elements of its original architectural features. One was a short wooden pillar that most likely had either stood at the beginning or at the end of one of the brownstone's three staircases; the other was a set of weathered but beautiful oak Dutch door panels. My nephew had accompanied me to my friend's home to load the items into our van to take them to our home. He certainly knew the significance of them to me, since I had related to him their personal value to me in no uncertain terms.

Returning to our house in a small town in New Jersey across the river from Manhattan, I reveled in being the recipient of the gifts my longtime black feminist friend had given me. Most of all, I felt deeply honored that she had given me that desk. I knew the spirit of the work she had done at it and all the African artifacts that once sat open upon it would inspire me in the daunting writing tasks that lay ahead of me. After my nephew and I had gingerly carried the desk down the back stairs to my office space in the basement of our house, we stored the column and the door panels in the garage. All was bliss—until some weeks later. Time had come for our yearly garage cleaning, always a massive task. As time and age have moved on, my wife and I more and more have assigned this labor-intensive task to our sons, both of whom aspire to become world-class weightlifters (in their dreams). They had spent a Saturday summer's morning exercising muscles and the authority we had given them about what should stay and what should be discarded. We assumed all was well.

Several weeks later, I was working at the desk, which had, indeed, been an unfailing source of inspiration for the "soul writing" that came forth during my daily marathon sessions at the computer. During one session, a little past midday, it suddenly occurred to me that I should check the garage to be certain that our sons had secured the column and door panels in a safe place. I ran up the stairs, hurried out the back door of the house, lifted up the garage door in one swift movement, and discovered with amazement that the garage was completely empty. Nothing remained except the column. Where were the Dutch doors? Surely, they had not been thrown out. My nephew, the "son" who had helped me to store them, knew exactly how much they meant to me, so I thought. With a rush of emotion (anger, sadness, disbelief, helplessness), all I could think about in that moment was that something of such great personal value to me now had been thrown away weeks ago at our local dumping yard. What were my plans for the doors? I have no idea.

Much more than their historical value, the panels with their faded veneer represented tokens of abiding friendship. Like these pieces, our relationship had endured many things. To me, the panels were beautiful things, treasured objects from my friend's home where (over the course of a decade) I had come and gone. That home had been a place of ceremonies and rituals—"spiritual" birthdays, political strategizing sessions, "house cleanings" and repairs, festive times of food and comradery among some of the best and brightest young folk I have come to know. Over the years I had come and gone to my friend's "yard," seeing it as a kind of sanctuary. I had come to know my feminist "sister" as a woman of great intellectual, spiritual, and political conviction, and to have lost something of hers—given me at a time when she was leaving New York City to take up residence in another country—symbolized a deeper internal loss. My "sister" friend had left me.

The doors were gone. Tears flooded my eyes; I could hardly see my way back into the house. I rushed into it, emotions at a high pitch, looking for answers from my sons. No one was on the first floor. I hurried up the stairs to the second floor with tears streaming down my face like water overflowing a dam. In the first room at the top of the stairs, a common family space, stood my biological son and his college roommate. There was no time to hide the obvious. I could not have held back my tears at this point if I had desired. My son looked at me with eyes filled with unbelief. "Where are the doors?" I blurted out. "What are you talking about?" "The doors that were in the garage, where are they?" "I don't know." My son knew nothing about the door panels. He had been away at college when my nephew and I brought them home. "Do you remember taking anything out that looked like two big wooden cabinet doors?" I struggled miserably to describe them. "Oh yeah, I remember something like that. I think they did get thrown out." "Why would he [my nephew] do that? Those doors were given to me as a gift," I said as the reality began to set in.

They really were gone. It never occurred to me that my son's roommate was still in the room during the heated exchange on that hot summer day. With my nephew nowhere in the house to be found, my son (and his roommate) witnessed a side of me he had not seen before. "How could he do this? He knew how much those things meant to me," I shouted, bolting up the steps to the bedroom my wife and I had created in the attic. "He threw away the doors. Can you believe he threw away the doors?" I cried as my wife and my daughter looked at me in disbelief at the top of the stairs. They tried to calm me, tried to make sense out of what I said. Nothing they said could have made any difference at this point. The pain of loss tied my stomach in knots. A heavy feeling of defeat came over me. I did not recognize myself. As quickly as I had rushed into the house from the garage seeking answers, I ran down three flights of stairs to the basement—past my family (and my son's roommate), past the last day in my friend's house, past our first meeting ten years earlier at the university in New York City where we had been colleagues, past years of malehood exile on the margin of masculinity, to my past as a black boy outsider.

In the basement, I sat before the massive wooden desk of my "sister" friend, laid my head on it and wept for all the times in my life I hurt—but held back the tears to be *manly*, in control. "Real men don't cry." Later that day my nephew returned home, came downstairs to the basement, and apologized profusely (his "auntie/mom" having called him earlier about the trauma of the day's events). While my nephew (who remains as close to me as a son) and I worked through the emotional fallout of that day, it would be weeks before my son could come to grips with what he witnessed that day. He had little to say around me other than giving a perfunctory yes or no in response to a question. One night, before the end of the summer, he, his mother, and I happened to be sitting together watching TV. I do not recall what we had been watching, but the subject matter of the show prompted a conversation that led me to revisit the Dutch door incident. When I asked him if his weeks of cool demeanor toward me had anything to do with it, he resoundingly asserted, "Yes." He said it was one thing for me to "lose it" among our family, but to have broken down in front of his roommate was another. "That just wasn't cool." "But couldn't you understand how devastated I was in the moment?" "Yes, but you shouldn't have done it." "You were embarrassed?" "Yes." "The truth is," I asserted," "if it happened again, I would react the same way." He was not at all pleased with that response, nor did I take kindly to what felt like his mother's agreement with him. To her my reaction had seemed more like an expression of wrath than of sadness.

She was right. In truth, my tears were filled with unbridled anger bordering on rage. But that was not really what bothered our son. It was the fact that a close *male* friend had seen his father crying uncontrollably. I had lost control and shown myself to be unmanly, vulnerable, weak. When are men *and* boys allowed to feel deeply, to hurt enough to shed tears? My son and I have not revisited our positions, even though his roommate would later share with me that he still respected me, explaining that his own father "cries at the drop of a hat." What my son has come to realize is that "that is the way Dad is." He still does not understand that my crying on the day the Dutch doors were mistakenly thrown away was not a sign of weakness but a signifier of personal manhood liberation.

The more vocal I am about my gender-progressive position, attitudes, and actions as a pro-feminist man, the more personally accountable I must be in defending them. I maintain that that the gender-progressive legacy of Frederick Douglass and W. E. B. Du Bois laid a solid foundation for contemporary pro-feminist black male activism. Beverly Guy-Sheftall asserts the importance of knowing the history of black male gender progressivism and its implications for the future of the black liberation struggle: "At a time when there is controversy among academics and activists alike over whether blacks should be fighting for the liberation of women *or* the liberation of the race, one can look at the lives of Frederick Douglass, Sojourner Truth,

Du Bois, and Mary Church Terrell, to name a few, and resolve this seeming dilemma rather easily" (2001, 86).

In confronting my childhood as a survivor of domestic violence, I realize that my father was a victim. Himself a survivor of domestic violence as a child, he learned the ways of patriarchy. It taught him to adopt a form of machismo in which as a black male not only did he have to fight white supremacy to survive, he believed he had to follow the masculinist dictates of male supremacy. While the performance of machismo may have made him feel more powerful as a black man against the power of white male hegemony, ultimately it did more harm than good for the people he loved. It did not protect him nor his family from the years of rage he surely held within in a culture of white male supremacy, nor did it ameliorate feelings of abandonment he surely must have felt toward his own father. I wish he could have shared his feelings of abandonment with my brother and me. Neither my brother nor I have become our father of those years when he believed it more important to show his power in violent ways in our family than represent a loving model of fatherhood to his sons. Only years later, after we had already become fathers—struggling to overcome the childhood psychological wounds he inflicted upon us—did he realize the benefits of being a loving (grand)father. Against the history of white supremacist patriarchy that denied the humanity of my father, and generations of black fathers before him, I continue to fight for feminist fatherhood as a strategic location for my own self-re(dis)recovery.

The Health Difference Black Male Feminist Thought Makes

> In this society, the Black man feels he can never rest, he can never relax, or just be himself. Many of us have developed a 'What difference does it make' attitude. Racism has forced a lot of Black men to sit on top of their pain. They feel there are very few outlets to share their feelings of frustration with the system. When we [Black men] don't feel we can provide for our families or protect our children, we feel worthless, depressed and we begin to turn on each other. This society only values what you do and not who you are. In this society, many of us feel alone. Who can we turn to?
>
> —The Black Mental Health Alliance for Education and Consultation (2003)

As long as patriarchal atonement is promoted as the goal of black male self determination, many black men *and* women will continue to interpret it as a positive measure. It only reinforces thinking that reinscribes the myth of black machismo, a seductive power trip for black male feelings of disempowerment. Rather than legitimize our right to be men and fathers, if we so choose, we disconnect ourselves from authentic expressions of love for members of our families. In the performance of machismo, we turn away from our own humanity in favor of a vacuous and nihilistic manhood. In this way, we do not act as men but as willful agents of our own demise.

Black men willing to engage in earnest dialogue about ways they are hurting and have been wounded by racism and patriarchal notions of manhood, masculinity, and fatherhood must create spaces of healing, locations for their own "gender talk." Identifying as a black feminist professor in my practice as a teacher in majority-white college and university classes for over a decade, I emphasize race as a critical feature in black feminists' critiques of sexism and patriarchy. Much of the work I have done on black men and patriarchal thinking has happened outside the classroom. Involved in faith-based recovery meetings with men in black communities over the years, I have found them a critical location for engaging in dialogue about our gender relations and our mental and emotional health.

When we look at statistical records on black male mental and emotional health, we must begin to link our gender trouble to masculinist inscriptions of who we are (or should be as men) in a culture driven by male supremacy and white supremacy. Many of us cannot justify our male existence when we see all around us white malehood continuously associated with patriarchal power and heteromasculine privilege. And for many of us our mental health is bound up in the damaging effects of patriarchy grounded in white male supremacist thinking. The (hetero)sexist, misogynist, and patriarchal game of male supremacy is killing us. According to the findings of the Black Mental Health Alliance for Education and Consultation in "Souls of Black Men: African American Men Discuss Mental Health," we are in some deadly gender trouble. There is a rising rate of depression among black men, and there are death rates "at least twice as high as those for women for suicide, cirrhosis of the liver, and homicide." The article reports that "[f]rom 1980 to 1995, the suicide rate for African American male youth (ages 15–19) increased by 146%. Among African American males ages 15–19 years, firearms were used in 72% of suicides, while strangulation was used in 20% of suicides" (Black Mental Health Alliance 2003). Even more devastating are its findings on the effects of alcohol abuse by black men in large cities "when compared to statistics for white men, white women, or African American women." Moreover, the article points out that "[w]hen mental disorders aren't treated, African American men are more vulnerable to incarceration, homelessness, substance abuse, homicide, and suicide."

A decade and more after the Million Man March, black men continue to face an immense challenge physically, emotionally, and spiritually.

Against a history of economic and social disenfranchisement, we organized and came together en masse at the nation's capital to restate our claim to humanity. Yet collectively, we have not responded to questions related to gender oppression, patriarchy, sexism, and homophobia in our movement to end racial oppression. Black men continue to disavow the existence of sexism, ignoring its pervasiveness and its harmful effects on black women and children in our communities. The masculinist rhetoric of the Million Man March suggests that once again we have failed to recognize the interlocking nature of oppression. Once again, with our masculinist blinders on, we have placed the evils of racism over the insidious ways male supremacy and white supremacy function interconnectedly to devalue black womanhood. Once again, we have acted as if racism is the only form of domination black women experience. We have, once again, decided that the agenda for black liberation rests on our right to be patriarchal men.

Critiquing black sexual politics of the 1960s in "The Black Movement and Women's Liberation," Linda La Rue argues that "[u]nless we realize how thoroughly the American value of male superiority and female inferiority has permeated our relationships with one another, we can never appreciate the role it plays in perpetuating racism and keeping black people divided" (La Rue 1995, 169). Black people's movement for liberation can never be emancipatory as long as black male self-interest lies at the center.

Contemporary black men struggling to contest white male hegemony only on the grounds that it keeps us from asserting patriarchal power fail to account for the privileged status we already hold as men—despite racism. Today, more and more gender-progressive black men are putting forward an analysis of racism that exposes the inextricable relationship between white supremacist thinking and ideas of male supremacy. Such an analysis resists the uncritical tendency to privilege the effects of racism over the combined impact of racism and sexism on black women. The progressive black male struggle to end sex and race oppression in the United States rejects the ideology of manhood that insists upon the patriarchalization of masculinity. Gender-progressive black men reject a romanticized, masculinist fantasy of royal African antiquity invoked to serve as a model for contemporary black gender relations. The representation of black women as African queens functions as another form of patriarchal control. In this version of utopian sexism, the power relation between black men and women does not change: black women remain subjugated.

Until masses of black men comprehend the interconnection between sexism and racism, we will continue to behave as if sexism (like homophobia) is not a problem that black people need to confront. Many black men claim that the injustices we suffer under white supremacist power is tantamount to racist castration (or "high-tech lynching," as Clarence Thomas so self-servingly protested). Thus, we cling to the ideas that antiracist resistance must be about defending our manhood. When black women critique masculine bias in our communities, we accuse them of the same crime against our manhood. Do we remain trapped by a self-absorbed, self-defeating quest to measure up to the litmus test of white supremacist patriarchy, as if we have no identity as black men outside the limits legally codified in slavery? Or do we acknowledge ways it continues to inform the male supremacist beliefs and behavior we have internalized as a form of antiracist resistance?

Recognizing heteroblack male privilege as inextricably bound up in heterowhite male hegemony begins a process of gender/sexual self-inventory. In it, we critically reflect on the *self*-sacrificing cost of black antiracist struggle for manhood, for we cannot imagine our liberation outside it as human beings. Racist decolonization exempt from antisexist intervention leaves black men (*and* women) in a no-win, zero-sum position. As I have argued, womanism offers an inclusive vision of human rights predicated upon the simultaneous liberation of the individual and the collective. To further ignore the ways (hetero)sexism is counterproductive to the eradication of racism, as well as profoundly dehumanizing to black women, is the worst form of racial genocide.

In a culture where white supremacist, patriarchal initiatives continue to deny the humanity of black people, there can be no substitute or excuse for black men and women not affirming each other's humanity through a vision of antiracism grounded in gender progressivism. A model of beneficent black patriarchy can never stand in as an acceptable compromise. Reflecting upon BMES's call for a total rejection of black machismo, I hear the voices of Frederick Douglass and W. E. B. Du Bois declaring the necessity of women's liberation. In their pro-woman(ist) words, we hear the voices of the young African American men who organized the first black male, gender-progressive conference at Morehouse. The passionate manifesto of Black Men for the Eradication of Sexism illuminates a visionary path of liberated manhood away from the dictates of patriarchal atonement. Our willingness to be womanist-identified men means that we must redirect our attention toward the pressing realities of female oppression in black communities. It means that we must nurture progressive ideas of black manhood and masculinity. The very existence of black men dedicated to the eradication of sexism, publicly advocating an end to the oppression of women, refutes the notion that feminism has no place in the lives of black males. We dismantle myths of black machismo. What is at stake in its perpetuation? It has not saved us. In actuality, it contributes to our (self-)destruction through a form of "stylish nihilism" (bell hooks's phrase) where who we are has become synonymous with a vulgar materialism. We have fashioned our bodies into salable commodity for a culture of white-supremacist capitalist consumption of the black male other. We are at once frightening and entertaining. We know it and we are working it. At what price? Our communities, ourselves, our souls? But isn't that what stylish nihilism is all about?

Practicing What I Preach *and* Teach: Pro-womanism as a Personal, Divine Calling

Pondering the academic implications of my professional concerns as a pro-woman(ist) professor (in the tradition of Frederick Douglass and W. E. B. Du Bois) and ordained Pentecostal preacher, I must make a confession that lies at the core of my practice of both. It is a confession held tightly in the grip of my memory as a little black boy whose understanding of Divine Providence was steeped in Christian teachings about faith and love. Today, I hold it even more tightly in my heart. As a child, I believed in angels—spiritual messengers assigned to aid an individual toward the completion of a divine mission. Like Fraedo, the transracial child protagonist in Harriet Wilson's fictional autobiography *Our Nig*, I was also filled with white supremacist notions of heaven formed from pictures in the family Bible. Heaven existed high in the sky, and was the place where Jesus, God, and all the angels dwelled. In my mind, the one thing they all held in common was *whiteness*. Everyone and everything in heaven was *white*. If heaven is the place for white people, I thought, where will I (and all other black people) go "if should die before I wake"? This was the one line in the prayer I prayed nightly that concerned me most. Devils are black and angels are white. Much like "the little black boy" in William Blake's poem of the same title, I believed that while my skin was black, my soul *had to be* white—or else I would not go to heaven if I should die.

That was years ago. But even today, as a black man in continual struggle to free myself from the internalization of white supremacy as a (normalized) way of thinking in the world, I still struggle to erase the mythology of "white" angels from my mind. Still steeped in the religious teachings from Sunday school teachers long passed away, I continue to believe in angels. Today, however, I think of them as black. *Black* angels? What a thought! On the surface, my "need" to believe in black angels may be interpreted as a simple mental act of racial reversal in response to a long history of white supremacist Christian iconography. In reality, the need touches something deeper and much more powerful within me, something related to inner racial self-recovery. In the representation of Christian saints in icons, why are they usually portrayed as beings with white skin? It was a really simple question, but one I never asked anyone as a child. In a radical (re)vision of heaven in my mind, I want to imagine angels as having black skin. If, after all, Europeans have imagined and worshipped the Madonna as black for hundred of years, then black angels should not be a stretch of the imagination for either white people or people of color.

I have talked at length about my childhood belief in angels and the racist conception of their whiteness with the man I call my "therapist," Rev. James Howard. Once I told him that I thought of him as a *black* angel, whose divine mission as a spiritual messenger was to aid me in completing this book. Having realized (after working earnestly on the manuscript for nearly a year) that I needed help to openly engage the pain of my childhood wounds, I perceived his "healing" entrance into my life as the answer to my prayer. After a long period of writing in circles, "Dad," as I came to refer to him fondly, pushed me to a crucial breakthrough in the writing process. As a spiritual guide and loving father figure, he counseled me through the hard places in the writing, places I had repressed. He was a man of deep faith, and his nurturing spirit inspired me to write through the pain of my wounded past. He helped me forge a critical link between my profession as a feminist educator and as a "preacher" possessing a religious background that had functioned significantly in my pedagogical development. Consistently, he compelled me to honor both callings.

"Dad" was a pastor, a preacher, and a chaplain ordained in a black Pentecostal church. Part of his work as a chaplain was his nine-year tenure at the Women's Detention Center when it was located in Greenwich Village. With vivid recall, he told me about having talked with Angela Davis and Assata Shakur during the times each of them was being detained there. He spoke of both with utmost respect, remembering the exceptionally mild-mannered ways of each woman. While the media represented them as scurrilous outlaws, he portrayed them as women of great integrity and conviction in the causes to which they were committed. He did not tell stories about his work at the Women Detention Center to boast about having engaged (in)famous black female political prisoners. Rather, I believe he shared these stories with me to make a critical connection between his profession as a black "man of the cloth" and the stand as a politically progressive believer in the rights of women one must uphold.

At the end of one of our afternoon counseling sessions, "Dad" spoke insistently on the necessity of foregrounding the spiritual in a book that seeks to represent the complex, intertwined "callings" of the academic and religious professions. Without being dogmatic, interpreting scriptural principles in the most compassionate light, he read the manuscript (and its numerous revisions) with the eyes of a sage. He turned eighty in January 2006. He died in September 2007.

Would he have called himself a feminist, a man with a long history of pro-woman advocacy? It is a moot question, considering the progressive views on the equality of women he held for most of his life. When I began my search for black feminist forefathers years ago, I discovered them symbolically in the pro-feminist writings of Frederick Douglass and W. E. B. Du Bois, and I have written of them in this book. But while writing this book, I also found Rev. James Howard. His pro-woman(ist) values, deep spiritual insight, and social consciousness revealed him to be one of the most gender-progressive black men I have known. Possessing keen insight into my struggle for self-recovery, he helped me transform personal trauma into a foundation for self-liberation. Pushing me beyond barriers of shame and self-denial, "Dad" would say, as many times as I needed to hear it, "What if all of the 'negative' things that happened in your life prepared you to write this book?" Shoring up the breaches in my confidence to face wounds of race and gender, he would gently chide me to repeat these words: "I have something to say."

Thinking about the influence of Howard on my writing *and* my life, I conceive the familial bond we held for one another in womanist terms. He was my feminist father. He nurtured me, restored my self-esteem, and made me believe that my writing mattered. He gave me the love I needed to feel from the father that had been absent during my childhood. His love was the gift that enabled me to recover from the wounded black boy in me—a boy so deeply scarred by internalized racist and heterosexist myths of black male identity, schooling in majority-white classrooms that perpetuated myths of white superiority, and the traumatizing impact of domestic violence as a child (that left me afraid of black men in general and of myself as a black male in particular). As I have said, for years I thought I would become the man my biological father had been during those awful years when he wreaked havoc upon the lives of my brother and me. We were defenseless against his brutal tyranny against our mother. We all survived—we all got "saved" in the church. But at what cost? While I loved my biological father for the religious conversion he made long before he passed away, I struggled to forgive him for the childhood he denied me. Rev. James Howard became the father I yearned for during my childhood and teenage years. The therapeutic relationship with him not only promoted inner healing that allowed me to embrace the little black boy in me, but also helped me to see (for the first time) some profound connections between my public feminist declaration in the classroom and the *ministry* of recovery I practice outside it. "Dad" helped me understand that both professions are rooted in "love" and "faith." For me, professing to be a pro-feminist black man has become an act of faith in my spiritual calling and love of teaching. I have come to believe that my public declaration of feminism represents a continual process of returning to a place of self-transforming love.

In *Black Male Outsider*, I wrote about my journey toward becoming a pro-feminist black man and the feelings of loneliness associated with it, feelings of not quite ever really fitting in, not anywhere. Often I felt, and still sometimes feel, like the quintessential black male outsider. In so many ways, identifying as a black male professor of feminism threatens to deepen the already existing fissures of my race and gender anxieties, with and apart from other black people. When I have been the only black male in all-white or majority-white classrooms where I have taught, feelings of race and gender insecurities have flooded my mind. More often than not over the years, teaching in these spaces (even with "professorial" rank), I still feel self-doubt regarding my position in them. "I am the black man passing as a feminist masquerading as the real thing—the black woman feminist who should be teaching a course on black feminism." More often than not, when teaching critiques of black male (hetero)sexism by black women feminists in white classrooms, I feel like a race and gender traitor. During those moments, I have wanted to pack my bag and quickly exit these spaces. But I tell myself that, whether in white spaces or places where people of color dominate, being a black professor of feminism is an inherently traitorous position to occupy.

In moments like these, I tell myself that I have a responsibility as a survivor of racism and (hetero)sexism to uphold my gender-progressive self-proclamations, and that I will not defend the subjugation or mistreatment of any female on the grounds of any man's "need" to feel self-empowered (because of masculine insecurity). I tell myself that I will not promote the dehumanization or mistreatment of any person who is not heterosexual—whether lesbian, gay, transgender, bisexual, or simply someone questioning heterosexual privilege. As a self-proclaimed race and gender traitor, I tell myself that I must hold on to my experience of (hetero)sexist self-transformation. I tell myself that it can be a strategic location for resistance struggle where faith and love in my recovery process serve as continual sources of self-liberating reinforcement. After consciously embracing womanist thinking as a mode of male self-recovery in the late 1980s, it took me more than a decade to understand what my work is as a black male professor of feminism and nearly the same number of years to translate its personal, social, and political meanings onto the paper of a book. Before writing it, I never imagined my "profession" would ultimately compel me to write publicly about its complexities. (Pro)claiming my position as a "brother" outside the script of patriarchal black manhood has enabled me to confront my own internalized myths about it. In the documented history of black male support for the eradication of gender oppression, I theorize a black male outsider standpoint conceptualized in the work of a new generation of contemporary gender-progressive black men. Rejecting the nationalist rhetoric of manhood invested in patriarchal atonement, we claim a vision of black fatherhood and "brotherhood" forged in womanist thought. In it, I see clearly the liberating possibilities of feminist manhood for black men willing to acknowledge the *self*-wounding effects of patriarchal domination.

A Theory Well-Suited for Black Male Self-Recovery

From the memoir writings of Frederick Douglass and W. E. B. Du Bois to those composed by some of today's most vocal black male advocates of feminism and/or womanism, what remains clear is a profound connection between the personal and the political struggle they embody. Examined together, Douglass and Du Bois unequivocally produced an amazing body of writings dedicated to gender justice focused on female equality and women's political autonomy. Through an activist-based discourse, traversing terrain between the confessional mode and social/political critique, each man demonstrated the power of a discursive strategy in which black male self-representation was integrally woven into the fabric of public political discourse on women's rights. As illustrated in the pro-woman(ist) autobiographical/political writings of these men, an ongoing tension exists between theory and practice. At times, this tension is unsettling, especially when male self-interest undermines the articulation of an integral pro-woman(ist) standpoint. In reclaiming the gender-progressive legacy of Douglass and Du Bois, my aim has not been to represent them as flawless icons of male feminism. But it is undeniable that today they offer gender-progressive black men a personal/political space to imagine a pro-woman(ist) male standpoint that negotiates the complex dynamics involved in the struggles for gender and racial justice. As asserted from the beginning, this book heralds the emergence of a new generation of black men committed to gender justice founded upon feminist/womanist principles.

Today, black males promoting female equality and women's rights employ memoir as a strategic site of self-recovery, healing, and political empowerment grounded in the rejection of patriarchy. These men have written about the transformative influence feminist/womanist thought has had in their daily lives. Michael Awkward claims that the power of male feminist autobiography lies in its strategic attempt to link confessional narrative to "professional concerns." As he theorizes in his memoir, autocritography serves as a "critical concept" to explore the formative relationship between the origin and evolution of black male feminist consciousness in the material condition of the (black) mother. Long before reading Awkward's memoir, I had already begun thinking about how the black maternal figure operates in the critical evolution of Douglass and Du Bois's pro-woman thought. Today, in the memoirs of gender justice by black men such as Awkward, Mark Anthony Neal, and Kevin Powell (as well as my own), it is clear that the gender-progressive beliefs they possess are inextricably linked to a transformative black *maternal* presence. Neal certainly illustrates this in the "letter" in *New Black Man* to his feminist mentor, Masani Alexis DeVeaux.

Black men for gender justice publicly writing and speaking about the impact of black feminist women in our lives constitute a testament to the power to transform the heteropatriarchal ways we think and act as men. Moreover, they have enabled us to come to grips with the sexist and misogynist behavior we have internalized, thereby masking the wounding effects of patriarchy in our lives and the lives of females in the private and public worlds we inhabit. They have birthed in us paths toward our self-re(dis)covery—not only as antisexist men, but as full human beings. In our journey toward wholeness, we lay the groundwork for a politics of black male vulnerability that supports our self-healing and gender healing in black communities. Ultimately, at its core, pro-woman(ist) memoir writing by black men is about personal recovery work toward black male liberation. Rooted in a progressive politics for gender justice aimed at eradicating sexism, autocritography for these men embodies a vision of womanist "profession." It echoes the insightful antisexist thinking Frederick Douglass and W. E. B. Du Bois so passionately exhibited in memoirs and political speeches in defense of female equality and the necessity of women's rights. They bequeathed to us a legacy of activism for gender justice linked to the *personal*. While not totally free from patriarchal notions of fatherhood, the legacy of pro-womanism they engendered framed a discourse of black male self-recovery. Openly acknowledging the power of gender-progressive thinking in their lives was, indeed, an act of self-(re)possession in terms that transgressed the boundaries of manhood thinking during their respective times. In our rejection of patriarchal manhood, we advance the pro-womanist legacy of Douglass and Du Bois.

Epilogue

"This Is What a (*Black Male*) Feminist Looks Like" Time Has Brought about a Change

> We're at a unique moment in history where there can be transformational change, and we want to make sure that in that transformational change, there is real change for women.
>
> —Ellie Smeal (2009 qtd. in www.democracynow.org, 2)

> The narratives of [the] men [in *Ain't I a Feminist?*] made me laugh, cry, frown, smile, scream, sigh, and (I believe) grow. After reviewing and analyzing their stories, I am convinced that some men can appropriately be called feminists because they are committed to correcting, through public *and* private actions, the imbalance of power between men and women that is built into the structures of American society. As a perspective, feminism can be accepted or rejected by anyone, male or female. *In my analysis, if one actively accepts that perspective in belief and practice, one is a feminist* [emphasis added].
>
> —Aaronette White (2008, ix)

My aim in this book has been as much about articulating what it means to be a *black male feminist*, as it is about reclaiming the historical legacy of Frederick Douglass and W. E. B. Du Bois as pro-women's rights men. Yet, against the history of racism and sexism in the United States, I continually struggle to rid myself of internalized wounds of white supremacy and patriarchy to imagine (as a black man) the self-healing power of feminism. Daily, it requires letting go of systemic and institionalized baggage I carry bound up in myths of white supremacy and male supremacy. I know the personal benefits of becoming a self-identified feminist/womanist man. I have whole-heartedly embraced the idea of a *black* man becoming a feminist. Moreover, I have come to believe it a critical imperative for *every* black to possess the transformative power of feminism as a critical form of physical, emotional, and mental self-recovery—free from the bonds of patriarchal manhood and masculinity. I can be my*self* and be for women. In my own process of becoming a pro-feminist man toward my own self-healing, it called for me—

- To affirm the humanity of all black men (across class and sexual difference);
- To contest the racist and sexist belief that all black men are inherently misogynist and homophobic;
- To struggle against the sexist image of the "strong black man" rooted in machismo;
- To critique the heterosexist notion that black self-determination is preeminently about the liberation of black manhood and masculinity;
- To call into question ideas of patriarchal atonement as the antidote for issues facing the black family (particularly as it pertains to the presence or absence of the father);
- To protest publicly the idea that "feminism" is a racist plot to emasculate/feminize the black man.

As a "professor" of feminism for nearly 20 years in the college classroom, my pedagogical aim has been to close the gap between the theory and practice of liberatory education grounded in womanist thought. In my classes, students come to know the praxis of feminist intersectionality conceptualized in black women's simultaneous struggle against racism, sexism, and classism. As a black man teaching feminism in majority white female classrooms, simultaneously, I must always be critically conscious of my male privilege *and* my race as potentially divisive elements in these spaces. I also know that as a black male professor in these classes, white privilege (most often demonstrated in the form of colorblind thinking) will undermine students' will to connect across our racialized gender difference. Nevertheless, I challenge myself and my students to confront differences of gender, race, class, and sexuality to enable community building in and beyond the classroom. Fostering a politics of difference at the center of liberatory pedagogy, I hold on to an inclusive vision of feminism where all persons committed to social justice work together to advance a coalitional approach to ending all forms of domination. Ending this book, reflecting upon the historic legacy of black male feminism in the lives of contemporary black men, I marvel at President Barack Obama's level of commitment to social change strategically linked to the struggle for women's rights.

To be Black, Male, Feminist, and the 44th President of the United States

Before and after the historic election of Barack Obama as the 44th President of the United States, photographs of him appeared on the cover of every major newspaper and magazine in the nation. However, one cover image of him stands out from the rest. It is the illustration of him on the cover of *Ms. Magazine*.

The magazine's decision to feature Obama on its 2009 winter cover edition created a firestorm among feminists, focusing attention on the admittedly provocative idea of a feminist man. Reactions were mixed, from those who thought the cover was a joke to others who seriously took the message to heart. As male and female feminists have documented, the history of the feminist movement in the United States is one in which men for social justice have been ardent supporters of women's rights since the "first wave" campaign for woman suffrage. Yet for people still struggling to comprehend the idea of a black man as President, the idea of a black man who self-identifies as a feminist may be even more difficult to imagine. Despite some people's refusal to divest themselves of a sexist and racist imagination, not only is it possible for a man to embrace feminism as an active, self-liberating rejection of patriarchy and sexism, as this book demonstrates, there exists a documented history of black male womanist activism. Today, for a black man of African descent who self-identifies as a womanist and/or feminist, opposing sexism in and outside black communities, the *Ms.* representation of President Obama is both creatively provocative and evocative. According to Ellie Smeal, publisher of *Ms.*, as well the co-founder and president of the Feminist Majority Foundation, "[W]e wanted to tell the world that he [Obama] self-identifies as a feminist and that he's run on the strongest platform of any major party for women's rights. And we also wanted to capture both the national mood and the feminist mood of high expectations and hope for his presidency" (Smeal 2009 qtd. in www.democracynow.org, 2).

When I saw the *Ms.* "Special Inaugural Issue" cover for the first time, it provoked in me an incredible, overwhelming feeling of personal joy and affirmation. At the same time, the representation of Obama evokes imagery that disrupts the history of male supremacy and white supremacy. Viewing the cover for the first time, I immediately zeroed in on its subversive power. Having grown up watching the masculine exploits of white male superheroes on TV and in movies, I joyously imagined Obama's gender and race reimagined within the gender, racial, and (white-woman-only) feminist politics *Ms.* calls into question. Can a black man *really* be a feminist? What must he believe and do to be considered a feminist? By whom? Who possesses the power to bar him from being "black," "male," and "feminist" simultaneously? The representation of President Obama on the *Ms.* cover clad in a suit and tie ripping open his shirt to reveal a black t-shirt imprinted with the sentence—"THIS IS WHAT A **FEMINIST** LOOKS LIKE"—compels the viewer to have to question centuries of racist and sexist mythologies in this country associated with the black male body (historically exempt even of the power to defend itself). Much more than a simple riff on the image of "Superman" (pop icon of white male, *super-human* power), *Ms.* magazine's feminist (not efeminizing) exposure of Obama's progressive gender politics signifies a revolutionary reimagining of black manhood and masculinity.

For all women and men invested in an inclusive, pro-woman(ist) coalition politics, the *Ms.* cover provokes a moment of serious reflection about who our allies are (or might become) in the struggle to end sexism. For gender progressive black men and self-identified black male feminists, in particular, Obama on the cover of *Ms.* invites a critical moment of personal and political self-reflection about the place(s) of black men in feminist movement. On multiple levels, the *Ms.* representation of President Obama is affirming for a vision of black manhood and masculinity free from the traps of white supremacy and male supremacy. If anything, the feminist image of Obama invites imaginative personal and political play galvanizing the possibility for—

- Affirming, first of all, that black men can, in*deed*, be pro-woman(ist)/feminist;
- Renewing investment in building a broader more inclusive coalitional base in movements for women's rights forged across gender, racial, class, and sexual difference(s);
- Adding strength to the struggle for *all* men not only to comprehend, but to implement strategies to reject the (self-)wounding effects of patriarchy;
- Making a stronger case for feminist/womanist thinking as a strategic location for liberatory self-recovery and anti-sexist healing for men as allies to women.

In black communities, more now than ever before, with Obama's ascendancy to the Presidency, his unapologetic commitment to human rights for all women and individuals across class and sexual difference has opened a new space for dialogue between black women and men about the ways patriarchy, sexism, misogyny, and homophobia continue to undermine the liberation of *all* black people. At this historical juncture, the state of black gender politics is caught up in a drama of patriarchal, capitalist manipulation predicated upon the sexual devaluation of the black female body. As object of sexual commodification for capitalist consumption, in particular, the body of any young black woman (most ruthlessly spectacularized in hip-hop culture) has become representational grist for one of the most violent, self-deprecating forms of toxic racist and sexist dehumanization—misogynistic nihilism. Many black women and men, cross-generationally, are experiencing an unprecedented level of psychic and spirit woundedness, exacerbated by the normalized myths of black machismo and black family dysfunctionality. I began the prologue to this book theorizing the possibility of a renewed engagement in the "Debate on Black Sexism."

It has been 30 years since the *Black Scholar* in 1979 devoted an entire issue on sexism in the lives of black women and men. It has been over 160 years since the Seneca Falls convention in New York in 1848, where Douglass cast the deciding vote which officially began the campaign for woman suffrage. According to Aaronette White, in *Ain't I a Feminist?: African American Men Speak Out on Fatherhood, Friendship, Forgiveness, and Freedom* (2008), self-identifying as a feminist (whether one is a woman or man) is about what one *does* to end sexist oppression. Obama is an advocate for women's health research, investment in small businesses owned by women, stronger anti-domestic violence laws, defense of Title IX (guarding against discrimination of female students and employees in education), equal pay for women in the workplace, and reproductive rights for women. On January 29, 2009, Obama signed the Lilly Ledbetter Fair Pay Act. Advancing his pro-choice commitment, with an executive order during his first weeks in office, he overturned the Bush administration's policy banning international funding for a wide variety of groups focused on family planning, reproductive counseling, and abortion related issues.

While the *Ms.* cover representation of President Obama conjures up an immediate association with the identity of Superman, as noted earlier, it does not readily evoke a connection to the history of black male feminism. Yet upon closer historical examination, one uncovers a revolutionary bond between this image of Obama and those of Frederick Douglass and W. E. B. Du Bois that grace the cover of this book. In word and deed as an equal rights activist for women, the President carries forward the legacy of Douglass and Du Bois's work for race and gender justice. I represent Obama as a "womanist son." At the same time, I mark another link between these men: their vision of pro-feminist fatherhood. What is the President's vision of feminist fatherhood? On the Sunday, January 18, 2009 cover of *PARADE* magazine, below the full-page color photograph of the Obama family (including Barack, Michelle, and their two daughters, Malia and Sasha), the headline reads: "'What I Want for You—And Every Child': A Letter to My Daughters."

After reading the letter, I came away with the distinct impression that more than a "feminist" approach to fatherhood, Obama had articulated for his daughters a call to a future of activism grounded in a vision of human rights directed toward all children. Framed in a list of "wants," he asserts: "I want all our children to go to schools worthy of their potential…I want them to have the chance to go to college—even if their parents aren't rich. And I want them to get good jobs: jobs that pay well and give them benefits like health care, jobs that let them spend time with their own kids and retire with dignity. I want us to push the boundaries of discovery… that improve our lives and make our planet cleaner and safer. And I want us to push our own human boundaries to reach beyond the divides of race and region, gender and religion that keep us from seeing the best in each other" (Obama 2009, 4–5). It is, however, the specific directives he passes on to his daughters that encompass the imperatives of human rights that governed Douglass's support for women's rights. Charging his daughters to a future of activism founded upon shared nation-building principles of personal accountability and social responsibility, Obama writes,

> I hope both of you will take up that work, righting the wrongs that you see and working to give others the chances you've had. Not just because you have an obligation to give something back to this country that has given our family so much—although you do have that obligation. But because you have an obligation to yourself . . . it is only when you hitch your wagon to something larger than yourself that you will realize your true potential . . . I want [you] to grow into compassionate, committed women who will help build [a] world . . . [where] every child [has] the same chances to learn and dream and grow and thrive [as] you girls have. (Obama 2009, 5)

Without compromising the intimacy the father seeks to maintain even in an open letter strategically written for public consumption, it is through this framework that he expresses his Presidential vision of social justice. Considering the letter's visionary gender politics, the father's personal (feminist/womanist) hope for his daughters' future, embedded in his desire for social change, aims to touch the life of every child in the nation.

In the two magazine cover images of President Obama examined here, my aim has been to uncover the pro-woman(ist) ideas that inform them and their representation in his public and "private" life. As his feminist ideals demonstrate, the progressive standpoint he holds on women's rights, sexuality, and gender equality clearly echoes that of other gender progressive black men. In the President's words and deeds on behalf of all women and children's welfare, I hear the resolute voices of pro-womanist black fathers and "brothers" that came before him. I hear them saying, "Time has brought about a change."

Listening to the Echoes of Our Womanist Heritage Urging Us to Hold Our Ground

Remembering those pro-womanist fathers and "brothers" who have come before us is critical to the project of black male self-restoration. From the prologue through part 1 of this book, I laid both a personal and a political claim to the history of black men who wrote and spoke publicly about their allegiance to feminist principles. In part 2, I sought to illustrate the efficacy of those principles in the lives of contemporary black men.

Reclaiming the legacy of Frederick Douglass and W. E. B. Du Bois as the antipatriarchal fathers of today's outspoken antisexist black men involves the crucial task of *re*-membering—"putting the bits and pieces of our lives together again" (bell hooks). Thinking about the thematic thread binding the book's two parts, I am drawn again to the power of womanist memory as a strategic tool of critical consciousness in the self-recovery work of gender-progressive black men across time and space. During the historic debate on black sexism sponsored by the *Black Scholar* in 1979, as I first noted in the prologue, one black male voice stands out—that of Kalamu Ya Salaam. In his argument that "women's rights are human rights," he claimed solidarity with the history of black male pro-womanism—despite the (e)masculinist name-calling he knew it would incur. Considering the historical importance of Kalamu Ya Salaam's words for feminist-identified black men today, his reference to Douglass bears repeating: ". . . I hear the echoes of our heritage urging me to be firm. I hear Frederick Douglass, who . . . spoke out strongly in support of women's rights. Douglass was vilified and shunned by former friends who could not understand his concern for the rights of women. I hear Douglass being called an 'hermaphrodite' and other terms which questioned his sexuality because of his stand on sexism. But in the spirit of Frederick Douglass, I do declare that I too should rather be called 'hermaphrodite' and other names because of my support for women's rights . . ." (Ya Salaam qtd. in Byrd and Guy-Sheftall 2001, 114).

Just as Kalamu Ya Salaam has looked back to history, hearing the voice of Douglass standing for women's rights against sexual vilification, so many contemporary pro-feminist black men have heard Ya Salaam. One among them is Thandabantu Iverson, whose poetic tribute to him represents a powerful testament to the black male heritage of his pro-woman(ist) stand. Recalling the first time he met Ya Salaam, who was inspiring people with his antisexist images of critical resistance, Iverson tracks the evolution of the "patriarchal rebellion" sparked in him by this transformative meeting. I would like to cite Iverson's "Poems Can Be Weapons, Too!"[1] as an amazing illustration of the radical force of black male pro-woman(ist) memory and its power to change the lives of black men:

   I did not know
you
   who you would be/come
to me
   in my patriarchal rebellion against injustices
that I saw.

I was blinded by my own silences
   and could not speak what I had seen
   in my mother's bloodshot eyes
I was closeted from my own pains
   so rebellion did not include the personal/political
in my life—it was the masses for whom I spoke
in the silence that could not save

when we met you were awakening and spoke in notes
I now can sing
   sounding alarms of what will be if we refuse to see
what is here
in the weekend beatings that so personally punctuate our political lives
yet remain unseen by eyes that cannot see
ears that will not hear
tongues that remain tied in the knots of
un remembered abuses—which of course are stories about power.

when we met I did not know
that the way ahead to which
you pointed was a pathway to my past and the present in which
I perpetrated the beginnings of a future . . .
I did not know what you meant
but now I see.
When we met you spoke with weeping willow breezes
that connectedmeto the painsofmymothersisterand myself.

You sounded an alarm and now I am a fireman.
Now I am running for my life telling all who will listen that the smoke
in our eyes is not about romance it is the acrid truth about abuse that
we oppress even as we burn oppressed.
While there is time I am running like Sojourner to win others from the
plantation
To gather as many as we can to leave all the injustices and run on
to make new paths to justice.
We wade in the water to elude the dogs that follow.
We run so others won't get too weary, so others will not faint,
so others will stand so others don't have to crawl.

When you stood and spoke at first I did not know,
Amazing Grace (how sweet that Sound) that saves the wretch I was
I once was blind but now hear and see and feel and run for justice.
You spoke and I thankyouforlettinmebe my (better) self.

As a professor of feminism in the academy whose background outside it as a minister often clashed with the pro-woman pedagogy I practice, the one thing that has remained constant in my struggle against patriarchy rooted in sexist religious dogma is the belief that there are no accidents—that things happen just as they should. While waiting for permission to reprint in this book material I had previously published, I began making certain minor revisions to the manuscript. Just before sending it off to the publisher, I received the poem above from Thandabantu Iverson. To my amazement, as stated earlier, it is dedicated to Kalamu Ya Salaam. Acknowledging the importance of his voice in the historic "Black Sexism Debate" at the close of the 1970s, I had already positioned his voice strategically in the prologue to reinforce my case for the influence of pro-womanist forefathers in the lives of contemporary black men.

After reading Iverson's poem, I knew that the book was not only waiting for the permissions to come through, it had been waiting for this poem—for it to take its place as the center of this epilogue. As a coming-to-consciousness piece about breaking silence about the oppressive nature of patriarchy, particularly in his mother's life, "Poems Can Be Weapons, Too" condemns domestic violence. For Iverson, Ya Salaam's commitment to the eradication of female oppression "sounded an alarm." Representing himself as a "fireman," he declares:

Now I am running for my life telling all who will listen that the smoke
in our eyes is not about romance it is the acrid truth about abuse that
we oppress even as we burn oppressed.

Like Iverson, and many of the men in the second part of this book, I have come to know the power of black men in the service of gender justice. Against the blinding effects of patriarchy that would have us believe that black manhood and masculinity are, first and foremost, about antiracist struggle, we publicly denounce the subjugation of women, heterosexism, and homophobia. Iverson ends the poem in a moment of heartfelt gratitude to Kalamu Ya Salaam for having led him to a pro-woman(ist) path of self-consciousness. Drawing inspiration from the lyrics of a well-known hymn to articulate the sight, "Sound," and emotional transformation experienced in meeting Ya Salaam, Iverson is able *to see* the "(better)" *self* Kalamu helped him recover:

> Amazing Grace (how sweet that Sound) that saves the wretch I was
> I once was blind but now hear and see and feel and run for justice.
> You spoke and I thankyouforlettinmebe my (better) self.

From the pro-feminist lessons in black male self-recovery we have learned from outspoken gender-progressive black men like Kalamu Ya Salaam and from Frederick Douglass and W. E. B. Du Bois as our "womanist forefathers," we write and speak without public shame about our rejection of patriarchy. The existence of contemporary black men for gender justice openly sharing our stories of self-recovery from the wounds of patriarchy advances my belief that womanist thinking is healing for women and men—personally *and* politically. Recovering the wounded self in us calls for black men to reclaim the little boy hidden away in childhood, where repressed feelings of boyhood pain lie covered over in the experience of patriarchal fatherhood.

Re(dis)covering the little black boy in us, we reclaim the self that was never meant to be. In a culture of white supremacist capitalist patriarchy—where who we are as black males is most valued and/or devalued for commercial profit from commodified (self)images of misogyny, (hetero)sexism, and homophobia—black men committed to gender justice forge a radically new vision for who we are and desire to become. In the "autocritographies" of contemporary gender-progressive black men, confessional writing functions not as patriarchal atonement but as a critical instrument of self-re(dis)covery. Reclaiming the woman's-rights discourse of Douglass and Du Bois enables us to sharpen tools of critical antisexism, toward dismantling the patriarchal tenets of the master's house many of us have internalized. Toward the building of nonoppressive, liberating gender relations in black communities with our own hands, we galvanize *the power of the black female within* us. With it, we construct a radical vision of pro-womanist black manhood, masculinity, and fatherhood full of emancipatory possibility for the antisexist work to which we have committed our*selves*.

Notes

Prologue

1. The participants in the debate included: Robert Allen, S.E. Anderson, Bonnie M. Daniels, Harry Edwards, Sarah Fabio, Chidi Ikomme, Terry Jones, June Jordan, M. Ron Karenga, Audre Lorde, Julianne Malveaux, Mark D. Matthews, Rosemary Mealy, E. Ethelbert Miller, George Mosby, Jr., Alvin F. Poussant, Kalamu Ya Salaam, Andrew Salkey, Ntozake Shange, Sabrina Sojourner, Robert Staples, Pauline T. Stone, Askia Toure, and Sherley Williams.

2. This quote comes from the editorial statement in the *Black Scholar* that served as an introduction to the debate.

Chapter 1

1. William McFeely (1991) cites several instances where Douglass's physical features were critical to his reception publicly.

Chapter 2

1. bell hooks (*Ain't I a Woman*), Paula Giddings (*When and Where I Enter*), Angela Davis (*Women, Race, and Class*), Hazel Carby (*Reconstructing Womanhood*), Patricia Hill Collins (*Black Feminist Thought*), and Patricia Morton (*Disfigured Images*), among a number of other black feminist scholars, have documented this phenomenon with remarkable accuracy.

Chapter 3

Sections of this chapter originally appeared in two publications: (1) *Traps: African American Men on Gender and Sexuality* (eds. Rudolph P. Byrd and Beverly Guy-Sheftall) under the title " 'When and Where [We] Enter': In Search of a Feminist Forefather, Reclaiming the *Womanist* Legacy of W. E. B. Du Bois"; and (2) *Phylon:*

The Journal of Art and Culture under the title "Womanism in the Name of the 'Father' and the Feminist Problematics of Patriarchy, Race and Art."

1. The fact that "The Damnation of Women" situates itself in a non-Western perspective indicates Du Bois's political interest in Ethiopianism as a transformative vehicle for black female liberation. Its ideological framework was frequently represented in the works of many black writers during the time (Henry Highland Garnet, Frances E. Harper, and Paul Lawrence Dunbar, to name a few). Fundamentally, it put forth the notion of Africa as "the mother of all civilization" and the primacy of all things African.

2. Michele Wallace offers a provocative analysis of the superwoman myth in her groundbreaking book *Black Macho and the Myth of the Superwoman*.

3. In the December 1912 issue of *The Crisis*, he wrote a brief essay entitled "The Black Mother" as a commentary on the myth of the black woman as a mammy figure heard through the voice her elite white female mistress. Though the white female voice we hear is a fictive one, Du Bois suggested it approximated with historical accuracy the racist positionality of those white women who possessed the power to create and control such an arrangement. The essay concludes with the assertion that once black women achieved economic self-sufficiency, the mammy as a racist stereotype would cease to exist. He sought to reclaim the dignity of black womanhood through the validation of its maternal power. But society, Du Bois argued, would have to undergo radical reform before motherhood could assume its rightful place.

4. The questions Du Bois posed in the "Questionnaire" would act as the theoretical springboard for his aesthetic principles of black art.

5. Arnold Rampersad (1985) notes Davis's assertion that Du Bois's representation of Zora Creswell ended the predominance of the light-skinned female hero in African-American literature. It supports the claim that Du Bois consciously worked to redefine black female physical beauty through a "dark-skinned" heroine.

Chapter 4

1. This statement appears on the back cover of *The Quest of the Silver Fleece* as a promotional advertisement.

Part II: Black Feminist "Sisters," "Brothers," and Fathers

Chapter 6

1. This phrase appeared in the subtitle of the conference "Poets on Location: A Tribute to a New and More Possible Meeting," held March 3–4, 2000, sponsored by the Department of Gender and Women's Studies at Connecticut College, then chaired by Jacqui Alexander.

Epilogue

1. This previously unpublished poem appears with the permission of the author.

Works Cited

Andrews, William L., ed. 1985. *Critical Essays on W. E. B. Du Bois*. Boston: G. K. Hall and Co.

Aptheker, Bettina. 1982. *Woman's Legacy: Essays on Race, Sex and Class in American History*. Amherst: University of Massachusetts Press.

Awkward, Michael. 1999. *Scenes of Instruction, A Memoir*. Durham, NC: Duke University Press.

Baker, Houston. 1987. *Modernism and the Harlem Renaissance*. Chicago: University of Chicago Press.

Bell, Derrick. 1994. *Confronting Authority: Reflections of an Ardent Protester*. Boston: Beacon Press.

Black Men for the Eradication of Sexism. [1994] 2001. In *Traps: African American Men on Gender and Sexuality*, ed. Rudolph P. Byrd and Beverly Guy-Sheftall, 200–204.

Black Mental Health Alliance for Education and Consultation. 2003. "Souls of Black Men: African American Men Discuss Mental Health." July. www.communityvoices.org.

Black Scholar. 1979. "The Black Sexism Debate." *Black Scholar: Journal of Black Studies and Research* 10, nos. 8–9 (May–June): 14–67.

Blassingame, John W., et al., eds. 1982. *The Frederick Douglass Papers*. Vol. 2. New Haven, CT: Yale University Press.

Braithwaite, William Stanley. 1985. "What to Read." In *Critical Essays on W. E. B. Du Bois*, ed. William L. Andrews, 38–40. Boston: G. K. Hall and Co. (Review of *The Quest of the Silver Fleece*, W. E. B. Du Bois.)

Brawley, Benjamin. 1919. *Women of Achievement*. Nashville, TN: Women's Home Mission Society.

Byrd, Rudolph P. 2001. "Prologue, The Tradition of John: A Model of Black Masculinity." In *Traps: African American Men on Gendered Sexuality*, ed. Rudolph P. Byrd and Beverly Guy-Sheftall. Bloomington: Indiana University Press.

Carbado, Devon W. 1999. Epilogue to *Black Men on Race, Gender, and Sexuality: A Critical Reader*, ed. Devon W. Carbado. New York: New York University Press.

Carby, Hazel. [1893] 1987. Introduction to *Iola, Leroy, or Shadows Uplifted*, by Frances Harper. Repr. Boston: Beacon Press.

———. 1987. *Reconstructing Womanhood: The Emergence of the Afro-American Novelist*. New York: Oxford University Press.

Chideya, Farai, and David Gates. 1993. "Making a New Home on a Mean Dead-End Street." *Newsweek*, August 30, 18–19.

Cleaver, Eldridge. 1968. *Soul on Ice*. New York: Dell.

Cole, Johnetta B., and Beverly Guy-Sheftall. 2003. *Gender Talk: The Struggle for Women's Equality in African American Communities*. New York: Ballantine.

Combahee River Collective. 1983. "A Black Feminist Statement." In *This Bridge Called My Back: Writings by Radical Women of Color*, eds. Cherríe Moraga and Gloria Anzaldúa, 210–18. New York: Kitchen Table/Women of Color Press.

Davis, Angela. 1983. *Women, Race and Class*. New York: Random House.

Davis, Thulani. 1987. "Family Plots: Black Women Reclaim the Past." *Voice Literary Supplement*, March, 14–17.

Democracy Now! The War and Peace Report. 2009. "*Ms. Magazine* on Barack Obama: 'This is What a Feminist Looks Like.' " January. www.democracynow.org.

Diedrich, Maria. 1999. *Love across Color Lines: Ottilie Assing and Frederick Douglass*. New York: Hill and Wang.

Diggs, Irene. 1974. "Du Bois and Women: A Short Story of Black Women, 1910–1934," *Current Bibliography on African Affairs* 7, no. 3 (Summer): 260–303.

Douglass, Frederick. [1845] 1982. *Narrative of the Life of Frederick, an American Slave, Written by Himself*. New York: Penguin Books.

———. 1845. *My Bondage and My Freedom*. New York: Miller, Orton & Mulligan.

———. [1855] 1994. *My Bondage and My Freedom*. In *Frederick Douglass Autobiographies*, 103–452. Repr. New York: Library of America.

———. 1881. *Life and Times of Frederick Douglass, Written by Himself*. Hartford, CT: Park Publishing Co.

———. [1892] 1962. *Life and Times of Frederick Douglass, Written by Himself: His early life as a slave, his escape from bondage, and his complete history to the present time*. New rev. ed. Repr. New York: Collier Books.

Du Bois, W. E. B. [1903] 1994. *The Souls of Black Folk*. Repr. New York: Dover.

———. 1907. "A Song of Smoke." *Horizon* 1 (February): 4–6.

———. [1911] 1989. *The Quest of the Silver Fleece*. Repr. Boston: Northeastern University Press.

———. 1915. *The Crisis* no. 9 (April): 285.

———. [1920] 1969. *Darkwater: Voices from within the Veil*. Repr. York: AMS Press.

———. [1920] 1999. *Darkwater: Voices from within the Veil*. Repr. New York: Dover.

———. 1922. *The Crisis* 23, no. 5 (March): 201–2.

———. 1926. "Criteria of Negro Art." *The Crisis* 32 (October): 290–97.

———. 1928. "So the Girl Marries." *The Crisis* 15, no. 4 (June): 192–209.

———. 1940. *An Essay Toward an Autobiography of a Race Concept*. New York: Harcourt, Brace.

———. 1968. *The Autobiography of W. E. B. Du Bois: A Soliloquy on Viewing My Life from the Last Decade of Its First Century*. Ed. Herbert Aptheker. New York: International Publishers.

Elder, Arlene. 1985. "Swamp versus Plantation: Symbolic Structure in W. E. B. Du Bois' *The Quest of the Silver Fleece*." In *Critical Essays on Du Bois*, ed. William L. Andrews, 201–10. Boston: G. K. Hall and Co.

Flexner, Eleanor. 1970. *Century of Struggle: The Woman's Rights Struggle in the United States*. Cambridge, MA: Belknap Press of Harvard University Press.

Foner, Phillip. 1950. *The Life and Writings of Frederick Douglass*. Vol. 1. New York: International Publishers.

———. 1955. *The Life and Writings of Frederick Douglass*. Vol. 4. New York: International Publishers.

———, ed. [1976] 1992. *Frderick Douglass on Women's Rights*. New York: De Capo Press.

Franchot, Jenny. 1990. "The Punishment of Esther: Frederick Douglass and the Construction of the Feminine." In *Frederick Douglass: New Literary and Historical Essays*, ed. Eric J. Sundquist, 141–65. New York: Cambridge University Press.

Friar, Kimon, and John Malcolm Brinnin, eds. 1951. *Modern Poetry: American and British*. New York: Appleton-Century-Crofts.

Gates, Henry L. 1990. "From Wheatley to Douglass: The Politics of Displacement." In *Frederick Douglass: New Literary and Historical Essays*, ed. Eric J. Sundquist, 47–65. New York: Cambridge University Press.

Giddings, Paula. 1984. *When and Where I Enter: The Impact of Black Women on Race and Sex in America*. New York: William Morrow.

Guy-Sheftall, Beverly. 1990. *Daughters of Sorrow: Attitudes toward Black Women, 1880–1920*. Brooklyn, NY: Carlson Publishing.

———. 2001. "Epilogue: Reflections on Black Manhood." In *Traps: African American Men on Gender and Sexuality*, ed. Rudolph P. Byrd and Beverly Guy-Sheftall, 342–48. Bloomington: Indiana University Press.

Harper, Ida Husted, ed. 1969. *History of Woman Suffrage, 1900–1920*. Vol. 6. New York: Arno and *The New York Times*.

Harper, Phillip Brian. 1996. *Are We Not Men? Masculine Anxiety and the Problem of African-American Identity*. New York: Oxford University Press.

Harris, Luke Charles. 1999. "The Challenge and Possibility for Black Males to Embrace Feminism." In *Black Men on Race, Gender, and Sexuality: A Critical Reader*, ed. Devon W. Carbado, 383–86. New York: New York University Press.

Heath, Stephen. 1987. "Male Feminism." In *Men in Feminism*, eds. Alice Jardine and Paul Smith, 1–32. New York: Methuen.

Hernton, Calvin. 1965. *Sex and Racism in America*. New York: Grove Press.

hooks, bell. 1981. *Ain't I a Woman*. Boston: South End Press.

———. 1984. *Feminist Theory: From Margin to Center*. Boston: South End Press.

———. 1989a. *Talking Back: Thinking Feminist, Thinking Black*. Boston: South End Press.

———. 1989b. *Yearning: Race, Gender and Cultural Politics*. Boston: South End Press.

———. 2004. *The Will to Change: Men, Masculinity, and Love*. New York: Atria Books.

hooks, bell, and Cornel West. 1991. *Breaking Bread: Insurgent Black Intellectual Life*. Boston: South End Press.

Huggins, Nathan Huggins, ed. 1986. *W. E. B. Du Bois: Writings*. New York: Literary Classics of the United States.

James, Joy. 1997. *Transcending the Talented Tenth: Black Leaders and American Intellectuals*. New York: Routledge.

Jardine, Alice, and Paul Smith. 1984. *Men in Feminism*. New York: Methuen.

Kostelanetz, Richard. 1985. "Fictions for a Negro Politics: The Neglected Novels of W. E. B. Du Bois." In *Critical Essays on W. E. B. Du Bois*, ed. William L. Andrews, 173–93. Boston: G. K. Hall and Co.

Kraditor, Aileen. 1968. *Up from the Pedestal: Selected Writings in the History of American Feminism*. Chicago: Quadrangle Books.

———. 1971. *The Ideas of the Woman Suffrage Movement, 1890–1920*. Garden City, NY: Doubleday and Co.

La Rue, Linda. 1995. "The Black Movement and Women's Liberation." In *Words of Fire: An Anthology of African-American Feminist Thought*, ed. Beverly Guy-Sheftall. New York: New Press.

Lazarre, Jane. 1996. *Beyond the Whiteness of Whiteness: Memoir of a White Mother of Black Sons*. Durham, NC: Duke University Press.

Lee, Chanel. 2007. "Homos 101: Premier Black College Is a Study in Anti-Gay Discrimination." April 2. http://www.villagevoice.com/news.

Lemons, Gary L. 1998. "A New Response to 'Angry Black (Anti)Feminists': Reclaiming Feminist Forefathers, Becoming Womanist Sons." In *Men Doing Feminism*, ed. Tom Digby, 275–89. New York: Routledge.

———. 2002. "Toward the End of Black Macho: Revisioning Black Manhood." In *A Man's World? Changing Men's Practices in a Globalized World*, ed. Keith Pringle and Bob Peace, 150–62. London: Zed Books.

———. 2008. *Black Outsider: Teaching as a Pro-feminist Man*. New York: State University of New York Press.

Lerner, Gerda. 1971. *The Woman in American History*. Menlo Park, CA: Addison Wesley.

Lewis, David Levering. 1979. *When Harlem Was in Vogue*. New York: Oxford University Press.

———. 1993. *W. E. B. Du Bois: Biography of a Race*. New York: Henry Holt and Company.

Lorde, Audre. 1984. *Sister Outsider: Essays and Speeches*. Trumansburg, NY: Crossing Press.

Lutz, Alma. 1959. *Susan B. Anthony: Rebel, Crusader, Humanitarian*. Boston: Beacon Press.

Majors, Richard, and Janet Mancini Billson. 1992. *Cool Pose: The Dilemmas of Black Manhood in America*. New York: Lexington Books.

Marable, Manning. 2001. "Grounding with My Sisters: Patriarchy and the Exploitation of Black Women." In *Traps: African American Men on Gender and Sexuality*, ed. Rudolph Byrd and Beverly Guy-Sheftall, 119–52. Bloomington: Indiana University Press.

Martin, Waldo E. 1984. *The Mind of Frederick Douglass.* Chapel Hill: University of North Carolina Press.

Matthews, Mark D. 1979. " 'Our Women and What They Think': Amy Jacques Garvey and 'The Negro World.' " *Black Scholar* 10, nos. 8–9 (May–June): 2–13.

McDowell, Deborah E. 1999. Introduction to *Narrative of the Life of Frederick Douglass: An American Slave,* by Frederick Douglass. New York: Oxford University Press.

McFeely, William S. 1991. *Frederick Douglass.* New York: W. W. Norton.

McKay, Nellie. 1985. "W. E. B. Du Bois: The Black Women in His Writings—Selected Fictional and Autobiographical Portraits." In *Critical Essays on W. E. B. Du Bois,* ed. William L. Andrews, 230–52. Boston: G. K. Hall and Co.

———. 1990. "The Souls of Black Women Folk in the Writings of W. E. B. Du Bois." In *Reading Black, Reading Feminist: A Critical Anthology,* ed. Henry Louis Gates, 227–43. New York: Meridian.

Morgan, David. 1972. *Suffragists and Democrats: The Politics of Woman Suffrage in America.* East Lansing: Michigan State University Press.

Moses, Wilson J. 1985. "The Poetics of Ethiopianism: W. E. B. Du Bois and Literary Black Nationalism." In *Critical Essays on W. E. B. Du Bois,* ed. William L. Andrews, 92–106. Boston: G.K. Hall and Co.

———. 1990. "Writing Freely? Frederick Douglass and the Constraints of Racialized Writing." In *Frederick Douglass: New Literary and Historical Essays,* ed. Eric J. Sundquist, 66–83. New York: Cambridge University Press.

Ms. Magazine. 2009. Special Inaugural Issue. "Visions for Change." (Winter): 34–39.

Neal, Mark Anthony. 2005. *New Black Men.* New York: Routledge.

Obama, Barack. 2009. " 'What I Want for You—and Every Child in America.' " In *PARADE* (18 January): 4–5.

Powell, Kevin. 2003. *Who's Gonna Take the Weight? Manhood, Race, and Power in America.* New York: Three Rivers Press.

Rahman, Laura L., producer and director. 2006. *Breaking Silences: Violence against Women on College Campuses.* www.utube.com. Documentary film.

Rampersad, Arnold. [1911] 1989. Foreword. *The Quest of the Silver Fleece,* by W. E. B. Du Bois. Repr. Boston: Northeastern University Press.

———. [1976] 1990. *The Art and Imagination of W. E. B. Du Bois.* Repr. New York: Schocken Books.

———. 1985. "W. E. B. Du Bois as a Man of Literature." In *Critical Essays on W. E. B. Du Bois,* ed. William L. Andrews, 57–72. Boston: G. K. Hall and Co.

Ross, Marlon B. 2004. *Manning the Race: Reforming Black Men in the Jim Crow Era.* New York: New York University Press.

Ruddick, Sara 1989. *Maternal Thinking: Toward a Politics of Peace.* New York: Ballantine Books.

Sinclair, Andrew. 1966. *The Better Half: The Emancipation of the American Woman.* London: Jonathan Cape.

Spillers, Hortense J. 1987. "Mama's Baby, Papa's Maybe: An American Grammar Book." *Diacritics,* Summer, 65–80.

Staples, Robert. 1979. "The Myth of Black Macho: A Response to Angry Black Feminists." *Black Scholar* 10, no. 8 (March–April): 24–32.

Terborg-Penn, Rosalyn. 1978. "Black Male Perspectives on the Nineteenth-Century Woman." In *The Afro-American Woman: Struggles and Images*, eds. Sharon Harley and Rosalyn Terborg-Penn, 28–42. Port Washington, NY: Kennikat Press.

Terrell, Mary Church. 1908. "Frederick Douglass." In *Frederick Douglass on Women's Rights*, ed. Phillip Foner, 175–81. New York: Da Capa Press.

Walker, Alice. 1983. *In Search of Our Mothers' Gardens*. San Diego, CA: Harcourt Brace Jovanovich.

Walker, S. Jay. "Frederick Douglass and Woman Suffrage." *Black Scholar* 4, nos. 6–7 (March–April): 24–31.

Wallace, Maurice O. 2002. *Constructing the Black Masculine: Identity and Ideality in African American Men's Literature and Culture, 1775–1995*. Durham, NC: Duke University Press.

Wallace, Michelle. 1978. *Black Macho and the Myth of the Superwoman*. New York: Dial Press.

Watkins, Mel. 1986. "Sexism, Racism and Black Women Writers." *New York Times Book Review*, June, sec. 7, p. 36.

White, Aaronette. 2006. "African American Feminist Fathers' Narratives of Parenting." *Journal of Black Psychology* 32, no. 1 (February): 43–71.

———. 2008. *"Ain't I a Feminist?" African American Men Speak Out on Fatherhood, Friendship, and Freedom*. New York: State University of New York Press.

Wideman, John Edgar. 1995. *Fatheralong: A Meditation on Fathers and Sons, Race and Society.*. New York: Vintage Books.

Ya Salaam, Kalamu. 1979. "Revolutionary Struggle/Revolutionary Love." *Black Scholar* 10, nos. 8–9 (May/June): 20–24.

———. 2001. "Women's Rights Are Human Rights." In *Traps: African American Men on Gender and Sexuality*, ed. Rudolph Byrd and Beverly Guy-Sheftall. Bloomington: Indiana University Press.

Yellin, Jean Fagan. 1973. "Du Bois' *Crisis* and Woman's Suffrage." In *The Massachusetts Review* 14 (Spring): 365–66.

Index

abolitionist (struggle): Douglass as, 51; women's role in, 16
accountability, personal and social: in relation to author's beliefs and the church, 170
"Address of the Anti-Slavery Women of Western New York," 18
"African American Feminist Fathers' Narratives of Parenting," 10, 146, 156
African mythology, 8–9, 97
African nationalist stance, 56
Ain't I a Feminist? African American Men Speak Out on Fatherhood, Friendship, Forgiveness and Freedom, 10, 191
"Ain't I a Woman?" 38
Alexander, M. Jacqui, 114
all-American man: heterosexist and homophobic image of, 140–143
all-American Morehouse Man(hood). *See* Morehouse Man(hood)
Allen, Robert, 137
Alwyn, Bles, 70, 78, 87–112
American Anti-Slavery Society, 19
American Equal Rights Association (AERA), 35–36, 42
American Moral Reform Society, 16
"Angel Gabriel Christian Center," 171
Anthony, Aaron, 40
Anthony, Susan B., 21, 32, 49: against negro male suffrage, 35–38, 49; in dialogue with Douglass, 33–34
antiracist: agitation, 38; movement, 55; resistance, 54; teaching, 159
antisexist thinking, 7
antislavery movement: and suffrage issues, 44; white women in, 19
Aptheker, Bettina, 19
Are We Not Men? Masculine Anxiety and the Problem of African-American Identity, 135
Art and Imagination of W.E.B. Du Bois, The, 70
Assing, Ottilia, 21
autocritographical writing, 115–117: as practice in and out of university, 164
"autocritography," 9, 115
Awkward, Michael, 1, 5–6, 115–118, 127–129, 148–149, 162, 189–190

Bailey, Harriet, 39
Baker, Houston, 69, 115
Bamboozled, 132
Barnum, Phineas T., 30–31
Bell, Derrick, 129
Bertie, 110
Betsy, 39
Bible, The, 185
Billson, Janet Mancini, 133
Biography of a Race, 82
black American family, 120
black fatherhood/fathers: impact on black boys, 121; patriarchy, manhood and, 6–7, 9, 118
black female abolitionists, 16
black female oppression, 3, 118
black feminine, 51
black feminist, 25: pedagogy, 171; profession, 115; struggle against

black feminist *(continued)*
gender and racial oppression, 13; woman as target, 128
black feminist fathering(hood): 156, 159; author's approaches, 156–157, challenges of, 173
"Black Feminist Statement: Combahee River Collective, A," 124
black feminist/womanist thought: healing power of, 123, 151, 154, 156; self-transforming power of, 4; through memoir, 115
Black Feminist Thought, 123
Black Flame Trilogy, The: Ordeal of Mansart, The; Mansart Builds a School; and Worlds of Color, 70
black humanism, 66
black intelligentsia, 67
black liberation, 22, 30, 35–38; and racism, sexism and classism, 33, 119; struggle, 135, 180; "Woman suffrage" as allegory for, 44
black machismo, 7, 120: myth of, 134
Black Macho and the Myth of the Superwoman, 134–135
"Black Male and Feminist/Womanist, To Be," 129, 132
black male empowerment, 125
black male feminist, 5, 128: antipatriarchal ideas of parenting, 10; critique of, 9; historic legacy of, 192; nationalism, 71, womanist thought, 9
black male gaze, 142–143
black male identity, 7, 119: in white supremacist heteronormative culture, 160, 164
black male outsider, 118, 154, 164
Black Male Outsider, 130, 163, 180
black male professor of feminism, 188
black male self-re(dis)covery: against wounds of white supremacist patriarchy, 10; linked with recovery of black family, 3; power of autocritography, 116; pro-womanist, 4; womanist thinking as a mode of, 7
black male subjectivities, 117
black manhood: Douglass as model of, 41; new vision of, 146; sexist notions of, 118–119
black masculinity: America's fear/fascination with, 132–133; homophobic notions of 9; nationalism, 125
"Black Men are Also Raping Black Women," 139
Black Men for the Eradication of Sexism (BMES), 129, 137–138, 184
Black Men on Race, Gender, and Sexuality, 129, 160
Black Mental Health Alliance for Education and Consultation, The, 181–182
black mother, 15: "Damnation of Women," 59; Du Bois's regard for, 51, 55–62; healing power of, 2; image of, 29, 51; material condition of, 5; place in black male feminism, 9
"Black Movement and Women's Liberation, The," 183
black patriarchal atonement, 199
black patriarchal domination, 6
black Pentecostal church, 156, 186: as spiritual anchor and place of gender othering, 169; and gender hierarchy (hetero)sexist patriarchy, heteronormativity and homophobia, 163
black patriarchy, 123
black recovery, 111
Black Scholar, The, 136, 195–197
Black Sexism Debate, 132, 199
black socialist commune, 106
black struggle, 106
black women feminists, 153, 155
black womanhood: and "Damnation of Women, The," 53, 58; defense against white supremacy and white female superiority, 8, defined in nationalist terms, 56; dignity, 108; and Du Bois, 55, 66, 81–83, 95–102; gender, race and class politics of, 14; libratory ideas of, 7, 68; masculinist

ideas of, 95; representation, 110; Yolande (Du Bois) as example of, 65
Blake, William, 185
Blassingame, John, 42
Braithwaite, William Stanley, 86–87
"Breaking Silences:Violence Against Women on College Campuses," 138–140
Browning, Bess, 17
Burnett, Zaron, 152–153
Bush Administration, 195
Byrd, Rudolph, P., 129, 146, 149–150, 154, 197

Cane, 69
Carbado, Devon, 129, 160
Carby, Hazel, 48, 84
Cary, Mary Ann Shadd, 20, 37, 61
"Challenge and Possibility for Black Males to Embrace Feminism, The," 159–160
Chideya, Farai, 121–122
Cleage Pearl, 138, 140, 152
Cole, Johnnetta B., 10, 136, 138–139, 147–148, 152–153, 162
Colored America, 19
Collins, Patricia Hill, 123
comradeship, 107–108
Condition, Elevation, Emigration, and Destiny of the Colored People, 18
confessional mode, 4, 147
"Confessions of a Recovering Misogynist," 150
Confronting Authority: Reflections of an Ardent Protestor, 129
"Conservation of the Races, The," 82
Constructing the Black Masculine: Identity and Ideality in African American Literature and Culture, 134
conversion; pro-feminist, 149; of Zora, 105–106
Cooper, Anna Julia, 45, 48, 54, 64
Council of Congregationalist Ministers of Massachusetts, 19
Creator, The; myth-laden vision of, 173
Crenshaw, Kimberle, 160
Creswell, Colonel, 110
Creswell, Harry, 97–100
Creswell, Mary (Taylor), 103
Creswell Plantation, 98
Creswell, Zora, 9, 66, 70–72, 74, 78–80, 81–84, 85–86
Crisis, The, 55, 67, 73, 86
"Criteria of Negro Art," 8, 65–67, 85, 110
Crow, Jim, 70
Crummel, Alexander, 8
Cullen, Countee, 78
"Cult of Motherhood," 62
"Cult of True Manhood," 31
"Cult of True Womanhood," 19, 45, 46, 58, 62

"Damnation of Women, The," 8, 15, 55, 57, 66, 70–74, 77, 79. and absence of fathers, 61; defense of black womanhood, 53, 85; for feminist commitment, 149; and hair, 104; as inspiration for *Daughters of Sorrow*, 54; as praise of black women/mothers, 59; as pro-woman suffrage text, 62; and Tubman, 106; and womanist politics/manifesto, 58, 61, 68
Dark Princess, 70
Darkwater, 15
Daughters of Sorrow: Attitudes toward Black Women, 54
Davis, Angela, 7, 22, 34–38, 153, 186
Davis, Arthur P., 71
De Mortie, Louise, 61, 86, 110
De Veaux, Masani Alexis, 147, 190
"Debate on Black Sexism," 195
degendered parenthood, 158
Delany, Catherine, 20
Delany, Martin R., 8; on connection between women's rights and black male oppression, 18; on getting women seated at the National Convention of Colored Freedmen (*see* Douglass), 20; at Seneca Falls, 21–23

Diedrich, Maria, 40–41, 48
Digby, Tom. *See* "Men Doing Feminism"
Divine Providence; childhood understanding of, 185
domestic violence, 5, 10, 118, 122, 147–149, 164, 167–169, 172: author's recovery from, 154–157; survivor, 181; "wife beaters" and television, 176–177
"Don't Be Like Your Father," 115
Douglass and Du Bois: antisexist thinking, 190; autobiographies of, 115, 117; being "called out of their names," 128, 137; connection of women's and black liberation, 14; defense of woman suffrage, 7; denouncing subjugation of women, 13; father's absence and family violence, 150; foundation for contemporary pro-feminist black male activism, 180; gender progressive thought, 7, 10; heteromale subjectivity, 123; legacy of, 3, 4, 6, 8, 185, 189–190, 197, 200; memoirs as black male self-libratory narrative, 9; personal and historical contexts, 7; as pro-feminists, 118; pro-womanist thoughts of, 9, 190; pro-women's rights men, 191; risks of being a feminist identified black man, 10; on women's oppression through firsthand witnessing, 14
Douglass, Anna, 40, 76
Douglass, Frederick: on black males in women's rights agitation, 18; and the case for woman suffrage, 8, 26, 29; as compared to Du Bois in linking race and woman suffrage, 55; on connection of women's liberation and abolition of slavery, 14, 18, 20, 22, 25, 32; and continued fight for woman suffrage, 38; critique of Southern white women's racism, 46; critiques of racism and sexism, 8, 14; and the deciding vote at Seneca Falls, 21–23; as father of black intellectual expression, 29; on female education, 18; in final book of trilogy, 24–26; and gender coalition, 22; gender politics of, 25–26; on getting women seated at the National Convention of Colored Freedmen, 20; importance of literacy, 28; and the line between women and Negro suffrage, 47, 49; as male feminist, 53; on notions of race and class in a culture of white supremacy, 40; portrait on Du Bois's *The Crisis*, 55; pro-feminism and pro-womanism of, 63; pro-Negro suffrage, 37; pro-womanist writings of, 8, 26–27; questioning privileges gained from woman suffrage movement, 49; and radical Republican support for Negro suffrage, 48; and recognition of male gender privilege, 48–49; in relation to mother, 27; relationships to women, 39–48; repression of feminine in autobiography, 28; "Rights of Woman, The," 14; on self-determination, emancipation, and human rights, 41–48; and self-promotion, 30–31; and struggle for gender and racial liberation, 32, 49; and Tubman, Harriet, 106; uncertainty of support for black women from white woman suffragists, 48; woman suffrage man, 20, 23, 51; woman's rights man, 24, 29; women in writings of, 7, 25
Douglass' Paper, 18
Du Bois, Nina, 73–78
Du Bois, W.E.B.: and the absence of fathers, 61; And the Afrocentricity of *The Quest*, 71–72,; autobiographical approach to the defense of black women's rights, 8–10, 14; on black arts, 67; on black female sexuality, 95–101, 181; on black humanism, 66; on black motherhood, 51, 73; on black womanhood, 74, 84–87;

critique of black female racial and class oppression, 15; and the cult of motherhood, 62; "The Damnation of Woman" on motherhood, 56–62; and (domestic) feminism, 62; on family and feminism, 73–74; feminist nationalism, 56; on ideal womanhood, 73–78, 81–83; on the inseparability of Negro and woman suffrage, 54; as male feminist, 53; and masculinism and patriarchal imperatives in writing, 7; and masculinist egocentrism, 63; and Nina, 76; pro-feminism and profeminist standpoint of, 63; publication of *The Quest*, 81; in role of *feminist* mother/father, 79; similarity to Douglass in use of antiracism in push for woman suffrage, 55; sociological essays of, 70; and womanism, 73; and Yolande, 73–78
Du Bois, Yolande, 9, 65, 73–78
"Du Bois' *Crisis* and Woman Suffrage," 55
Dumas, Alexander, 104
Dunbar, Paul Lawrence, 71–72
Dyson, Michael Eric, 145–146

Elder, Arlene, 86–87
"elf-girl," 87
Eliot, T.S., 166
Elspeth, 86–87, 91, 95–101
emancipation, 50–51
emancipatory faith, 174
Emerson, Ralph Waldo, 30–31
Emma, 57–58, 110–111
Ester (Hester), Aunt, 26, 28, 40
Ethical Culture School, 75
Ethiopianism, 70 72, 78, 86
"Evolution of Negro Leadership, The," 69

Farrakhan, Louis, 120, 125, 131, 131
Fatheralong: A Meditation on Fathers and Sons, Race and Society, 119
fatherhood: antisexist manhood, 10; manhood and masculinity in black community, 146; pro-womanist/feminist benefits, 10
female equality: black male advocates of, 5; Douglass's discourse on, 26; masculinist or patriarchal thinking about, 7
feminism: *male*-identified notions of, 173; power of in men's lives, 13; self-transformative possibilities of, 7
feminist activism, 114
feminist consciousness, 117
feminist fatherhood, 173, 181
"feminist father," 83
Feminist Majority Foundation, 193
Feminist Majority Leadership Alliance (FMLA), 139–140
feminist manhood, 189
feminist politics, 122
feminist subjectivity, 117
feminist/womanist scholars, 55
Ferguson, Kate, 61
Fifteenth Amendment, 35–38, 48
Folger, Rebecca, 17
Foner, Phillip, 38, 42–43, 44–47
Ford Foundation, The, 152
Forten: family, 7, 16, 22; James, Jr., 8, 16; James, Sr., 8, 16; Margaretta, Sarah, Harriett, and Charlotte, 16
Fraedo, 185
Franchot, Jenny, 26–29, 40
"Freedmen's Bureau, The," 69
"From Wheatley to Douglass: The Politics of Displacement," 29
Fuller, Ida, 57–58

Garnet, Henry Highland, 22, 71–72
Garvey, Amy Jacques, 56
Garvey, Marcus, 56
Garrison, William Lloyd, 19–21, 41
Gates, David, 121–122
Gates, Henry L.: and autocritography, 9, 115; regarding Douglass and manhood, 29
gender healing, 146

gender justice, 10, 15, 124, 148: Douglass and Du Bois as advocates of, 126; and interrogating heterosexual privilege, 160
gender oppression: and black female oppression, 118; "The Damnation of Women" as denunciation of, 53; eradication of, 180; Douglass and, 18; race and, 8; struggle to end, 10, 128
gender-progressivism: black male scholars and, 25; and black males, 4, 7, 13–14; black males and heteromale subjectivity, 123; as compared to patriarchal gender norms, 183; connection to domestic violence, 157; contradictions of Du Bois, 64; Douglass's views, 24; Du Bois's views, 8; fathering, 157; herstory of, 126; husband, 10; ideas of in elite black families, 7–8; labeling associated with feminism, 9; in parenting, 153, 156–157; proponents of, 123; and thinking, 116; and writing, 118
gender slavery, 138
Gender Talk: The Struggle for Women's Equality in African American Communities, 136, 147–150, 152, 154
Giddings, Paula, 7, 14, 16–17, 19–20, 34, 36–37, 45, 53
Griffing, Josephine, 38
Griffiths, Julia, 21
Grimke, Angelina, 19
Grimke, Sarah, 19
Guy-Sheftall, Beverly, 10, 13, 54, 57, 59, 61, 129, 136–140, 146–149, 152–153, 162, 180, 197

Harlem Renaissance, 56, 65–67, 79–80, 112
Harper, Frances, E., 35–38, 71–72, 84–85, 112
Harper, Philip Brian, 135
Harris, Luke Charles, 145, 159–160
Harvard Law School, 129
"Having Their Say: Conversations with Brothers and Sisters," 148
Historically Black Colleges and Universities (HBCUs), 141–143
Heath, Stephen, 173
Herald of Freedom, 19
heteroblack male privilege, 184
heteronormative black male identity, 116
heteropatriarchy, 118
(hetero)sexist self-transformation, 180
heterosexual privilege, 188
hetereowhite male hegemony, 184
High John the Conqueror, 146
hooks, bell, 25, 32–35, 115, 125, 137, 145–146, 153, 163, 197
homophobia in black communities 3, 124
Hot Springs, Arkansas, 164–167
Howard, Rev. James ("Dad"), 186–189
Hughes, Langston, 76
human rights: Douglass; beliefs in, 31; Lockean contractual view and woman suffrage, 43; suffrage for women as, 44–47; standing up for, 171; women's rights as part of, 14
Hurston, Zora Neale, 112

Inez, 57–58
institutionalized homophobia, 141–143
insurgency: radical antipatriarchal, 4
Iola Leroy or Shadows Uplifted, 84
Iverson, Thandabantu, 137, 148, 153–154, 198–200

Jacobs, Harriet, 48
James, Joy 7, 62–65
Jason and the quest for the Golden Fleece, 68; and Zora's education, 93
Jesus (Christ), 105

Katy, Aunt, 27–28
Kelly, Robin, 152
King, Mark, 139
King, Dr. Martin Luther, 140

Kostelanetz, Richard, 91

Ladies Anti-Slavery Society of Philadelphia, 16
LaRue, Linda, 183
Lazarre, Jane, 175
Lee, Chanel, 141
Lee, Spike, 132
Lemons, Gabriel, 171
Lemons, Gary L., 114
"Lemons" street, 172
Leroy, Iola, 84–85, 112
"Let Woman Take Her Own Right," 41
Lewis, David Levering, 61, 81–85, 112
liberal racism, 103
liberal white feminists: and racist attitudes in abolition movement, 8
liberated black man, 24
liberation struggle: Zora's role in, 93
Liberator, 19
Life and Times of Frederick Douglass, written by himself: His Early Life as a Slave, His Escape from Bondage and His Complete History, 23–24, 39
Lilly Ledbetter Fair Pay Act, 195
Lincoln, Abraham, 30–31
"Little Black Boy, The," 185
Logan, Celia, 21
Logan, Jermain W., 22
Lorde, Audre, 138, 153–154, 177
Lutz, Alma, 34

machismo: black patriarchal, 120, 151; fallacy of, 130; myth of black, 123, 177, 182
Madhubuti, Haki, 149–150
Major, M.A., 30
Majors, Richard, 133
male feminism: Douglass and Du Bois as leading male feminists of their times, 14; idea of, 173
male identity, 119
male *self* representation Douglass and Du Bois's drive for, 7
male supremacy: autocritography as opposition to, 115, 118; bondage of ideology, 149; Douglass in opposition to, political implications in a culture founded on ideology of, 8, 13
male woman suffragist, 49
"Mama's Baby, Papa's Maybe: An American Grammar Book," 2
"Man Child: A Black Lesbian Feminist's Response," 153
manhood: demons, 173; heteronormative ideas of, 117, 170; notions of rooted in sexism, patriarchy and white supremacy, 4
Manning the Race: Reforming Black Man in the Jim Crow Era, 135
Marable, Manning, 127–128, 153
Martin, George, 120–122
Martin, Valerie, 122
Martin, Waldo, E., 23, 42–45
masculine self interest, 117
masculinist thinking, 7
Massachusetts Abolition Society, 19
Massey, Walter, 141
Maternal Thinking, 73
Mayers, Isaac, 20
McDowell, Deborah, 7, 15, 25–27, 29
McFeely, William, 21, 26, 29, 38, 39
McKay, Nellie, 9, 54, 70, 81–84, 100, 108, 110
"Meaning of Progress, Of the," 69
"men doing feminism," 117
Men in Feminism, 173
Messengers of Black Cultural Awareness (MOBCA), 176
Million Man March, 120, 125, 132, 135, 137, 139, 182–183
misogyny, 117; black, 151; culture of, 175; as measure of the man, 172
"Moon, The," 72
Morehouse College, 129, 132, 137–143, 184
Morehouse Man, The, 138, 140–143; and heteronormative patriarchy, 143
Morton, Patricia, 64
Moses, Wilson, J., 30–31, 33, 71

mother, 73–74; African mythical, 61
motherhood: image of, 51; ideology of, 58–60
Mott, Lucretia, 19, 21, 41
Moynihan, Daniel Patrick, 139
Ms. Magazine, 193–195
My Bondage and My Freedom, 27

Narrative of the Life of Frederick Douglass, An American Slave, 21, 35–36, 39, 39
National American Woman Suffrage Association, 34–35
National Association of Colored Women, 45
National Colored Labor union (NCLU), 20
national Convention of Colored Freedmen, 20–21
National Convention on Women's Rights, 38
National Immigration Convention, 38
National Women's Rights Convention, 41
Neal, Mark Anthony, 116–117, 127, 130–132, 137–140, 146–148, 162, 190
"Negro artist and the Racial Mountain, The," 67
Negro (male) suffrage, 8, 24–25, 32–39, 42, 47–50, 54
Negro *male* woman suffragist, 31
Negro World, 56
"Negro Question, The," 24
"Negro Schoolmaster in the New South, A," 69
"Negrohood," 33
Nell, William C., 8, 17
"NewBlackMan (hood)," 116, 129, 131, 145–146, 147, 162
New England Anti-Slavery Convention, 19
New England Convention of Colored Citizens, The, 20
New England Freedom Association, 17
New National Era, 42
New York Herald, 21
New York Statewide Woman's Rights Convention, 22
Newsweek, 120–121
Nineteenth Amendment, 70
Norris, Frank, 84
North Star, 18, 22
Notable Negro Women, 30

Obama: family, 196; President Barack, 193–196; Malia, 196; Michelle, 196; Sasha, 196
Octopus, 84
"Old Miss" (Sarah Smith, Miss Smith), 89
Oliver, Joann, 155–156, 162
Our Nig, 185

PARADE Magazine, 196
paternal abandonment, 6, 181–182
patriarchal atonement: nationalist rhetoric of manhood in, 181–184, 188–189; "won't do," 125; wounding effects of, 6
patriarchal domination: women's innocence in, 50; wounding effects of, 189
patriarchal father, 113
patriarchal thinking, 7
patriarchal victim: father as, 173; son as, 147
patriarchy: in agitation for woman suffrage but not negro suffrage, 47; critique of, 7, 51; wounds of, 146
Paul: family, 7, 16; Susan, 16
Phelps, Rev. Amos A., 19
Philadelphia Female Anti-Slavery Society, 19
Philips, Wendell, 31, 35
picking cotton, 93; as children's game, 174
Pit, The, 84
"Poems Can Be Weapons, Too!" 198–199

"Poetics of Ethiopianism: W.E.B. Du Bois and literary Black Nationalism," 71
politics: of black women's hair, 102; of family identity for black men, 7; of gender and class for Douglass and Du Bois, 7
Powell, Kevin, 116–117, 127–132, 148–151, 162, 190
pro-feminist autobiography, 129
pro-feminist "brothers"/black men: narratives, 10, 118, 152
pro-feminist teacher and preacher, 174
"professor" of feminism, 163, 192
pro-woman(ist) black forefathers, 55, 118, 149
pro-womanism: history of, 4; "profession" of black man, 9
"Property Rights of Women, The," 41
Purvis: family, 7, 22; Charles, 37; Hattie, 16; Robert, 8

Quest of the Silver Fleece, The, 9, 57, 65, 66, 68–72, 74, 78–85, 86–112
"Questionnaire, A," 67

Rahman, Laura, 139
Rampersad, Arnold, 9, 56, 67, 70, 82–84, 90–91
recovery, 155
"Relationship of the Negroes to the Whites in the South, The," 69
Remond: family 7, 16; Charles Lenox, 8, 19, 21, 37; Sarah, 16
Revolution, 36–37
"Right is of no Sex," 42
"Rights of Woman, The," 14, 22
Roger, Nathaniel, 19
Ross, Marlon B., 135
Ruddick, Sara, 73
Rustin, Bayard, 128

Scenes of Instruction, 5, 115–117, 129, 149
Seneca Falls (Convention on Woman's Rights at Seneca Falls), 21–23, 49, 116, 195
sexist oppression, 115
sexual purity, 109
Shakur, Assata, 186
Shukur, Tupac, 130
"Silver Fleece," 93
Sister Outsider, 153
Smeal, Ellie, 191
"So the Girl Marries," 9, 65–66, 73–78
"Song of Smoke, The," 82
Souls of Black Folk, The, 9, 15, 65–66, 68–71, 79
"Souls of Black Men: African American Men Discuss Mental Health," 182
Spelman College, 138–141
Spillers, Hortense, J., 1–3
Stanton, Elizabeth, Cady, 19, 21–23, 33, 38, 49–51
Starks, Janie, 112
"stylish nihilism," 184–185
"Superman," 194
"supportive social arrangements": in 'degendered parenting, 159; for homosexual black parents, 160–161
system of maleness: forgiveness of, 173

Talented Tenth Theory, 65, 75, 78–79, 85
Task Force on Tolerance and Diversity, 141
Tatum, Beverly, Daniel, 138, 140
Taylor, Mary (nee Creswell), 93–95
television: as education in white superiority, heteronormative gender identity and class, 165
Terborg-Penn, Rosalyn, 7, 17, 19
Terrell, Mary Church, 23, 181
"third eye," 152
"THIS IS WHAT A FEMINIST LOOKS LIKE," 194
Thomas, Clarence, 183
Toomer, Jean, 69

"Training of Zora, The," 103–104
Transcending the Talented Tenth: Black Leaders and American Intellectuals, 63
Traps: African American Men on Gender and Sexuality, 129, 149–150
Truth, Sojourner, 35–38, 41, 61, 86, 180
Tubman, Harriet, 61, 86, 106, 110

Underground Railroad, 16
Union Society of Africans of Newport, Rhode Island, 17
Universal Negro Improvement Association, 56
universal suffrage, 46, 59

Vanderpool, Mrs., 102–110
"Vision of Zora, The," 105
"Vision Splendid," 104

Walker, Alice, 4, 111
Walker, Rebecca, 137
Wallace, Maurice O., 135
Wallace, Michele, 133–135
Warren, Nagueyalti, 64
"Waste land, The," 166
Washington, Booker T., 70
Watkins, William J., 22
We Real Cool: Black Men and Masculinity, 146
Wells-Barnett, Ida B., 34, 64
"What I Want for You—and Every Child: A Letter to My Daughters," 196
Wheatley, Phillis, 29, 30, 61, 86
When and Where I Enter: The Impact of Black Women on Race and Sex in America, 14, 53
Whipper, William, 8, 16
White, Aaronette, 10, 145–147, 155–162, 191, 195
white male hegemony, 183
white male heteropower: culture of, 3
white male privilege: Douglass; critique of, 43–44
white supremacist patriarchy: black male recovery against, 3, 119
white supremacy: growing up in a culture of, 6; and male supremacy, 8; Zora Creswell's critique of, 92
white woman suffragists, 48
"Whiteness of Whiteness, The," 175
Who's Gonna Take the Weight? Manhood, Race, and Power in America, 116, 129–130
Wideman, John Edgar, 119–120
"wife beaters," 175–176
Will to Change, The, 125, 137, 146
Williams, James, 29
Wilson, Harriet, 185
"Woman and the Ballot, 44–49
"Woman Question, The," 24
woman suffrage: and abolitionists, 21; Douglass's campaign for, 42; Douglass and Du Bois in movement for, 3–8; Douglass justifies as above other movements, 50; man, 8, 20–22; movement, 7, 20, 22; passage, 53; texts, 9
"Woman Suffrage," 42, 44, 46, 48
Woman Suffrage Association, The, 14, 21–22, 31, 49–50
woman warriors, 114
Woman's Journal, 48
"Woman's Suffrage Movement, The," 48–51
womanist forefathers, 113
Womanist Forefathers, 4, 15–19
womanist liberation, 113
womanist nationalism, 110
womanist thought, 4, 7
woman's right to choose, 156
Women's Club Movement, 45
Women's Detention Center, 186
women's education: among elite families of the 19th century, 16
Women's Resource Center at Spelman, 140
Women's Rights Convention, 17–18, 21–22

women's systemic oppression, 117
World Anti-Slavery Convention, 19
"World without Fathers: The Struggle to Save the Black Family, A," 121
Ya Salaam, Kalamu, 127–128, 197–200
Yellin, Jean Fagan, 55

"Zora's Way," 88, 102, 106